TRUST IN SCHOOLS

TRUST IN SCHOOLS
A CORE RESOURCE FOR IMPROVEMENT

ANTHONY S. BRYK AND BARBARA SCHNEIDER

A Volume in the American Sociological Association's
Rose Series in Sociology

Russell Sage Foundation • New York

The Russell Sage Foundation

The Russell Sage Foundation, one of the oldest of America's general purpose foundations, was established in 1907 by Mrs. Margaret Olivia Sage for "the improvement of social and living conditions in the United States." The Foundation seeks to fulfill this mandate by fostering the development and dissemination of knowledge about the country's political, social, and economic problems. While the Foundation endeavors to assure the accuracy and objectivity of each book it publishes, the conclusions and interpretations in Russell Sage Foundation publications are those of the authors and not of the Foundation, its Trustees, or its staff. Publication by Russell Sage, therefore, does not imply Foundation endorsement.

Library of Congress Cataloging-in-Publication Data

Bryk, Anthony S.
   Trust in schools: a core resource for improvement / Anthony S. Bryk and Barbara Schneider.
      p. cm. — (The Rose series in sociology)
   Includes bibliographical references and index.
   ISBN 0-87154-192-0
   1. Schools—Decentralization—Illinois—Chicago—Case studies. 2. School improvement programs—Illinois—Chicago—Case studies. 3. Education, Urban—Illinois—Chicago—Case studies. I. Schneider, Barbara L. II. Title. III. Series.

   LB2862 .B79 2002
   371.2'009773'11—dc21   2002021849

Text design by Suzanne Nichols

RUSSELL SAGE FOUNDATION
112 East 64th Street, New York, New York 10021
10 9 8 7 6 5 4 3 2

To Sara Spurlark, whose life's work has been devoted to placing the interests of children first.

And, to our own children, Sara Greenberg Bryk and Dana and Lisa Schneider. Our hopes and dreams for them remind us daily why good schools really matter.

═ The Rose Series ═
in Sociology

The American Sociological Association's Rose Series in Sociology publishes books that integrate knowledge and address controversies from a sociological perspective. Books in the Rose Series are at the forefront of sociological knowledge. They are lively and often involve timely and fundamental issues on significant social concerns. The series is intended for broad dissemination throughout sociology, across social science and other professional communities, and to policy audiences. The series was established in 1967 by a bequest to ASA from Arnold and Caroline Rose to support innovations in scholarly publishing.

DOUGLAS L. ANDERTON
DAN CLAWSON
NAOMI GERSTEL
JOYA MISRA
RANDALL STOKES
ROBERT ZUSSMAN

SERIES EDITORS

= Contents =

═ About the Authors ═

Anthony Bryk is the Marshall Field IV Professor of Urban Education and Sociology and director of the Center for School Improvement at the University of Chicago.

Barbara Schneider is professor of sociology and human development and codirector of the Alfred P. Sloan Center on Parents, Children, and Work at the University of Chicago.

Sharon Greenberg is associate director for research at the Center for School Improvement at the University of Chicago.

Julie Kochanek is an advanced graduate student in the department of sociology at the University of Chicago and a research assistant with Consortium on Chicago School Research.

═ Foreword ═

T he Chicago School Reform Act of 1988 remains one of the most far-reaching efforts at school reorganization ever attempted. At a time when national attention was building around school restructuring to improve student learning, Chicago chose a particularly novel course: decentralization with parent empowerment. For some this reform harkened back to the community empowerment efforts of the 1960s; for others it represented the newest chapter in a long history of school wars over the control of education in America.

During the early 1990s, we spent over three years studying this reform in twelve different elementary school communities. A diverse research team, including scholars and urban school practitioners, conducted in-depth interviews with principals, teachers, parents, and community leaders about local school governance. We observed at key school meetings and events, and also spent time visiting classrooms and talking to teachers about how reform was influencing what they did there. Our field data on the early implementation of Chicago's reform contributed to a previously published collective synthesis on this topic by Bryk, Sebring, Kerbow, Rollow, and Easton entitled *Charting Chicago School Reform: Democratic Localism as a Lever for Change.*

As we pondered the results of these first analyses of Chicago's reform, we became increasingly convinced that the quality of social relationships was playing a powerful role in determining whether a school community made good use of their newfound authority and resources. Participants' own language—how they made sense of what was or was not happening in their schools—focused our attention on the salience of ideas about respect, trust, caring, and personal regard in school life.

Our interests were further piqued by emerging scholarship in social theory, economics, and political science about the role of social capital in the effective functioning of democratic governments, large-scale economic systems, and diverse social organizations. Multiple research strands were merging around a common theme: the quality of social relations in diverse institutional contexts makes a difference in how they function. This scholarship, together with field observations, directed our attention to a critical but often overlooked aspect of school reform. Schools are networks of sustained relationships. The social exchanges that occur and how participants infuse them with meaning are central to a school's functioning. Moreover, the character of these social exchanges is especially salient in times of broadscale change.

Our first serious test of these ideas occurred as we reanalyzed extant survey data, collected by the Consortium on Chicago School Research in 1991 and 1992, about the quality of social relations in Chicago schools. This led us, with the assistance of the Consortium, to develop, pilot, and administer new survey items in 1994 to directly tap this domain. By 1995, we had strong statistical evidence validating our field-based accounts. A relatively small number of survey items, on what we began to call relational trust, sharply distinguished schools moving forward under reform from those that were not. While our theoretical conceptualization and survey analyses would continue to evolve over the next four years, the basic theme for this book—the centrality of relational trust to school improvement—was now established.

The remainder of the work entailed "polishing the stone." Our deepening theoretical understandings of relational trust helped to further refine our survey measures for 1997. We also revisited preliminary analyses of the field data, now deliberately examining each school case through an increasingly detailed theoretical lens. Then, as the 1997 survey data became available, we at last had the capacity to link measures of developing relational trust over time within school communities with changes in the work life of these schools, and most importantly, with measured improvements in school academic productivity during the early to mid 1990s.

With this large-scale statistical evidence in hand, we embarked on the task of drafting this volume. The seven chapters combine insights culled from diverse academic literatures, with field-based reports from teachers, principals, parents, and community leaders, and statistical evidence from teacher surveys and individual student test scores. Taken together, these data afford an empirically grounded account of relational trust as a social resource for school improvement.

This book is organized into three parts. Part I (chapters 1 and 2) considers the social foundations of schooling and explores the extant scholarship on social trust in diverse organizational contexts. Since little formal research on this topic exists in sociology of education, we found it necessary to cast a broader net in looking for ideas to help us better understand the social dynamics we were observing. By joining this conceptual inquiry to ongoing reflections on field observations, we eventually developed a theory of relational trust for analyzing school operations.

Part II (chapters 3 through 5) systematically uses this theory to analyze the actual social dynamics at work in three different school communities. These cases allow us both to explore the utility of our conceptual framework as a practical guide for understanding change processes and to enhance the framework's specificity as it applies to urban schools and their reform. These chapters describe what relational trust (or its absence) looks like in urban school communities, how it influences the day-to-day dynamics of school life, and, most important, how it conditions the efforts of local actors to improve their school. These cases also offer insights about how trust is built and sustained in school communities, and identify some features of public school systems that can impede such development.

Part III focuses on formally evaluating the effects of relational trust on teachers' work and on long-term improvements in student learning (chapter 6). We also draw out some of the analytic and policy implications of these results (chapter 7). These chapters offer strong statistical evidence of relational trust as a social resource for school improvement, and identify some of the numerous ways in which the presence (or absence) of such trust is likely to interact with other efforts to reform our nation's schools. Diverse policy audiences, regardless of their particular orientation toward school reform, are likely to discern important issues here of concern to them.

= Acknowledgments =

A project of this magnitude involves the efforts of many individuals, and we gratefully acknowledge their hard work and support. First, thanks to our colleagues who assisted in developing our many field-research instruments as well as conducting interviews, observations, and focus groups. We especially thank Michael Bennett, Al Bertani, Sharon Greenberg, David Jacobson, Lisa Moultrie, Rachel Resnick, Sara Spurlark, and Josie Yanguas for their care and tenacity in pursuing high-quality data often under very difficult field circumstances. Their deep insights about the microdynamics of reform in the communities they were studying proved invaluable. We also appreciate the efforts of several other individuals who assisted in this field research, including Paul Deabster, Hal Gershenson, Daniel Maier, William Pink, and Sylvia Smith.

We also would like to thank the many individuals who transcribed and coded the field data. Shad Cesarz, Jennifer Cox, Bobby Durrah, Nancy Jennings, Lorraine Mudloff, Heather Palmer, Scott Salk, and Cora Smith coded pages and pages of interviews and observations into our qualitative software package. Valerie Corr, Kirsten Fink, Mong-ha Hoang, Janet Mezgolits, Charity Thomas, and Ann Webster listened to fieldwork tapes over and over in the process of transcribing them into usable files. Thanks also to Josie Yanguas, who translated our interview protocols into Spanish, and Jennifer Schmidt, who translated our Spanish interviews into English. We also thank Winnie Lopez, who recoded the field observations for our emerging concept of relational trust, and Jose Guitierrez and Maria Martinez, work study students who assisted with all these tasks.

Several administrators at the Center for School Improvement assisted us over the years, keeping us on track with our budget, personnel issues, and space concerns. We appreciate the efforts of Penny Davis, Janice Stroud, Carmen Valverde, and Ann Marie Willis for their patience and careful attention to the endless details of administering a complex research project.

We are extremely grateful to the twelve principals for their many hours of effort facilitating our work in their schools. We also thank the teachers, parents, local school council members, community and neighborhood association leaders whom we interviewed during the course of our study. These interviews often lasted several hours, and individuals graciously gave of their time to help us understand better the problems of reform in their school communities. In these conversations, we learned about the importance of social relationships in the formation of high-quality schools; indeed, their voices constitute our argument.

We also thank our Advisory Panel, who gave us important input on our sample design and cautions pertaining to the constraints and promise of local democratic processes. This panel included David Cohen of the University of Michigan, Thomas Cook of Northwestern University, Joyce Epstein of Johns Hopkins University, Marvin Lazerson of the University of Pennsylvania, Henry Levin of Teachers College, Columbia University, and Mary Metz of the University of Wisconsin at Madison.

We owe a special thanks to Fred Newmann and Gary Wehlage for inviting us to a 1994 conference on social capital at the University of Wisconsin at Madison, where we first presented our ideas about relational trust. We especially benefited from the critique offered by Robert Putnam, who attended this meeting. Subsequently, we presented our work at several conferences and national meetings and received helpful feedback from many individuals. We thank in this regard Janice Jackson, Charles Payne, Caroline Persell, Kent Peterson, and James Spillane. We also are very appreciative of the detailed comments offered on the penultimate draft by George Farkas, Maureen Hallinan, Valerie Lee, and Fred Newmann. Similarly, we appreciate the efforts of the anonymous reviewers who critiqued our manuscript for the American Sociological Association.

The quantitative analyses presented here draw on the collected contributions of several individuals. We were fortunate in that we were able to rely heavily on the analytic expertise at the Consortium on Chicago School Research in maintaining the data archive on the Chicago Public Schools, conducting the citywide surveys, preparing analysis files, and constructing specific measures. We acknowledge in this regard the assistance and expert advice of John Easton, Stuart Luppescu, David Kerbow, and Yeow Meng Thum. We also thank Bonnie Strakowski for her initial work on multivariate models.

We would like to acknowledge the extensive contributions of Sharon Greenberg (formerly Rollow) to the case studies presented in part II. Sharon led much of the original fieldwork in these schools and authored extensive case study analyses of each school as part of her dissertation research on the micropolitics of school reform. Although the cases presented here represent an independent reanalysis of these field data, we remain deeply indebted to her original insights about the schools, the communities, key actors, and local problems of reform. Her guidance proved invaluable as we drafted the cases presented here. Sharon also offered detailed, line-by-line comments on the earlier drafts of these chapters, which led to substantial final revisions.

Our greatest thanks is owed to Julie Kochanek. Without her assistance, it is doubtful that we ever would have managed to complete this book. Julie organized our analyses of the field data and worked with Barbara Schneider to prepare the first drafts of the cases presented here. She also undertook the bulk of the statistical analysis presented in chapter 6, with Tony Bryk's guidance. Julie reran models countless times, fine-tuning our novel analyses accounting for changes over time. Julie also reviewed the voluminous sociological literature on trust that contributed to the final revisions of chapter 2.

Finally, we thank the Spencer Foundation for their support for the original study of Chicago school reform from which the field data and ideas for this book arose. We especially thank Patricia Graham, past president of the Spencer Foundation, for her continuing belief in this work, even as it took our ideas some time to percolate and be refined. We also acknowledge supplemental support from the Center on the Organization and Restructuring of Schools at the University of Wisconsin at Madison, which received funding from the U.S. Department of Education, Office of Educational Research and Improvement. These resources allowed us to continue fieldwork into a fourth year in our study sites. Similarly, we thank the Joyce Foundation, the John D. and Catherine T. MacArthur Foundation, and the Spencer Foundation for their core support of the Consortium on Chicago School Research. Without this foundation, the quantitative analyses presented in chapter 6 would not have been possible.

Over the course of ten years, we worked together, meeting almost every week, talking, rethinking, and reformulating our ideas. While Tony Bryk took primary responsibility for chapters 1, 6, and 7 and for the final revisions of chapters 2 through 5, the book is truly our joint work. Our hope is that the academic and policy community will find useful guidance in these ideas for improving urban schools.

Anthony Bryk
Barbara Schneider

═ Part I ═

Framing Themes and Illuminating Theory

═ Chapter 1 ═

The Social Foundations of Schooling: An Overlooked Dimension for Improvement

Almost daily, some major conference, research report, or pronouncement from an important public official calls for fundamental change in schooling in the United States. A casual inspection of most any issue of *Education Week* may well leave the reader stunned by the intensity and scope of reform activity occurring across this country. Seemingly every aspect of our education system—how it is governed, the basic organization of schools, who teaches, how students are educated, what's being taught, and how we know what students actually are learning—are all subject to intense scrutiny and revision.

We confront today a transformative moment in the history of American education. Standing behind this proliferation of reform activity are fundamental economic and societal changes rivaling those precipitated by the industrial revolution at the turn of the twentieth century. During the last hundred years, U.S. society functioned adequately with only a modest portion of its students being well educated. Now, high-level academic achievement has become a universal aim.[1] Where just two decades ago we would have trumpeted an increase in student basic skills scores in reading and mathematics and a reduction in high school dropouts, reform rhetoric now emphasizes "World Class Standards" of academic attainment for all.[2]

Research has documented significant changes in the economic returns to education during the last two decades.[3] We are evolving rapidly into a two-tier economy where formal schooling becomes a strict gatekeeper between those who gain access to well-paying jobs and those who do not. Moreover, the "new basic skills" required for economic opportunity in the future are likely to be substantially higher

3

than they are today.[4] Equally compelling arguments are raised as we consider the intellectual demands for effective political participation in an increasingly complex democratic society.[5] That the vitality of a democratic government depends on the social intelligence of its citizenry has been long recognized.[6] The basic form of public education that served adequately on this account in the past, however, is also unlikely to suffice in the future. Similar themes arise internationally, where education is seen as key to economic and political development. It is widely assumed that countries with strong education systems are the ones most likely to prosper in the years ahead.[7]

Such analyses have major implications for our education system. At base here is a call for a fundamental transformation in the mission and operation of U.S. schools. To promote higher levels of academic attainment requires raising the quality of educational experiences for all students, pre-K to 12 and beyond. Within the past decade, we have seen the emergence of efforts at comprehensive school redesign.[8] States and districts are experimenting with various forms of decentralization, chartering, and contracting.[9] Also ongoing are efforts to restructure the basic organization of teachers' and students' work, intensive scrutiny of teachers' knowledge and skills, and efforts to systematically introduce research-based best practices into classrooms.[10] More generally, a broad array of new policy initiatives aimed at advancing student learning has emerged around professional development, accountability, and assessment.[11]

Two broad approaches to school improvement appear in these various reforms. On one side is a focus on structural change as witnessed in efforts to promote governance reform and restructuring of work conditions in schools. This strategy assumes that unless a fundamental reorganization takes place in the institutional arrangements of public schooling, significantly higher levels of academic performance—especially among very disadvantaged students—remains unlikely. These reformers claim that we must reframe the incentives and control mechanisms under which school professionals work in order to encourage the needed innovations and improvements.

Contrasting with this structuralist approach to reform is a more immediate, direct focus on instruction. These critics argue that if we want to promote higher standards of student work, then we must transform teaching practice. This necessitates a concerted effort to improve the knowledge and skills of current teachers, better preparation of their future colleagues, and support for continued development of the teaching profession. While these critics may acknowledge that the current work structures are problematic, they argue that the primary focus for reform should be on enhancing the human resources of schooling. If this occurs, they believe, the rest will follow.[12]

In our view, both perspectives have merit. Embedded in the current governance arrangements for public education are disincentives and constraints that seriously impede desired improvements.[13] Structuralists therefore are correct in arguing that fundamental institutional change is required. Equally correct, however, are those focused on enhancing teacher competence, who remind us that the classroom—where teachers encounter students around subject matter—is the primary context for instruction. If we wish to substantially improve student learning, we must transform the intellectual dynamics of the classroom.[14]

While acknowledging the significant insights embedded in each of these policy arguments, we have also concluded that both analyses remain incomplete. Within any formal arrangements for schooling, teachers must engage not only particular subjects and ideas about how to teach them, but also students, their parents, and professional colleagues. Important consequences play out in these daily social exchanges.[15] The personal dynamics among teachers, students, and their parents, for example, influence whether students regularly attend school and sustain efforts on the difficult tasks of learning.[16] The history of power relations between a principal and her or his faculty can strongly influence a staff's willingness to undertake some new reform.[17] Similarly, established norms about teacher autonomy can delimit a faculty's capacity to engage in broad-based organizational change.[18]

The Dynamics of Improving Urban Schools

In this book, we argue that the social relationships at work in school communities comprise a fundamental feature of their operations. The nature of these social exchanges, and the local cultural features that shape them, condition a school's capacity to improve. Designing good schools requires us to think about how best to organize the work of adults so that they are more likely to fashion together a coherent environment for the development of children. We have learned, based on our research on school reform in Chicago, that a broad base of trust across a school community lubricates much of a school's day-to-day functioning and is a critical resource as local leaders embark on ambitious improvement plans. Moreover, we maintain that this social trust is especially important as we focus on disadvantaged urban schools and their task of educating "other people's children."[19]

A Troubled Urban School-Community Context

Profound economic and social changes have swept over our nation's major cities in the last three decades. Many urban neighborhoods have been ravaged by the loss of basic institutions: businesses, churches, banks, health and social service agencies, and community organizations. Little of what we normally envision as communal life exists in some of the poorest neighborhoods.[20] Residential mobility is high, as many families move frequently in search of safe, affordable housing. Taken together, these developments have made some urban communities much less hospitable for raising children. High levels of violence, coupled with transience, tear at the basic social fabric that binds neighborhood residents together. This social fabric, normally considered a resource for child rearing, often is weak.[21]

Moreover, a steady stream of federal, state, and local policies aimed at promoting desegregation had the unintended consequence of distancing schools from the communities in which they are located. For example, almost 30 percent of Chicago elementary school students do not attend their neighborhood school. (At the high school level, the comparable figure is 50 percent.) Similarly, by a judicial consent decree in 1980, a massive redistribution of faculty was executed in the Chicago public schools.[22] On one day, the ties of thousands of teachers to families and local communities were severed. A residue of social distance between school staff and communities has been left in its wake, and is now normative in many places.

As a consequence of these large-scale societal changes, distrust now characterizes many of the social interactions that poor families have with local schools and other public institutions. Teachers often see parents' goals and values as impediments to students' academic accomplishments. Parents in turn believe that teachers are antagonistic toward them and fail to appreciate the actual conditions that shape their children's lives.[23] This lack of trust between teachers and parents—often exacerbated by race and class differences—makes it difficult for these groups to maintain a genuine dialogue about shared concerns.[24] The resultant miscommunications tend to reinforce existing prejudices and undermine constructive efforts by teachers and parents to build relational ties around the interests of children. Instead of working together to support the academic and social development of students, teachers and parents find themselves operating in isolation or, in the worst cases, in opposition to one another.

A Striking Contrast in Urban Catholic Schools

Our interest in the social dynamics of effective urban schools derives from prior research on urban Catholic high schools. Bryk, Lee, and Holland (1993) found that many parents who placed their children in these schools were neither well educated nor necessarily held a well-articulated conception of the academic experiences that they desired for their children. Parents selected a Catholic school because they trusted that these school professionals would provide their children with a good education. When it came to deciding what students actually did in school, parents relied on the judgment and expertise of the staff, who in turn worked under a moral obligation to act in the best interests of their students. It was understood that teachers' responsibilities included defining the specific content and methods of instruction and, at times, also counseling parents about what they had to do to advance their children's learning.

The support that Catholic schoolteachers received from parents helped them to sustain a high level of commitment to the difficult task of educating disadvantaged youth. Teaching in these schools not only was a technical act, it also was a moral imperative. Faculty felt a strong sense of responsibility for student learning and welfare, and this collective commitment was recognized and valued by parents. The reciprocal character of the trust relations between teachers and parents made demands on teachers to act ethically, and on parents to support and encourage the work of the school. Since parents trusted the intentions of the staff, many potentially contentious issues never developed into conflicts. When misunderstandings did occur, they often were resolved quickly. Overall, the absence of suspicion and distrust in these schools was a key element in their operations and played an important role in their special effectiveness.

Insights from Recent Efforts to Change Urban Schools

Surprisingly, there is relatively little acknowledgment of these relational concerns in either education policy or the more general education research literature.[25] The importance of this social dimension does emerge, however, as we examine more closely some actual efforts to change urban schools. A notable contribution is the work of James Comer. Comer's reform effort, the School Development Project, focuses directly on the social misalignment, described earlier, between urban school professionals and poor parents. Comer organizes his school development work around a community mental health perspective, maintaining that unless substantial attention focuses on strengthening the social relationships among school professionals and parents, efforts at instructional improvement are unlikely to succeed.[26]

Similarly, Deborah Meier (1995) devotes a whole chapter of her book, *The Power of Their Ideas*, to reflections on the centrality of social relationships in the highly successful middle school she created in Harlem.[27] By her account, building trust among teachers, school leaders, students, and parents was essential to advancing the academic mission of the school, which was to provide challenging intellectual work for all students. Other supportive accounts from New York City can be found in the efforts of Tony Alvarado and colleagues to build learning communities in District 2.[28] The importance of building respect, trust, and a collegial spirit are specifically cited as central to the positive developments that emerged there.

Further evidence about the significance of the social dimension to school improvement can be found in results from a five-year study of school restructuring efforts conducted by the Center on School Organization and Restructuring at the University of Wisconsin at Madison.[29] Researchers associated with the Center concluded, based on longitudinal studies of restructuring schools, that

> human resources—such as openness to improvement, *trust and respect*, teachers having knowledge and skills, supportive leadership and socialization—are more critical to the development of professional community than structural conditions . . . the need to improve the culture, climate, and *interpersonal relationships in schools* have received too little attention.[30] [emphasis added]

Additional support for these assertions can be found in a detailed study of nine districts' efforts to reform mathematics and science education.[31] Here, too, researchers concluded that norms of trust among local participants played a key role in whether teachers were able to make good use of external support and professional development opportunities to change their practice.

In sum, a growing body of case studies and narrative accounts about school change direct our attention to the social dynamics of schooling, and especially to the engaging but also somewhat elusive idea of social trust as foundational for meaningful school improvement.[32] At last, a fundamental feature of good schools comes into our field of vision. Yet what precisely is social trust and what does it mean in the context of a poor urban school community? What effects are actually associated with it? This book seeks to answer these questions.

Studying Trust in Chicago Elementary Schools

A unique set of circumstances evolved in the Chicago Public Schools in the early 1990s, which made systematic inquiry on this topic possible.

A Context of Decentralized Reform

Beginning in 1988, a major effort was launched in Chicago to transform the operation of its public schools. Then Secretary of Education William Bennett had characterized the city's school system as the "worst in America." Many Chicagoans agreed and in response embraced a radical school system decentralization. Relative to extant practices in other urban districts, the Chicago reform devolved an extraordinary level of resources and authority from the central office out to local school communities. Specifically, the Illinois legislature passed in 1988 the Chicago School Reform Act, which sought to bring about more direct involvement of local school professionals with parents and community members in the improvement of neighborhood schools.[33] Under this legislation, voters in specified residential areas elect Local School Councils (LSCs), each of which consists of six parents, two community members, two teachers, the principal, and for high schools, a student. These LSCs were granted considerable responsibility, including the hiring and firing of school principals, who no longer hold tenure in their respective buildings. LSCs annually allocate substantial funds for school improvements (that previously were controlled by the central administration), and nearly all aspects of the school's curriculum and management come under their purview. Similarly, principals gained substantial authority under the Reform Act, including the right to hire new teachers without regard to seniority.[34] Finally, in order to protect the newly established autonomy of local school communities, the Reform Act specifically delimited the central office's authority to intervene in local matters and sought to reduce their actual capacity to do so.

A basic premise of this reform was that improving urban schools required stronger social ties between local school professionals and the parents and community whom they are responsible for serving. By establishing school community governance and by devolving substantial resources and authority to it, a context and rationale for collective local action was enjoined. Although the reform created opportunities for improvement, it did not lay out an explicit blueprint for all schools to follow. Rather, an outburst of diverse local initiatives ensued. This created a natural experiment for investigating differences in school change processes and ultimately proved a good site for examining the significance of trust relations in efforts to improve school effectiveness. Not surprisingly, some school communities in Chicago dramatically moved forward, but others did not.[35] By examining this variability among school communities in their processes of reform and its effects, we were able to glean insights about how local actors effectively engage one another around improving their schools.

Unique Research Resources

The results reported here draw on a larger collegial effort to research school reform and improvement in Chicago. Through this extraordinary collaboration, a ten-year body of both quantitative and qualitative evidence has been assembled on school-community change and its impact on student learning. The basic conceptualization of social trust as a resource for school improvement, developed herein, draws on field observations from longitudinal case studies of twelve Chicago elementary schools, conducted by the Center for School Improvement at the University of Chicago. In addition to these systematic case studies, we also had access to clinical observations from center staff who were actively involved on a daily basis supporting change efforts in several Chicago public elementary schools over this same period.[36] This combination of field notes and informal clinical observations helped us to elaborate an empirically grounded theory about the nature and function of social trust in school communities.

Complementing this field-based evidence are the large-scale quantitative data resources assembled by the Consortium on Chicago School Research. Founded in 1990, the Consortium is a federation of Chicago-area researchers and policy advocates and their organizations who have committed collective efforts to ongoing research on the conditions of education in the city, the progress of its various reforms, and more generally, an agenda of research to inform reform. The Consortium has assembled a large, integrated, longitudinal database on the students, schools, and communities of Chicago. The database includes: Chicago public school data from both students' administrative records and test score files; school-community information assembled from the school system, other public agencies, and the U.S. Census; and periodic general purpose surveys developed and administered by the Consortium to track local school change efforts. The data resources of the Consortium allow us to rigorously evaluate our claims about social trust and its effects on teachers' work and student learning. Taken together, the practice-based observations of the Center for School Improvement and the data archive assembled by the Consortium create an unparalleled set of information resources for research on urban school reform.

═ Chapter 2 ═

Relational Trust

O UR INTERESTS in the role of social trust in improving schools emerged out of field observations in Chicago elementary schools as they engaged in a decentralization reform. Comments about trust arose frequently as school leaders sought to explain why some actions occurred—or more typically, failed to occur—in their particular school community. Although an analysis of social trust was not initially our primary research priority, we gradually came to recognize this as a powerful concept shaping the thinking and behavior of local school actors.

Our growing recognition of the salience of trust led us to explore the extant scholarship on this topic. As noted in chapter 1, although social trust in school communities has emerged in a few studies as a key element in improving schools, little systematic research existed on this topic as we began our work. Little attention has been focused on the nature of trust as a substantive property of the social organization of schools,[1] on how much trust levels actually vary among schools, and how this may relate to their effectiveness.[2]

Consequently, we broadened our search to consider the more general literature on trust and recent developments in the closely related concept of social capital. Insights from a diverse array of fields, including philosophy, political science, economics, and organizational behavior, helped us to construct a grounded theory of social trust in school communities. Through a combination of literature analysis and field note review, we developed an explicit focus on the distinctive qualities of interpersonal social exchanges in school communities, and how these cumulate in an organizational property that we term *relational trust*.

Much of the current interest in trust as an organizational concept has been inspired by recent developments around the theory of social capital. Of particular salience to our investigation is the research of Robert Putnam, who has drawn on these ideas to analyze the func-

12

tioning of democratic institutions. Harking back to Tocqueville's analysis of the emergence of American democracy, Putnam reminds us that the effective functioning of democratic institutions rests heavily on the willingness of citizens to associate voluntarily with one another to redress collective concerns. He argues that such civic engagement depends on the nature of social ties among community members, in particular their levels of interpersonal trust.[3] Putnam's studies have provoked concern about recent declines in civic participation and increased anxiety about the quality of American collective life.[4] His research is salient for our purposes because it posits that the effectiveness of democratic institutions depends on the quality of interpersonal ties across a community. Since Chicago's 1988 School Reform Act sought to create local democratic institutions to promote school improvement, a natural application of Putnam's argument is that level of social trust within a school community should influence the effectiveness of Chicago's decentralization reform.

In the economic realm, Francis Fukuyama used a social capital framework to examine the contribution of social trust in the efficient operation of national economies.[5] He argues that variations in national culture, in particular their degree of "spontaneous sociability," contribute to their capacity to sustain complex economic relations. Specifically, high levels of social trust among individuals and institutions create more efficient production arrangements than in situations where it is necessary to rely on direct monitoring and extensive legal mechanisms to regulate economic transactions. This research is significant for us because it links the effectiveness of workplace organizations to the quality of social ties that exist within and between institutions. While Chicago's 1988 School Reform Act regarded democratic localism as a lever for change, the ultimate aim was more effective schools.[6] The arguments raised by Fukuyama suggest that the quality of social ties across a school community might directly influence the effectiveness of its operations. In particular, where high levels of social trust exist, the cooperative efforts necessary for school improvement should be easier to initiate and sustain.

Both Putnam's and Fukuyama's research drew inspiration from James Coleman's theory of social capital.[7] Coleman conceptualized social capital as a property of the relational ties among individuals within a social system. He argued that the nature of these relationships play a key role in a wide range of social and behavioral phenomena. Like human capital, social capital is intangible and abstract, and accumulated for productive ends. Whereas human capital is acquired through education, social capital develops around sustained social interactions.[8]

According to Coleman, two general factors combine to create high levels of social capital. The first is social network closure. Coleman argued that a high degree of interconnectedness among individuals makes it easier for members to communicate. This social network closure also facilitates correction of any miscommunications that if left unaddressed, could lead over time to interpersonal rifts and, in extreme instances, even to a breakdown of the network. Second, Coleman pointed out that the presence of dense relational ties makes it easier not only to communicate basic information, but also to articulate mutual expectations among various parties and to ascertain whether individuals are actually meeting their respective obligations. Coleman referred to this property of a social network as *trustworthiness*. Networks with high levels of trustworthiness maintain socially desirable norms and sanction unacceptable actions.[9]

A conceptual key in Coleman's work is that he coupled his ideas about the structure and impact of social networks with an explicit theory about the social exchanges among individuals who comprise the network. We too sought to develop a multilevel theory that roots a consequential organizational property of a school community (defined as relational trust) in the nature of interpersonal social exchanges among members who comprise that community.

In terms of understanding the microdynamics of trust relations among pairs of individual actors, we were able to draw on an extensive behavioral and philosophical literature that bears on this topic. Rational choice theorists have focused on the conditions and incentives that motivate individuals to trust one another, and on how individuals assess potential benefits and losses associated with actions they might take in a particular situation.[10] From this perspective, trust constitutes a calculation whereby an individual decides whether or not to engage in an action with another individual that incorporates some degree of risk. The exchange is assumed to be primarily instrumental: How can I best advance my material interests given the conditions in this situation?

More specifically, in choosing to trust another individual, each party evaluates past benefits in the relationship, assuming some history of prior exchanges has occurred. In the absence of such direct exchanges, individuals may rely on personal reputations, or in their absence, more general social similarities (for example, he comes from our neighborhood or attends our church) in making judgments.[11] Each party in a social exchange has some personal disposition to trust (or not trust) the other. Similarly, some level of trustworthiness characterizes each individual. Influencing the general structure of the exchange is a power relationship between the two parties that conditions each individual's propensity and need to trust the other.

A different strand of social research, based on group theory, helped us to further expand our conceptualization of the microdynamics of trust.[12] When an individual sustains a relationship with some person or organization, these long-term social connections can take on value unto themselves. In part, a self-identification process is at work. Individuals come to define themselves as connected to that person or organization (for example, "these are *my friends, my school, my community organization*") and undertake subsequent actions because this identification is meaningful to them. Feelings of friendships evolve and alter subsequent exchanges. Individuals begin to take on the perspectives and interests of others in their social network. A personal sense of social status and esteem—being a valued member of a social group—accrues to participants. Thus, social participation entails not only material benefits to individuals, but also important social-psychological rewards.

Philosophical and religious writings on trust bring a third, even more distinct view. Rather than the calculus of return used by both rational choice and group theorists, this perspective roots trust in a shared set of primary beliefs about who we are as persons and how we should live together as a people.[13] Social exchanges now entail a moral-ethical dimension, where actions are justified in terms of an obligation to advance what is good or proper in some social setting. Individuals understand, by virtue of their socialization in families, religious institutions, and communities, that they have a responsibility to "do what is right" and expect others in their social group to do the same.[14]

Together with our preliminary field note analyses, these theoretical arguments convinced us that the microdynamics of trust entails a complex mix of individual motivations. At the most basic level, self-interest is directed toward securing some desired return, whether that is improved learning opportunities for children, more attractive work conditions for teachers, or employment possibilities for poor parents. Social-psychological considerations play a major role as well. Schooling entails long-term social relationships that often are quite intimate. Parents hand over the nurturance, care, and development of their children to school staff and depend on them to advance valued aims in their children's behalf. Teachers attach great importance to the psychic rewards associated with their work.[15] Furthermore, while discussing the aims of schooling today primarily in economic terms is common (getting a good job, producing qualified workers for a local economy, stimulating regional economic development), schools continue to serve important political, civic, and moral purposes. They form students' attitudes, values, and dispositions, and in the process contribute to the kind of society we are and will become. That moral considerations also shape social interactions among teachers, parents, and administrators therefore is not surprising.

School community members indeed attend to instrumental concerns. They value achieving desired personal outcomes and being able to influence core organizational procedures that affect their lives.[16] Yet they also attend to the intimate personal qualities of these social exchanges: Do they appear respectful, promote a sense of regard, affiliation, and self worth? And they bring a moral lens as well: Can the behavior of others be understood as advancing the best interests of children?

Alternative Forms of Social Trust

The form that trust takes depends on the nature of the specific social institution in which it is embedded.[17] We eventually came to conclude that a particular system of social exchanges—which we term *relational trust*—was key to advancing improvement in urban public school communities. We consider first two other forms of trust and the kinds of institutions where they are most likely found. This comparative context helps to illuminate the distinctive connection between a theory of relational trust and the institutional basis of public schooling.

Organic Trust

Organic trust is predicated on the more or less unquestioning beliefs of individuals in the moral authority of a particular social institution, and characterizes closed, small-scale communities. In such social systems, individuals give their trust unconditionally; they believe in the rightness of the system, the moral character of its leadership, and all others who commit to the community. The presence of organic trust creates strong social bonds among members, who share an ethical responsibility for the consequences of their behaviors to themselves and others. Day-to-day social exchanges provide members with a broad range of personal rewards. A strong sense of identity with the institution is fostered, and members believe that they enact in their daily lives a core set of beliefs that have moral value.

Fundamentalist religious schools, such as those described by Louis Peshkin, exemplify a contemporary social institution where organic trust operates.[18] Such schools are part of larger religious communities that embrace a moral vision that guides the actions of professionals. The shared beliefs of the community order and control much of the work of school staff. Since the truth of their vision is beyond doubt, complete obedience is demanded. The school is an integral part of a total institution, and is explicitly designed to realize its moral precepts. An extraordinarily high level of trustworthiness among individual members characterizes such contexts.

The applicability of organic trust rapidly breaks down, though, when we consider most modern institutions. Typically, institutional membership is much more open, and individuals are less likely to maintain lifelong affiliations. A limited set of institutional purposes, rather than an all-encompassing worldview, orders associative relations among participants. Given the natural diversity in individuals' family backgrounds and prior experiences, there are few core beliefs to which assent by all members can be automatically assumed. Moreover, the ability of a modern institution to compel consent, as a condition for participation, is also typically limited. Even nurturing such consensus is difficult, given the high value most Americans place on freedom and individual choice. To be sure, shared beliefs characterize effective schools, but they are much narrower than those of a total institution, and conscious sustained effort typically is required to rationalize even these beliefs in the context of daily school operations.[19]

Contractual Trust

Much more common in the context of modern institutions is a second form of social relations called *contractual trust*.[20] Here individuals and institutions stand in a much more constrained relation to one another. The basis for social exchange is primarily material and instrumental. Although personal friendships may arise over time through repeated interactions, social-psychological motivations remain modest, and the moral-ethical dimension is weak or nonexistent. A contract defines basic actions to be taken by the parties involved. The terms of the contract explicitly spell out a scope of work to be undertaken, or a product or service to be delivered. As a result, it is relatively easy to ascertain whether the parties have acted in accordance with the agreed-upon terms. If one party fails to uphold the contractual agreement, legal actions can be taken by the aggrieved party to seek redress. Much of modern social life, including virtually all commercial transactions, are shaped at least implicitly by this form of trust.

The social relations around schooling, however, do not fit well within this framework for several reasons. First, the aims of schools are multiple and interrelated. Education is not a single product, good, or service to be procured. Parents expect schools to care for the safety and welfare of their children as they might themselves. Parents also typically expect schools to teach basic academic skills, develop more complex intellectual capacities (for example, to synthesize information, analyze competing claims, and articulate compelling arguments), nurture a diverse array of individual student interests (for example, arts, music, technology, sports), promote students' social and emotional development, and inculcate a core of values for responsible personal and civic life. Moreover, parents' priorities among these various outcomes are dynamic, depending on the evolving attributes, interests, and behavior of each child as he or she progresses through schooling. Some of these outcomes are relatively easy to produce and document (for example, whether the student has acquired basic academic skills in decoding a text or can undertake simple mathematical computations). Others, however, represent complex intellectual, personal, and interpersonal dispositions that develop over long periods and are difficult to assess accurately. As a result, objective evidence on many of the desired outcomes of schooling, which might form the basis of a contract, cannot be easily attained.

Second, the specific mechanisms that contribute to the production of these diverse student outcomes are complex and diffuse. While a substantial body of research has accumulated on effective schools and instruction, it still does not constitute an explicit knowledge base for detailing best schooling practices. Although instances of problematic practice may be relatively easy to specify (for example, chronic teacher absenteeism, lack of appropriate classroom materials, arbitrary adjudication of discipline problems), no universally accepted standards for good professional practice currently exist. For example, even though primary reading has been intensively studied for several decades, considerable disagreement still exists over appropriate methods for teaching different kinds of students. Without clear standards, however, it is not easy to make definitive judgments about the proper execution of school practice.

This latter observation is important because contractual trust is predicated either on specification of a particular product or outcome to be delivered (that is, outcome specificity), which, we have argued, does not readily apply to schooling, or on the use of established processes to affect some desired outcome which itself might not be assurable (that is, procedural specificity). Unfortunately, the basic nature of schooling is not consistent with this second condition, either. Drawing on a medical analogy, no doctor can absolutely assure a patient of the successful outcome of any given procedure. So even though in this instance it is possible to objectively measure the desired outcomes, outcome specificity cannot function as the exclusive basis of a contract. Yet contractual trust can function here through procedural specificity—that is, the demonstration of the proper choice and execution of an appropriate procedure. For example, a doctor may undertake open-heart surgery to correct a cardiac problem. Even though the patient's condition might not improve as much as desired, the appropriateness of the chosen procedure (that is, the particular surgical technique used) and the adequacy of its execution can still be established. Such procedural specificity, however, does not characterize most of schooling.

Third, even if best practice standards were established, to monitor whether such practices were regularly being used would be difficult in a logistical sense. Schooling extends over a substantial period and many different contexts. Much of this activity occurs behind the privacy of classroom doors, where little external oversight is the norm. No easily accessible records exist from which it is possible to determine what is actually taught and how well it matches school aims and acceptable teaching practices. While in principle it might be possible to establish an appropriate system of teacher record-keeping, coupled with direct classroom monitoring, the overhead costs attached to such formal policing mechanisms would be quite substantial.

Relational Trust

Schooling, an Intrinsically Social Enterprise

Although the arrangement of social exchanges is an important consideration in the overall productivity of any organization, these concerns take on a heightened salience for schools.[21] The social relations of schooling are not just a mechanism of production but are a valued outcome in their own right.[22] We recall, in this regard, John Dewey's long-standing observation that a good elementary school is more akin to a family than a factory. While families are organized to provide many "goods and services" for their members, participation in family life creates the deepest forms of personal meaning and identity. The quality of social exchanges that occur here, and how various parties understand and interpret them, are of great human significance. Similarly, social exchanges that occur around schooling also shape participants' lives in powerful ways. They provide opportunities for self-identification and affiliation around an enterprise of much social value.

Even if we focus just on the technical core of instruction, research on effective schools points to the importance of social relationships here as well. Teachers, for example, rely on maintaining good student rapport as a resource for teaching.[23] Teachers also need parental support to promote their children's sustained engagement in instruction.[24] While principals hold formal authority over teachers, principals nonetheless remain quite dependent on teachers' cooperative efforts to maintain the social order of the school and its reputation in the community.[25] Similarly, teachers must sustain cooperative relations with each other for coherent schoolwide instructional practices to emerge.[26]

In addition, as noted earlier, the aims of schooling are multiple, and the mechanisms for addressing them are complex, diffuse, and not simply specified. Organizational operations under these circumstances demand frequent context-specific decision making, and success depends heavily on cooperative efforts around local problem solving.[27] The social dynamics of such workplaces are much more important, from a productivity perspective, than in settings characterized by a well-defined and routinized production process.

Thus, both philosophical arguments and behavioral research findings lead us to an important conclusion. A complex web of social exchanges conditions the basic operations of schools. Embedded in the daily social routines of schools is an interrelated set of mutual dependencies among all key actors: students, teachers, principals and administrators, and parents. These structural dependencies create feelings of vulnerability for the individuals involved.[28] This vulnerability is especially salient in the context of asymmetric power relations, such as those between poor parents and local school professionals. A recognition of this vulnerability by the superordinate party (in this instance, the local school professionals) and a conscious commitment on their part to relieve the uncertainty and unease of the other (that is, poor parents) can create a very intense, meaningful social bond among the parties. Unfortunately, neither organic nor contractual trust captures adequately this social dynamic. We argue that a third, alternative conceptualization of interpersonal exchange—relational trust—better represents this phenomenon.

Theory Overview

Relational trust views the social exchanges of schooling as organized around a distinct set of role relationships: teachers with students, teachers with other teachers, teachers with parents and with their school principal.[29] Each party in a role relationship maintains an understanding of his or her role obligations and holds some expectations about the role obligations of the other. Maintenance (and growth) of relational trust in any given role set requires synchrony in these mutual expectations and obligations. For example, parents expect that teachers will take the necessary actions to help their child learn to read. Teachers feel obligated to work in a professionally appropriate manner and are willing to commit extra effort, if necessary, in seeking to respond to the parents' expectations. Parents in turn are obligated to make sure that students attend school regularly and, more generally, to support the teachers' efforts at home.

Schools work well as organizations when this synchrony is achieved within all of the major role sets that comprise a school community. In many schools, however, the behaviors of "others" do not conform to expectations. In the previous example, if teachers' actual classroom practices appear grossly inconsistent with parental expectations, many parents are likely to withhold support. Similarly, when the expected parental support is absent, the teachers' sense of responsibility may become more circumscribed. Interestingly, unlike contractual trust, violations of relational trust are not easily subject to legal redress. Rather, individuals typically withdraw their trust when expectations are not met, leading to a weakening of relationships and, in more extreme instances, a possible severing of ties.

In a sense, relational trust represents an intermediate case between the material and instrumental exchanges at work in contractual trust and the unquestioning beliefs operative in organic trust.[30] Like contractual trust, relational trust requires that the expectations held among members of a social network or organization be regularly validated by actions. Yet the criteria for drawing judgments about others now expand. As social interactions occur, individuals attend simultaneously to the behavior of others (that is, the outcomes occurring and the observable processes being deployed to advance those outcomes), to how they personally feel about these interactions, and to their beliefs about the underlying intentions that motivate all of this.

Formally, we posit that a discernment of the intentions of others is a fundamental feature of day-to-day interpersonal exchanges.[31] A complex mix of considerations enters here: instrumental concerns about achieving valued outcomes; hedonic concerns about self-esteem, social status, and institutional identification; and moral-ethical concerns about advancing the best interests of children. Similarly, a mix of motivations—from self-interest–based, to taking into account the needs and feelings of others, to enacting one's moral duty—operates as well. Relational trust diminishes when individuals perceive that others are not behaving in ways that can be understood as consistent with their expectations about the other's role obligations. Moreover, fulfillment of obligations entails not only "doing the right thing," but also doing it in a respectful way, and for what are perceived to be the right reasons.

We further posit that these judgments of intentionality are grounded in each individual's historical perspective on the institution, personal and cultural beliefs rooted in his or her family and community of origin, and prior workplace socialization experiences. For this reason, relational trust entails a personalistic account of action where normative judgments are made about how and why others go about the process of fulfilling their obligations. If desirable outcomes are advanced, but the processes by which this occurs leave individuals uncertain as to another's real intentions, trustworthiness may not be achieved. For example, whether teachers embrace a reform depends in part on how they perceive their principal's motives in advocating change. Teachers may ask, Is the intent really to improve opportunities for the children, or rather to bring the principal some public acclaim and perhaps career advancement?

Thus, relational trust differs from organic and contractual trust in that it is founded both on beliefs and observed behavior. The focus on analyzing intentions contrasts with organic trust, which is based on the presumption that individuals and institutions will consistently act in ways believed to be right and good. In such situations, there is simply less need for discernment. Interestingly, intentions also play a minor role in contractual trust relations, where expectations primarily are outcome- or procedure-based. If the desired products or services are delivered, individual motives remain largely irrelevant.

The basic conceptualization of relational trust presented thus far is essentially a three-level theory. At its most basic (intrapersonal) level, relational trust is rooted in a complex cognitive activity of discerning the intentions of others. These discernments occur within a set of role relations (interpersonal level) that are formed both by the institutional structure of schooling and by the particularities of an individual school community, with its own culture, history, and local understandings. Finally, these trust relations culminate in important consequences at the organizational level, including more effective decision making, enhanced social support for innovation, more efficient social control of adults' work, and an expanded moral authority to "go the extra mile" for the children. Relational trust, so conceived, is appropriately viewed as an organizational property in that its constitutive elements are socially defined in the reciprocal exchanges among participants in a school community, and its presence (or absence) has important consequences for the functioning of the school and its capacity to engage fundamental change.

Criteria for Discernment

Participants bring several lenses to bear as they observe and interpret the behavior of others in school settings.[32] Drawing on both the extant scholarship on trust relations and our own school observations, we posit a dynamic interplay among four considerations: respect, competence, personal regard for others, and integrity. Individual school community members simultaneously analyze the behavior of others through all four lenses. A serious deficiency on any one criterion can be sufficient to undermine a discernment of trust for the overall relationship.

Respect As noted earlier, schooling entails a long-term process of social exchange among students, teachers, parents, and school administrators. Maintaining a modicum of respect in these exchanges is a base condition for sustaining civil social interactions within a community. Such respect needs to be reciprocated by parties in each role set.

In the context of schooling, respect involves recognition of the important role each person plays in a child's education and the mutual dependencies that exist among various parties involved in this activity. Key in this regard is how conversation takes place within a school community. A genuine sense of listening to what each person has to say marks the basis for meaningful social interaction. In many public meetings that we observed, the communication among individuals was regulated through formal parliamentary procedures. These procedures may grant someone a right to speak but do not necessarily mean that anyone actually attends to what is said.[33] Such exchanges are quite different from those where individuals intently listen to each other and in some fashion take others' perspectives into account in future action. Genuine conversation of this sort signals that each person's ideas have value and that the education of children requires that we work together cooperatively.

Concerns about respect apply in all of the role relations around schooling. Parents must be able to talk with teachers and perceive opportunities to influence the education of their own children. Teachers need to be able to voice their workplace concerns and feel that the school administration will take them into account in subsequent actions. The administration in turn needs to feel that the faculty shares its concerns for the effective functioning of the school and will give serious consideration to any proposals offered to improve it. In each case, the process of genuine listening fosters a sense of personal esteem for participants and cements their affiliation with each other and the larger institution.[34]

Competence Competence in the execution of an individual's formal role responsibilities represents the second criterion for trust discernment. This consideration connects directly to instrumental concerns about the ability to achieve desired outcomes. We recognize that in the context of the social exchanges operative around schooling, outcomes tend to be broadly defined to include not only learning objectives for children, but also effective work conditions for teachers, and administrators' needs to maintain positive school-community relations.

Interestingly, applications of the competence criterion in school settings often involve significant asymmetry. Judgments about high standards of performance are hard to validate. As discussed earlier, the fundamental character of schooling—its multiple aims, the complex mechanisms needed to advance them, and the lack of good data on actual practice—makes it exceedingly difficult to answer such questions as: Is a principal really exemplary at leading school improvement? Is a teacher employing best practice in reading instruction? Are parents doing all they can to support schoolwork at home? While managerial aspects of principal competence are somewhat easier to ascertain (much of this behavior is easily visible), this is generally less true for teachers, whose practice typically occurs in the privacy of their classrooms. To be sure, parents want good teachers and good schools for their children, but discerning goodness remains difficult. This is especially so for poor parents who may have only a weak evaluative standpoint for making these determinations.[35] For these reasons, we expect judgments about expert practice to play only a modest role in discernments of trust relations in school settings.[36]

Yet teachers, administrators, and parents can and readily do make judgments regarding issues of incompetence. Principals, parents, and other teachers quickly recognize when a teacher is unable to control student behavior in his or her classroom. They also can discern whether a teacher's approach to discipline demeans students. Similarly, teachers who offer little meaningful classroom instruction are noticed too (for example, a teacher whose regular classroom practice consists of handing out worksheets and sitting in front of the class reading a newspaper).[37] Likewise, negative judgments about principal competence are quick to form when buildings are not orderly and safe, and when individuals interact in a disrespectful manner. Other obvious signals of principal incompetence might include the absence of standard organizational routines (for example, agreed-on routines for how students will enter and exit the building), allowing gross student misconduct to go unaddressed, or failing to provide basic supplies and materials for instruction. Similarly, parents who routinely yell at teachers and cannot seem to provide for children's most basic learning needs (such as getting them to bed at a regular hour and getting them to school on time) signal to professional staff that a relationship cannot be trusted.

In short, relational trust may exist even in the presence of considerable variation as to how well each individual actually carries out his or her role. Gross incompetence, however, is corrosive to trust relations. Allowed to persist in a school community, incompetence will undermine collective efforts toward improvement.

Personal Regard for Others   Recall our earlier observation that mutual dependence and personal vulnerabilities characterize the social exchanges of schooling. Any actions taken by a member of a role set to reduce others' sense of vulnerability affects their interpersonal trust. Such actions typically are interpreted as an expression of benevolent intentions, and understood as signaling personal regard for the other.[38]

In general, interpersonal trust deepens as individuals perceive that others care about them and are willing to extend themselves beyond what their role might formally require in any given situation.[39] Principals, for example, show personal regard when they create opportunities for teachers' career development. Expressing concern about personal issues affecting teachers' lives is another way in which principals reach out to their staff. Correspondingly, teachers who exhibit caring commitments toward students internalize obligations more encompassing and diffuse than is typically specified in collective bargaining agreements or school board work rules. Such teachers are willing to stay extra hours to work with colleagues on program improvement efforts, meet with parents after school, and participate in local community affairs. They may even become personally involved in some of their students' lives outside of school.

Personal regard thus represents a powerful dimension of trust discernment in school contexts. As noted earlier, the social encounters of schooling are more intimate than typically found in associative relationships within most modern institutions.[40] Expressions of regard for others in this context tap into a vital lifeline and, consequently, important psychosocial rewards are likely to result. When school community members sense being cared about, they experience a social affiliation of personal meaning and value. Such actions invite reciprocation from others and thereby intensify the relational ties between them.[41]

Integrity   In our daily social encounters, we listen to what people say and watch what they do. In a basic sense, we think of individuals as having integrity if there is consistency between what they say and do. This criterion applies, for example, as teachers evaluate their principal. Can she be trusted to keep her word? Such reliable interpersonal behavior is fundamental to advancing the basic instrumental aims of any collective activity. Not surprisingly, it operates as another core criterion for trust discernments in all of the role relation sets around schooling.

In a deeper sense, integrity also implies that a moral-ethical perspective guides one's work. The previous discussion about expressions of personal concern for others pushes in this direction. A school community, however, consists of many individuals with varied interests. Conflicts often will arise among competing personal needs. In adjudicating these disputes, integrity demands resolutions that reaffirm the primary principles of the institution. In the context of schooling, when all is said and done, actions must be understood as about advancing the best interests of children. Teachers demonstrate such integrity to their colleagues when they willingly experiment with new forms of instruction to improve student learning, even though this entails additional work and the risk of failure can be high. Similarly, principals do the same thing when they are willing to speak out, for example, against a central office policy that they believe will not help the children. Behaviors of this sort publicly affirm an individual's commitment to the core purposes of the school community. Such actions tend to promote solidarity among participants by conveying the message, "Our work together is rooted in important shared beliefs and values, and members of this school community will do whatever is necessary to enact them." Embedded in this microlevel behavior is a manifestation of relational trust as a moral resource for action.

Role Set Relations: Obligations, Expectations, Dependence, and Vulnerability

The social organization of schooling structures distinct relations among teachers to other teachers, teachers to students, teachers to parents, teachers to administrators, and administrators to parents. Particular expectations and obligations characterize each role in these relation sets. Moreover, these understandings take on a distinctive coloration in large urban school districts serving highly disadvantaged student populations.

In general, the power base held by each individual directly affects the nature of relational trust in any given role set. Although gross variations exist in the power distribution across roles in an urban school community, the most significant structural feature here is that no one person typically exercises absolute power. Even the school principal—the single most influential actor in a given school community—remains dependent on both parents and teachers. For example, principals must secure a base of parental support to maintain their jobs. Similarly, as principals seek to engage change efforts in their schools, they are dependent on the good intentions and efforts of their faculty, if new initiatives are to have any chance of succeeding.

Thus, while an asymmetric power distribution characterizes urban school communities (that is, principal power > teachers' power > students' and parents' power), no single role enjoys complete dominance. This is quite different from the more absolute power exercised in a patron-client arrangement or in the case of a despotic leader.[42] As a consequence, all parties in school role relations remain vulnerable to each other. Moreover, as will be shown, these dependencies and vulnerabilities exist even in situations where the power distribution is relatively equal, as in teacher-teacher interactions.

School Professional–Parent Relations Strong asymmetry characterizes teacher-parent relations. Poor parents typically do not have the educational knowledge and skills that teachers have to help children learn. This imbalance places poor parents in a subordinate status vis-à-vis their children's teachers in terms of selecting appropriate actions to advance student learning. As a result, poor parents are highly dependent on the efforts of school staff if meaningful opportunities are to be afforded their children. Even so, teachers also remain dependent on parental support to achieve success in their work.

At minimum, parental support entails ensuring that their children attend school regularly and arrive ready to learn; it also means parental assistance if classroom behavior problems emerge. This dependency is particularly salient at the primary grade level, where the school is an extension of the family. If learning is to occur, the trust relation developed between a parent and child during the first years of life must be transferred to school staff.[43] Teachers need parents to signal to their children that the teacher has a special role in the child's life, akin to that of an extended family member.

In addition, much research on teaching details the personal and intimate character of this work. Good teaching "touches the soul" of those who practice it.[44] While most discussions in education policy today focus on the technical dimensions of teaching and its enhancement, that teachers' humanness is very much a part of their practice is important to remember, and teachers need expressions of personal regard and support as much as anyone else does. Thus, for instrumental reasons regarding effective instruction and for teachers to derive psychic rewards from their personal interactions with students, teachers remain quite dependent on parental support to feel good about their work.

The dependency and vulnerabilities in the principal-parent role set follows along similar lines. Here too parents remain highly dependent on the good efforts and intentions of a school's principal to advance learning opportunities for their children. For the principal, job tenure and role success entails maintaining good parental rapport. Thus, even though principals are not as directly involved as teachers in the education of children, their basic structural dependency with parents remains comparable.

Owing to the substantial power asymmetry in all of the professional-parent relations, the onus falls on the professionals to initiate actions that reduce parents' sense of vulnerability in these exchanges. Common initiatives in urban schools toward this end include: creating a parent center at the school; developing support activities that parents can do at home to assist student learning; designing parent and family programs in response to local needs (for example, intergenerational literacy initiatives or GED programs); and, more generally, welcoming parents at the school and showing a personal interest in their children. Such initiatives are especially salient for poor immigrant families for whom the local public school is a foreign institution. As parents apprehend a wide range of behavior intended to make them feel more comfortable, they come to understand that school staff have genuine regard for them and truly care about their children.[45] Such discernment of intentions can have very positive effects on the overall quality of these role relations.

Further complicating parent-professional relations are the class, race, and ethnic differences that frequently exist between families and professional staff in urban contexts. As noted earlier, prior research on interpersonal trust documents that social similarities by race, ethnicity, and class offer an initial basis for trusting another until specific evidence has accumulated on a particular relationship. By extension, the absence of social similarity signals a possible reason for withholding trust. Thus, to effect relational trust in urban school contexts may require more conscious attention than might be the case in more culturally homogeneous contexts.[46]

Teacher-Principal Relations   In general, lower-status individuals in work relationships (in this case, teachers) are concerned about exploitation and unfair treatment. Those in higher positions of organizational authority (for example, the principal) worry that their subordinates will shirk their responsibilities and possibly undermine the work of the organization.[47] These reciprocal vulnerabilities are inherent in hierarchical work arrangements, but they can be lessened by trust relations that create opportunities for jointly beneficial out-comes.[48]

The combination of the principal's isolation from instruction and the procedural ambiguity associated with this activity makes it difficult for a principal to closely supervise all aspects of teachers' work. As a result, principals largely have to trust that teachers will make good efforts at advancing student learning, will go the extra mile in helping to improve the school, and work to sustain positive relations with parents. A reciprocal dependence exists for teachers as well. They generally expect procedural fairness in adjudicating competing interests among the faculty, a predictable environment governing basic school operations, adequate resources to conduct instruction, and professional support from their principal.

Like professional-parent role relations, teacher-principal relations are characterized by distinct power asymmetry. Principals exercise considerable role authority that directly affects teachers. Typically, they control major aspects of teachers' work conditions, including decisions about which students will be assigned to a teacher, the location of a teacher's classroom (for example, whether in the main building or a mobile unit), and the kinds of instructional materials available, such as computers, books, or other supplies. Moreover, these allocative decisions not only affect work quality, they also signal status and personal regard within the school community. As a result, teachers who perceive benevolent intentions on the part of their principal are more likely to feel efficacious in their jobs.

Any actions taken by the principal that reduce teachers' sense of vulnerability are thus highly salient. Establishing inclusive procedures for decision making affords teachers real opportunities to raise issues and be heard. When such routines are implemented effectively, teachers come to understand that they have a meaningful voice in influencing important decisions that affect their lives. At a more fundamental level, the principal's articulation of a compelling vision for "our school community" and corollary actions that can be interpreted as enlivening that vision, go a long way toward fostering a collective sense of engagement among a faculty in social activity of moral value. Such behavior speaks directly to the integrity dimension in teachers' discernments about trusting their principal.

Teacher-Teacher Relations   A novelty about this particular role set is that it is the only one in a school community grounded in a relatively symmetric distribution of power. Nonetheless, the institutional structure of schooling still imposes substantial interdependency among a faculty. Classroom teachers, for example, rely on the good efforts of teacher colleagues in earlier grades to develop students' prerequisite knowledge, skills, and dispositions in order for grade-level appropriate work to occur in their classrooms. Serious student deficiencies in this regard make a teacher's job more difficult and may thwart her success. Similarly, common policies crafted by a faculty around concerns such as student discipline, textbook selection, and instructional objectives introduce additional constraints on individual teachers' work.

At a basic level, teachers need each other's help in carrying out the day-to-day routines of schooling. A norm of generalized reciprocity therefore is important to trust discernments in this role set. For example, playground duty might be shared among a group of teachers in a particular elementary school. If one teacher cannot supervise the playground on her designated day, she might ask another teacher to cover for her. The colleague who picks up the extra day of supervision expects some unspecified future favor in return. While at any given time these exchanges may be imbalanced, an expectation is that this imbalance eventually will be redressed. Stated simply, the assumption is that "Someday you might stand in my shoes and I anticipate that you would do for me what I am now doing for you."[49] In addition to solving instrumental needs in the daily work of schools, such exchanges also afford opportunities for expressions of personal regard and extend some psychosocial rewards to both parties.

At a deeper level, relational trust within a faculty is grounded in common understandings about such matters as what students should learn, how instruction should be conducted, and how teachers and students should behave. For teachers to sense integrity among colleagues they must not only share common views but also perceive that actions taken by others are consistent with these views. The social structure of most elementary schools, however, delimits the opportunities for these shared norms to develop. Teachers typically work alone in their classrooms most of the day and have few occasions for meaningful interaction with colleagues. In addition, little control exists over the entry and exit of teachers into and from the school. Bumping privileges in urban districts where teachers are entitled to positions solely by virtue of their seniority mean that faculties usually are not assembled with the specific purpose of creating coherence around a shared school vision. Indeed, the idea of a faculty as a deliberately formed instructional team or high-performing work group simply does not enter into this equation.[50] Rather, teaching slots typically are filled based on an individual's holding the appropriate teaching certificate and in accordance with seniority rights.[51]

Absent then the typical organizational mechanisms for promoting collegialism, few opportunities exist for teachers to work out personal differences and develop common understandings. Instead, differences in beliefs, values, and prior work experiences may stay unexamined and the corollary interpersonal tensions remain latent. Social exchanges may appear respectful, but little of consequence happens in them. Teachers may say good morning to each other and generally act in a friendly manner. They may collaborate with colleagues around a few decisions, such as the organization of major field trips and assemblies, but the core work of teaching is either carried out privately in individual teachers' classrooms or externally controlled by central offices and state bureaucracies. The latter is especially significant in urban contexts, where much in the organization of the instructional core is decided externally. This further reduces the opportunities for teachers to act as a faculty to address collective problems.

All of these factors have important consequences for relational trust among teachers. Since the articulation of common beliefs and the demonstration of actions consonant with them are not routine, we are unlikely to see a deep sense of professional integrity develop within a faculty.[52] Interestingly, this is another instance of an asymmetry embedded within the institutional structure of schools. As noted in the discussion of discernments of professional competence, the same appears true for teachers' discernments of their colleagues' integrity. While faculties may not share deep professional understandings that shape a common practice, teachers indeed discern and attend to behavior by other teachers that appears grossly inappropriate. Examples include the teacher who uses punitive and demeaning disciplinary practices with children, the teacher who constantly refuses to try new approaches to improve achievement, and those who are regularly out the school door as soon as students leave. Such actions say to teachers that some of their colleagues lack integrity and cannot be trusted.

In general, moral and ethical concerns are salient in the life of classrooms and central to teachers' thinking about their individual work.[53] Most individuals who enter this profession tend to express strong sentiments about "really caring for the children." As a result, any teacher behavior that signals a flagrant disregard for the children, as illustrated in these examples, is likely to have profound effects on others.

Teacher-Student Relationships   Trusting student-teacher relations are essential for learning. These exchanges take on a distinctive form in the early grades, resembling parent-child interactions. For successful learning to occur here, the trust built up in family life must be transferred to the classroom teacher. Assuming this happens, elementary grade teachers will hold diffuse affective power over their students. Given this power asymmetry in the student-teacher role set, the growth of trust depends primarily on teachers' initiatives. Such initiatives include both establishing a familylike climate in the classroom that builds on students' affective experiences at home, and engaging parents in a supportive relationship around their child's learning.[54]

As students progress through the grades and gradually become more responsible for their own learning, the role dependency between teacher and student changes. By middle school, the mutual obligations for learning become more explicit between students and teachers. This change continues through high school, closely paralleling adolescents' self-identity development. In addition, powerful peer group influences emerge at this point. Thus, a theory of trust in secondary schools would also have to conceptualize trust as a collective concern among students rooted in prevailing student norms.

Since the focus of this book is on organizational change in elementary schools, we offer only limited attention to the teacher-student role set. Our substantive focus on structural school change naturally directs attention toward adults rather than students. While students are significant school actors, changes in the operation and organization of schools are primarily an adult game. In addition, although student-teacher trust relations are an important social resource in elementary instruction, their impact at the organizational level is more modest. In contrast, in high schools, peer influences and student norms are quite powerful, and these forces must be engaged directly by any school reform effort.

Nonetheless, our analysis does take students into account in two important ways. First, we view student-teacher trust in elementary schools as operating primarily through parent-teacher trust, where students are the implied "third" party. At a base level, then, in attending to parent-professional relations we also are attending to student-professional relations.[55] Second, and more significant, advancing the interests of children represents in our theory the primary standpoint for evaluating individual integrity across all role relations regarding schooling. Thus, although students may not be direct actors in our theory of relational trust in elementary schools, we indeed attend closely to how their interests permeate all adult social interactions in a school community.

Organizational Consequences of Relational Trust

As noted in the introduction to this chapter, our claims about the impact of trust relations in schools draw on a growing body of scholarship in diverse fields, including work on organizational behavior and management. Writings in this latter area suggest that trust is especially important for organizations that operate in turbulent external environments, that depend heavily on information sharing for success, and whose work processes demand effective decentralized decision making.[56] All three of these factors characterize the day-to-day functioning of schools. In addition, organizational research also suggests that trusting relations are especially important in times that call for major structural changes, as was demanded by the Chicago School Reform Act of 1988.[57] Taking these various considerations together therefore gives us good reason to suspect that trust relations can have a profound effect on the processes of school reform.

Specifically, we see relational trust operating as a resource for school improvement in four broad ways. First, organizational change entails major risks for all participants. Teachers must take on new practices that may not work. Parents are asked to support initiatives whose value has yet to be demonstrated. Principals must commit substantial personal effort to an uncertain change process. In addition, school reform movements often are accompanied by external pressure to improve quickly and considerable external scrutiny as well. In short, the stakes suddenly are high and the demands for change great. The presence of relational trust, however, moderates the sense of uncertainty and vulnerability that individuals feel as they confront such demands. When trust is strong, individual engagement with reform does not feel like a call for heroic action. In this sense, relational trust is a catalyst for innovation.

Second, the transaction costs associated with decision making are reduced in environments where individuals are predisposed to trust one another. This is especially important in times of reform because efforts at structural change entail intense collective decision making within the organization. In the context of high relational trust, teachers and parents believe in the good intentions of school leadership. As a result, they are more likely to afford principals a wider zone of discretionary authority. In addition, when arguments arise over the merits of some reform effort, these disagreements are more likely to be resolved in a straightforward fashion, again because of the assumed good intentions all around. Consequently, reform is likely to progress faster in high trust contexts because participants are more able to coalesce around a plan of action. In this regard, relational trust facilitates public problem solving.

Third, contexts with strong relational trust benefit from clear understandings about role obligations that are routinely reinforced in day-to-day behavior. Individuals understand what is expected of them and the consequences that may ensue if obligations are not met.

Relational trust thus undergirds a highly efficient system of social control where extensive supervision of individuals' work is not required, and shirking behavior remains minimal. This organizational feature is also especially significant in times of reform. Given the privacy of classroom practice, successful change efforts depend heavily on the voluntary initiative and goodwill of school staff. The presence of high relational trust increases the likelihood of broad-based, high-quality implementation of new improvement efforts. In this regard, trustworthiness across the organization helps coordinate meaningful collective action.

Finally, relational trust sustains an ethical imperative among organizational members to advance the best interests of children. Participants in schools with high relational trust enact an interrelated set of mutual obligations with one another. The normative understandings embedded here provide good reasons for engaging efforts that, from a purely self-interested point of view, might seem irrational. Why should teachers, for example, voluntarily agree to work longer hours and risk new practices that might fail, or engage in change processes with colleagues that may provoke misunderstandings and possibly conflict? From an individual perspective, it is quite natural to eschew such activity; yet all of these behaviors are central to meaningful organizational change. In this regard, relational trust constitutes a moral resource for school improvement.

═ Part II ═

Relational Trust in Three Urban School Communities

As noted in chapter 1, our interest in relational trust grew out of an intensive field study in the early 1990s of Chicago's school decentralization reform. This study focused on the micropolitical dynamics of twelve elementary school communities, the local forces that shaped them, and how together these influenced a school community's capacity to engage the opportunities provided by this reform. Our research directed considerable attention to the nature and quality of adult relations in these school communities.[1]

It became clear from a preliminary reading of field notes and interviews that concerns about respect, trust, personal regard, and caring were quite significant to local actors as they sought to make sense of the reform efforts of which they were a part. These emerging observations led us to review selectively the academic literature from a diverse set of fields that bore on these themes. The theory of relational trust formalized in chapter 2 resulted from continued reflections on how school participants' commentary, represented in field notes and interviews, interacted with key ideas culled from a review of the literature.

A first, qualitative test of the adequacy of this theory is whether it illuminates the actual social practice of urban school communities. More specifically, Chicago's decentralization reform assumed that school communities could engage in effective local problem solving if school professionals joined with parents and community leaders to harness their latent resources. Thus, a key question is whether relational trust actually helps us better understand why initial efforts at reform progressed more satisfactorily at some school sites than at others.

With this in mind, we returned to the corpus of field data and systematically reanalyzed participants' commentaries and our field observations about the social relations at work in three of the twelve school communities originally studied. Our theory of relational trust directed a focus on each major role set in these school communities, considering what informants told us about the expectations they held for others and the specific discernments they made about their behavior.

The three schools chosen for in-depth analysis capture much of the diversity in reform implementation observed across all of the sites initially studied. Taken together, they afford considerable detail about the social relations at work in urban school communities and their organizational consequences. The Ridgeway Elementary School (chapter 3) represents one of the most adversarial and conflictual school communities in Chicago during the early 1990s. Examination of this case reveals the seeds of distrust in a school community, and how such distrust continually frustrates efforts at collective social action. The Holiday Elementary School (chapter 5) represents a much more positive story. Holiday is especially interesting given the unusual nature of this school's context: a racially isolated African American school, with a white male principal, that sits in the shadows of a major Chicago public housing project. Making sense of this case of high relational trust in a most unexpected place challenged us to reconsider our tacit assumptions about the social dynamics at work in disadvantaged African American school communities. Finally, the Thomas Elementary School (chapter 4) represents a complex "middle" case, both in terms of the basic structure of the school's operations and the underlying beliefs and values of its diverse participants. Much in the daily social life of this port-of-immigration school community was deeply engaging. Nonetheless, it remained a difficult place for leadership to articulate a unifying school vision and promote its collective advancement. This school case defies simple analysis. Our theory of relational trust did help, however, to illuminate some of the complex contradictions at work here.

Chapter 3

Ridgeway Elementary School: The Costs of Conflicted Leadership

R IDGEWAY Elementary School is located in the northeast section of Chicago. The neighboring community had been in transition for some time. Beginning in the 1950s, an influx of newcomers initially from Appalachia and the rural South and later from Central America and several Asian countries gradually changed the social landscape. By the late 1960s, the previously white middle-class neighborhood had become racially and ethnically diverse, and primarily low income. In the 1980s, the Ridgeway neighborhood began to gentrify, with the pace of this activity accelerating in the 1990s. The renovation of old apartment buildings and the construction of new single-family town houses began displacing large numbers of low-income tenants.

The Ridgeway neighborhood had been a site of intense community organizing for some time. An Alinsky-style community-based organization (CBO), founded in the 1960s, actively focused on housing and school reform issues throughout the 1980s. As Chicago's decentralization reform began in 1989, the CBO's efforts to improve local schools for poor children now interacted with the interests of newer, less well-organized but more affluent residents who also were seeking greater influence over their neighborhood school. Dissatisfied with Ridgeway Elementary School, many of these newer residents enrolled their children either in private schools or magnet public schools around the city.

A slate of candidates assembled by the community-based organization won a majority of the parent and community seats on the first Ridgeway School Council in 1990. Politically savvy, these newly elected LSC members sought to increase their skills and knowledge about school reform by attending workshops and weekend seminars offered by a variety of organizations around the city. These parents and community members would prove formidable advocates for reform at Ridgeway School. They were well prepared to take on any school professional who they believed did not care about their children.

As reform began, Ridgeway Elementary School enrolled 875 students in grades pre-K through 5. The school's population consisted primarily of working poor, unemployed, recent immigrants, or homeless families. The student body was racially mixed with about one-third black, one-third Hispanic, approximately 20 percent white (primarily from the Appalachian region), 12 percent Asian, and 2 percent Native American. The majority of students scored well below grade level on standardized tests. Reading scores were particularly discouraging, with less than 10 percent of Ridgeway students above grade level on the Illinois Goals Assessment Program and only 13 percent scoring above grade level on the nationally norm-referenced Iowa Tests of Basic Skills.

Examining Role Relations

The principal at Ridgeway, Dr. Lionel Newman, was a twenty-four-year veteran in the Chicago Public Schools (CPS) system. He began his career as a teacher in the CPS. Later, he became principal at another Chicago school, a post he held for twelve years before assuming the principalship at Ridgeway. Dr. Newman had earned an education doctorate from a local university, and for several years he had been an adjunct professor at a local college, teaching courses in educational supervision and evaluation. Recognized by the Chicago Board of Education as a knowledgeable administrator, Dr. Newman served on a new principals' task force for the CPS. On paper, he certainly appeared to have the professional credentials and experience to lead the Ridgeway School.

A Humanistic Philosophy of Leadership

Dr. Newman saw the students as his first priority. "I represent—that is, I hope I represent—the students. You know, they [parents] always ask for a child advocate. I think I represent the students. I [also] represent the staff to a great extent" (Newman, 2: 42).[1] In placing priority on students first and staff second, Dr. Newman articulated a philosophical commitment to putting students' interests ahead of all others.

Dr. Newman knew that he needed to establish trusting relationships with all members of his school community to advance its improvement efforts. He was articulate about what this meant to him. "Trust is built by contact, by consistency, by doing what you say you're going to do, by showing concern, by acting on solutions, [but] mostly by doing what you say you're going to do" (Newman, 2: 47). Throughout our interviews, Dr. Newman talked at length about the importance of positive social relations in the functioning of a good school, and felt strongly that developing trust was critical within his school community.

In an effort to be responsive to different groups, Dr. Newman adopted a conciliatory leadership style. He sought to build a bridge between teachers and the local school council. "It's not them against us. It's not 'you're the bad guys and we're the good guys.' There can be a partnership and there can be a sharing and also there is a balance" (Newman, 2: 44–45). Seeking to minimize conflict among fractious parties, Dr. Newman was willing to put aside his own views about what should happen at Ridgeway. "I'm not the kind of person that beats my head against the wall if I see there is no chance. [For example], I've always wanted another counselor in this school. Someone who could talk to kids. Someone who could work with kids. Not a paper pusher. And I pushed for that in the last SIP and budget. Well I could see, last year, it wasn't going anywhere [on the LSC], so I dropped it" (Newman, 2: 42). Dr. Newman was willing to discard his plans, even when he believed they were best for the school, in order to promote goodwill with the LSC. This conflict avoidance also carried over into his interactions with teachers.

Dr. Newman's View of Teachers

Although generally supportive of his staff, Dr. Newman acknowledged that many teachers at Ridgeway were not especially committed to school improvement and some simply were not up to the task. "You can't impact the classroom or improve reading scores drastically overnight. . . . [S]ome of the people in the school really know what they are doing, and they are for the kids, but not all of them" (Newman, 2: 44–45). Dr. Newman openly questioned the willingness of some on his staff to place the needs of students first.

> [M]any of the teachers are basically concerned with maintenance factors [for example, orderly hallways and playgrounds, adequate supplies, and building repairs]. That's their basic concern. For others, the level of commitment is different. Some of the people are really committed to the kids and to what's going on, and some people have a level of commitment that "this is basically a job." Some people think in terms of the job, some people think in terms of the kids. (Newman, 1: 49)

Even though Dr. Newman recognized serious problems with some Ridgeway teachers, he made no mention in interviews of "counseling out" weak teachers or exerting pressure on "reluctant reformers" to get on board. This orientation distinguished him from some other school-site leaders in Chicago, who were using their newfound authority under the decentralization reform to actively restructure their schools.[2] Instead, Dr. Newman articulated a low-key approach of "leading by example. Getting in the classroom and doing it" (Newman, 1: 50). Dr. Newman was reluctant to directly confront individual teachers. He preferred to work with small groups of his faculty rather than singling out specific individuals as particularly problematic. He felt that this strategy minimized the likelihood of personal conflict with his staff.

Dr. Newman's View of Parents

Dr. Newman viewed the parent population at Ridgeway as composed of two distinct groups. The larger, general parent population was poor, undereducated, and tended to defer to the judgments of school professionals about the education of their children. Dr. Newman maintained that with this group of parents,

> I have a pretty good relationship, a close relationship. Most of [these] parents, a goodly number of them, I don't even know how aware they are of the local school council and what they do. I think their basic interest is, "How is my kid doing? What's my kid doing? Is my kid safe, secure? Is something positive going on in the school? Is he learning something? Do teachers care about my kid? [Does the] principal care about my kid?" (Newman, 1: 48)

A second, smaller group of parents were actively aligned with the LSC parent and community representatives who were supported by the community-based organization. In stark contrast to the general parent population, Dr. Newman saw these parents as constantly challenging the professional staff. Newman found their challenges disconcerting and worried that their efforts did not always advance the best interests of children at the school.

> [T]hey shouldn't come in and say, "Well, I'm a parent, and you do what I want you to do in every situation." . . . And some parents feel that's what they can do now. I think that's a problem. Because what they want to do is very much [a] self-motivated, self-interested kind of thing which is really not in the best interest of the kids. (Newman, 2: 55)

Dr. Newman perceived that these LSC parents sometimes misused their authority, pushing for programs that he felt would not benefit the students.

> What is the intent, you know, what is the overall intent [of the program]? Is it really in the best interest of the kids, as opposed to the best interest of the people on the council? . . . Everybody has their pet project, and everybody has what they want to see happen, and sometimes you don't see the whole picture, you just see what you want to see. And I think that's something that everybody needs to learn. (Newman, 2: 31)

Even though he expressed strong reservations about LSC initiatives in our private interviews, we observed little behavior consistent with this in Dr. Newman's actual interactions with his council. Publicly, he rarely voiced disagreement. Rather, he generally sought to placate council members, assuring that he would try to address whatever concerns they raised and implement whatever new program initiatives they passed.

Indecisive Leadership: Teachers' Views of Dr. Newman

Dr. Newman's leadership style did not go unnoticed by his staff. As a first-grade teacher commented, "[E]very time they [the LSC] say 'Jump,' instead of standing his ground, he jumps. He is a nice person, he is as nice as he can be, but he needs to stand up and be a man" (Teacher 1, 1: 10–11). Another teacher, who was a faculty representative on the LSC, discussed Dr. Newman's failure to lead the school.

> Sometimes, I just say, "Hey, they're [the LSC] supposed to be advising, not telling us, not setting policy." And I think because he lets them do it, they get away with it, and a lot of times, [my colleagues] and I are just saying, "No, they can't do this. This is not their job." And we have to fight, because he'll let them run everything. If we didn't step in, he would give away the candy store. (Teacher 2, 1: 25)

A telling episode in this regard occurred around a faculty decision to end the practice of kindergarten graduation. The teachers argued that kindergarten should be regarded as the beginning of a child's school career rather than an ending. They also felt that these ceremonies required a great deal of work and that their energies could be better spent elsewhere. Dr. Newman distributed a letter to the parents informing them that the last day of kindergarten would be celebrated with an open house for parents and their children rather than a graduation ceremony. Soon after, a contingent of about twenty parents raised this issue at an LSC meeting. They argued that kindergarten graduation was a school tradition in which parents enjoyed seeing the children dressed up and receiving awards, and the LSC endorsed their position. Dr. Newman quickly withdrew his support for the teachers' position, saying that he wished he had appointed a committee to look into the issue. He then decided that the school would hold both the graduation and the open house. The parents were given the task of organizing the graduation, while the teachers were asked to put together the open house.

Some teachers also called Dr. Newman to task over his reluctance to address the problem of weak teachers at the school. A teacher representative on the LSC, for example, expressed frustration when Dr. Newman failed to act on this issue.

> [W]e wanted him in the classroom. The teacher representatives, the parent representatives, and community representatives felt that he was going about it the wrong way, and consistently told him. . . . We wanted him to get to these teachers that everybody knows are a problem and focus on trying to improve their teaching methods. But instead of doing that, he decided to make it very, very general. And it was a waste of time to a lot of people, and it eventually fizzled out. (Teacher 2, 1: 6)

With a number of teachers expressing concerns about Dr. Newman, one might have expected significant teacher opposition as the LSC began consideration of his four-year performance contract. This was not the case, however. Regardless of his shortcomings, many teachers sensed that Dr. Newman truly cared about them and the children. In addition, teachers feared that they might be even more vulnerable under a new principal, hand-picked by the council. Contributing to this view was the unusual process adopted by the Ridgeway Council in its principal contract review. Generally, across the CPS, councils first made a decision about retaining their current principal, and only initiated a search process if they failed to reappoint that person. Instead, the Ridgeway Council required Dr. Newman to reapply for the principalship along with other new candidates. This protocol, while not illegal, appeared disrespectful to the professional staff. As one teacher stated,

> Every [sitting] principal had to be evaluated, which was understandable. But to have a vote and say "maybe," I thought was a horrible thing. I thought either say "yes" or "no." Either he's going to be principal, or you don't want him. But, to say "maybe," and let him dangle there and say, "We'll interview you with other principals," . . . I thought

this was a real slap in the face. I went to him, personally, and I told him how I felt about this. I wrote up a petition. I went around with it, and everybody in the school signed it, saying that they wanted his contract renewed, that he was a good principal, that he cared about the children. (Teacher 3, 1: 6)

Many teachers attended the LSC meetings at which Dr. Newman's evaluation was discussed. One teacher, who spoke during the public participation portion of these meetings, voiced strong support for Dr. Newman. She spoke of Ridgeway as a "professional environment" and described Dr. Newman as "a very visible principal" who is "compassionate" and "caring." She finished by saying that it would be "a big loss to the community if Dr. Newman does not remain at Ridgeway." Two months later, on the night of the LSC's official vote on the principal's contract, more than thirty-five teachers attended to show support for Dr. Newman. With a noticeable lack of enthusiasm, the LSC voted to renew his contract.

An Unprincipled Principal: LSC Parents' Views of Dr. Newman

LSC members clearly understood that they had both formal power over Dr. Newman in terms of his contract renewal, and informal power through their ability to mobilize other parents and community members.

> He understands that if something goes terribly wrong with that school, we could probably mobilize more parents than he would ever want to see inside of the school. So . . . he will cater to whatever it is that myself or a couple of us will present, only because we are part of the power structure. I mean we obviously are, . . . so, on one hand it's good, because then you can walk in at any time and say, "Well let's do this, this, this, and this," and if it is within his purview to be able to do that, he can do that. On the other hand, he rarely follows through on much of what we think he has agreed to do. (LSC Member 1, 1: 8)

This last comment is especially telling. The parent leaders on the Ridgeway LSC were elected officials. They expected Dr. Newman to implement what had been agreed to in their meetings. Their trust in him eroded as it gradually became clear that this was often not the case.

Observation notes from LSC meetings revealed constant pressure on Dr. Newman regarding LSC concerns. During a series of meetings focused on developing a schoolwide discipline policy, for example, Dr. Newman supported the Ridgeway faculty. Teachers felt that a uniform policy was already in place and rejected LSC members' claims that discipline varied from class to class and student to student. Undaunted, several LSC members continued to call for a new policy that would standardize punishments for misbehavior. Council members organized disgruntled parents to attend the next LSC meeting, where they again placed the discipline policy on the agenda for further discussion. After numerous parents presented a litany of specific complaints, Dr. Newman withdrew his earlier support for the faculty's position and conceded that a more standard policy indeed was necessary.

Dr. Newman's conciliatory response to pressure fostered a perception of him by both LSC parents and teachers as someone who was weak and "did not stand up for principles." As one LSC member said, "He always takes the path of least resistance. You may want something different than I want, so he will placate you and he will placate me. . . . I mean, he is just, I just find him kind of wishy-washy and really not a very strong leader" (LSC Member 1, 1: 8).

In addition, parent leaders, like some of the teachers, also raised questions about Dr. Newman's failure to replace weak teachers and provide instructional leadership for the faculty.

> It's like, "Let's make it a big, happy family here." An axe never fell on anyone's head. The teacher that's lousy, nothing was probably ever done to say, "You're going to have to improve or you're out of here." He didn't get rid of anyone. . . . In March, [a] parent called me and said, "My kid hasn't gotten homework all year." Well, you want to know why we have poor scores, well, you know, no one knows how to sit down and study here. No one is getting any homework. No skills are getting taught here. There are no expectations. (Parent 2, 1: 26)

The parents on the LSC saw Dr. Newman's tolerance of weak and incompetent teachers as evidence of a pact among school professionals to secure their jobs, and in so doing, maintain the dysfunctional status quo for children. One parent noted,

> The teachers have been there a long time, most of them, a long time. They came to me. . . . [T]hey said, "We like this school. We have paper and pencils and books and workbooks. I've been in a school where we didn't even have a pencil or a piece of paper. He really gives us this stuff and he's out on the playground before school and after school and recess and lunch." Gee, anyone should be able to provide paper and pencils and books to students. That should just be a basic for every school. (Parent 2, 1: 27)

In short, parents came to understand that while Dr. Newman said his first priority was the children, more often than not he seemed to act as if adult needs came first. Parent leaders expected and wanted more from their school leader.

Questioning the Intentions of Colleagues: Teachers' Views of Teachers

The faculty at Ridgeway held mixed views about the competence and commitment of their colleagues. Their comments echoed themes raised in the interviews with Dr. Newman. Some teachers appeared deeply committed to educating the children of the Ridgeway school community. A fourth-grade math teacher, for example, described her reasons for teaching at Ridgeway as "Helping children learn. That is the profession. That is what it is all about" (Teacher 4, 1: 8). Others, however, characterized their motivations in less altruistic terms. For example, when asked why she chose teaching as a career, another teacher commented,

> I decided to major in elementary education because of my aunt. . . . She told me, "When you are working with somebody, you always have somebody looking over your shoulder, but when you are in your own classroom, you can close the door and have peace and quiet and you are the boss." So this is what I did. (Teacher 1, 1: 13)

According to one of the faculty representatives on the LSC, Ridgeway was "a school that's very complacent," where many colleagues made little effort to improve their teaching (Teacher 2, 1: 14). Moreover, she perceived that at base, some teachers lacked personal regard for the children they were suppose to educate.

> I don't think a lot of our teachers have compassion for the children . . . and there are a lot of reasons, because you get tired after a while of administration screwing you around, wondering every year if you're going to go on strike. I don't think a lot of our people have had experiences [like our school families], and so therefore they can't even comprehend where these children are coming from. . . . We're getting a lot of homeless children. Now, these teachers will tell me that it's upsetting for them to get a homeless child because the child is only here a week, two weeks, and it's true. But where is the mind of these children in homeless shelters? They don't know where they're going to be staying tonight. How can you be concerned with math when you haven't had any food in your stomach, when your clothes smell because you've been living in an abandoned building? This is where I want the teachers to have compassion. (Teacher 2, 1: 19)

Several other teachers at Ridgeway raised similar concerns about the competence and commitment of their colleagues. For example, a first-grade reading teacher commented that many teachers at Ridgeway did not trust that their colleagues were really doing their job in the classroom.

> When you get kids from the lower grades and if they don't know everything that they should know, all the skills and everything, that means you are going to have to work double hard. So, you know, each level wants to go down into the lower level and make sure that they are teaching more, and teaching what they should be teaching. Because it puts so much pressure on you. . . . We have to check on these people, see what they are doing. (Teacher 5, 1: 9)

Another teacher, who managed the computer lab, raised questions about her colleagues' willingness to change. Although she had been teaching for fourteen years, she constantly sought to improve her teaching by learning new instructional techniques. As the second teacher representative on the LSC, she had embraced the council's push for whole language instruction and encouraged her colleagues in that direction as well. She arranged for teachers to attend a workshop on this topic and targeted in particular four teachers who especially needed help. Although at first they agreed to participate with her, all four canceled at the last minute. Such behavior led her to question these teachers' motives.

> There are teachers here that need to take a good look at their teaching. What you did twenty-five years ago does not work, and it won't work because I haven't seen scores jumping up. I haven't seen a lot of problems changing. I cannot understand somebody who wouldn't want to learn something new. (Teacher 6, 1: 9–10)

Unfortunately, she also understood that these teachers perceived little pressure from their principal to change. As she casually observed, "nobody here is afraid of the principal"—the implication being that some of them should indeed be (Teacher 6, 1: 9).

Failure to Care About Us and Our Children: Parents' Views of Teachers

Parents on the Ridgeway LSC felt that the faculty did not respect them or their children. One LSC parent described the staff's attitude toward students as disrespectful and pejorative. "I've heard one teacher's aide say, 'They're just animals. It's just a jungle. . . . You just can't do anything with them. They're wild'" (Parent 2, 1: 31). In response to this perceived lack of sensitivity among the faculty, the LSC pushed for implementation of a Respect Program that called for explicit standards regarding teacher behavior with parents and students. Not surprisingly, this program did little to alleviate the deep-seated distrust between parent leaders and teachers: teachers perceived the LSC's actions in pushing for the program as an attack on their professional competence and clear evidence of the LSC's disrespect for them. While the explicit goal was to establish a more supportive student-centered learning climate, many teachers and parents became more deeply entrenched in a reciprocal disdain.

LSC parents and community representatives believed that the job of improving instruction fell to them, since they observed little initiative from the school staff in this regard. An LSC parent talked about how the council had developed a strategy for evaluating teachers at Ridgeway.[3]

> You have to go in the classroom and investigate. I hate to say investigate, but you just have to know what's going on. . . . I'm not a teacher. I'm not trained in any of that to figure out exactly if this looks like an interesting classroom or not. . . . But I then turned to these people and said, "Well, we need to kind of pick a grade level and go into those classrooms on a regular basis. Get to know the teachers, and just meet and give your opinion about what's going on." (Parent 2, 1: 12)

During its first two years, the LSC devoted several of its meetings to concerns about instruction. They invited teachers at every grade level to report at LSC meetings on their curricula and classroom techniques. Council members questioned teachers about the amount of time students spent in reading groups per day, the types of questions teachers asked of students, the activities of these reading groups, and what the remainder of the class was doing while the teacher was occupied with each group. Teachers appeared visibly upset with these "inquisitions." The LSC, however, remained steadfast in its commitment to scrutinize their practices and to hold them accountable.

From the teachers' perspective, parents were intruding into their most sacred professional domain—what they do in their own classrooms—and this struck a very sensitive chord. The teachers at Ridgeway, like most other teachers, expected considerable professional discretion over the conduct of their work. Having parents—especially poor parents—be so vocal and critical was an egregious breach of the expectations that they held for their role relation with parents. One of the community representatives on the LSC recognized these teacher concerns.

> I think most teachers tend to look at me and one or two of the other council members thinking that . . . we think we know more than they

do. We don't work in a classroom five days a week for six hours a day or whatever it is, and how dare we think that we might know more. When we got elected, one of the first rumors that started was that we were going to fire everyone. (LSC Member 1, 1: 9)

For teachers to feel vulnerable in the uncertain days following the introduction of Chicago's radical decentralization reform was not unreasonable. Local school councils now held some unknown amount of power over them, and at Ridgeway at least, the LSC seemed intent on using it.

A subsequent article in a local newspaper acted as a lightning rod for this distrust. The article quoted the LSC chair as saying that the problems at Ridgeway stemmed from teachers who "wallowed in incompetence, did not teach, and held low expectations for their students." In response, the faculty composed a letter of protest that was read at the next LSC meeting. The LSC chair replied that she was misquoted and that the reporter had taken her comments out of context from a casual conversation that she believed was off the record. She did not, however, apologize for her views about the Ridgeway faculty. Instead, she reiterated that some teachers at Ridgeway were indeed incompetent and held low expectations for their students.

Looking for Professional Respect:
Teachers' Views of Parents

Many Ridgeway teachers took some issue with the larger parent population at the school. Teachers criticized parents for their lack of interest in education, family drug dependency, and unemployment. They complained that much in their students' home situations impeded learning, and they took a generally dim view of the quality of parenting that was occurring. One first grade teacher noted that "I really don't have any problems with the parents. I don't look down on anybody. I don't say, 'Well you are only an aide.' But yes, I am saying some people around here do that to parents all the time" (Teacher 1, 1: 7).

Like most teachers, the Ridgeway faculty expected parents to instill in their children the value of education and respect for their teachers. As one teacher commented,

When I was in school, it was the orientation of most of the parents in my neighborhood, if the teacher told you to do something, you did it because the teacher would never tell you anything wrong to do. The teacher was right. The teacher is to be respected. You don't talk back to the teacher. This type of thing. (Teacher 1, 1: 8)

Teachers also expected parents to support school efforts at home.

> I think parents should be involved and teachers should be involved. . . .
> Everybody needs to work together so that this child can succeed. You
> can't expect to send your child to school for five or six hours, and then
> you have them for nineteen hours, and you don't even talk to your
> child. (Teacher 1, 1: 11)

Faculty members at Ridgeway often blamed parents when their
expectations for support went unmet.

> I called a parent in this morning for a conference about her little girl
> and another little girl writing notes [that said] "Dear Mrs. Green, I hate
> you." And the parent and I talked. . . . You know, I have to call things
> like that to the attention of the parent, and not that I feel as though it is
> my place to suggest to her how to raise her child. That is her decision.
> But . . . the child does not show respect for the parent. So I mean, how
> is she going to respect me? (Teacher 5, 1: 10)

Another teacher lamented, "Parents are not into it, because they don't
talk to their children. We can only do so much. . . . There has to
be some help from the home. Kids have to read at home instead of
watching television. There has to be some interest" (Teacher 4, 1: 9).

While many faculty members expressed similar concerns about
parents at the school, they reserved their deepest outrage for the parent and community representatives on the LSC. A faculty representative on Ridgeway's council shared the following perceptions.

> I think the tone of lack of respect comes from the council, I really be-
> lieve that. . . . I'm telling them they're always talking about respect for
> parents and children but never respect for staff. We have to fight
> over this every single time there's something written down. The teach-
> ers met with them yesterday regarding discipline policy. I had to say
> the same thing again. I said, "But you have four pages of a document
> here, and you're saying that the teachers should apologize to the par-
> ents, the teachers should do this, and never once do you have it written
> down that they should get respect. How come we have to keep remind-
> ing you of that?" (Teacher 2, 1: 9)

This same teacher went on to complain that

> Every time they put out a piece of paper, it's like propaganda. They
> always portray teachers in a negative viewpoint, and that gets the
> teachers all riled up again. I told them yesterday, "Words have power.
> It's how you say things. So here you have this cartoon of a teacher

saying, 'I don't care!' like we all do that. Why would you print that?" (Teacher 2, 1: 28)

Many teachers at Ridgeway saw LSC parents as engaged in a grab for personal power rather than acting to advance the best interests of the entire school. The faculty representative on the LSC went on to explain,

> The problem is that everyone has their own agenda. One time I almost quit the council because I honestly sat there and saw that not one person really cared about the children. It was their own agenda. Inclusion came about because we had one parent with a special ed student. That's her total agenda, so now that's pushed through. Then we had the discipline issue come up because of one father, who's not on the council, but he's in with the group, the council slate, and so he's pushing all of this. Everybody has their own agenda. (Teacher 2, 1: 15)

Many teachers at Ridgeway felt that LSC parents did not respect their professional expertise. A fourth-grade math teacher commented on the LSC's questioning of another teacher's instructional methods.

> The council called the teacher into a closed meeting. . . . They didn't like the way he was teaching. . . . And from what I understand, they criticized such things as he was teaching from different grade level spelling books. Now his reasoning for that was that they couldn't all read on the same level. I think that is wonderful. I think that is a lot more work for the teacher than it is anything else. But if he is willing to do it, I think it is great. But they didn't like it. (Teacher 4, 1: 6–7)

Given this context, Ridgeway teachers were quick to reject any guidance offered by the LSC. As one primary teacher noted,

> They talk a big education thing, but really have no background. They think they have, and they question everything, everything that the teachers do, and everything that the teachers propose. Well, it's nice to ask questions, but there are different kinds of questions. It's how you say or ask the question that determines what the inferences are. I haven't heard them say one good thing about anything that's been proposed. It's never enough. . . . It sounds like they've heard this propaganda and they're repeating it. (Teacher 3, 1: 9)

Unmet Obligations and Pervasive Distrust

We have argued that the social exchanges of schooling are organized around distinct sets of role relations. Each participant in a role relation maintains an understanding of his or her obligations and holds some expectations about the role obligations of the other. Building and sustaining trust requires that the expectations that participants hold for others must subsequently be validated in the discernment of intentions that they make about the behavior of others. Relational trust atrophies when individuals perceive that others are not acting in ways that are consistent with their understanding of the other's role obligations. Moreover, the fulfillment of obligations involves not only doing the right thing, but also doing it for what are perceived to be the right reasons and in ways that are viewed as personally respectful.

It would have been extremely difficult for relational trust to develop at Ridgeway, given the pervasive concerns about respect and integrity across the school community. Parent leaders appeared to know better and ignored what even the most moderate teachers might have had to say. Correspondingly, teachers failed to acknowledge that the parent leaders had a right under the 1988 reform law to voice and act on school improvement issues. In this regard, parent leaders felt disrespected by school staff in their roles as elected officials. Although the principal appeared to listen to everyone's concerns, he rarely followed through on them. Similarly, while at least some teacher leaders acknowledged in private the legitimacy of many of the concerns raised by community activists, they too failed to act publicly on them. At base here was a crisis of professional integrity as well.

LSC leaders at Ridgeway sought to legislate a broad array of curricular and instructional changes without teacher consultation. The teachers, in response, viewed these LSC actions as an intrusion into their professional role responsibilities. While some teachers privately acknowledged the legitimacy of LSC concerns about the poor quality of instruction and unprofessional conduct in some classrooms, no one acted on this. Instead, teachers criticized LSC members for overstepping their roles and making judgments in a domain about which they lacked adequate knowledge and training.

Teachers, for their part, were defensive about the perceived attacks on their professional competence, even if in private they too questioned the competence and commitment of some of their own colleagues. The stronger teachers at Ridgeway limited their interactions with other staff whom they regarded as behaving unprofessionally toward their students. One teacher, for example, reported that a colleague disciplined misbehaving students by having them stand in the wastebasket. The message conveyed here—"you are trash"—is morally reprehensible. One might expect that such teacher behavior would at a minimum be officially reprimanded. Yet at Ridgeway, this classroom practice was allowed to persist. Not surprisingly, a few teachers confided to us that they hoped their students would not be placed in certain other teachers' classrooms in the next academic year. Given this weak collegial regard, also not surprising is that limited efforts around instructional improvement emerged at this school during the first four years of reform. Absent a base of collegial trust, a few individual teachers might attempt some innovations in their own classrooms, but larger initiatives that demanded coordinated teacher effort would remain frustrated. Ironically, then, LSC leaders were correct in their judgments that catalyzing improvements at Ridgeway fell largely to them.

The level of distrust at Ridgeway was so pervasive that even actions that most laypeople would see as reasonable were viewed as suspect. For example, several of the parents on the LSC advocated developing a multicultural reading and writing curriculum. Given that Ridgeway served a highly diverse population, selecting curricular materials that were sensitive in this regard seems imminently sensible. The response from the teachers to the LSC on this issue, however, was almost reactionary. Rather than focusing on what might actually be good for students in this proposal, all that teachers could see was yet another challenge to their expertise. A genuine discourse about the real issues was never enjoined.

The conflict at Ridgeway was exacerbated by the principal's inability to cope with the adversarial climate in the school community and to lead it in a more constructive direction. Dr. Newman had expressed a clear vision for Ridgeway School: how it should run, how people should relate to one another, and the type of professional community necessary to mount a major school improvement effort. In practice, though, he failed to enact the principles he espoused. The school principal created a leadership vacuum by waffling between the competing parties of parents and teachers. His position on any issue typically depended on whom he talked to last. While his words sounded good, teachers and parents eventually came to realize that he could not be counted on to follow through on his promises. As soon as the context changed, he was likely to change too.

Teachers voiced frequent complaints about Dr. Newman, remarking that he capitulated to the LSC on every issue, even when their actions compromised standards of good professional practice. As a result, in the teachers' minds, Dr. Newman lacked integrity. Moreover, given the politically tense circumstances at Ridgeway and general uncertainty about the real power possessed by the LSC during the early years of the Chicago reform, teachers felt vulnerable. They did not trust the principal to stand up for them and remained unsure about where he stood, since he appeared ready to compromise most any principle to avoid conflict.

LSC parents distrusted Dr. Newman for many of the same reasons. Although he generally agreed with their priorities, the principal tended to either disregard their suggestions or pursue them in a manner that was unlikely to promote real change. This was quite noticeable in Dr. Newman's approach to dealing with weak staff. Rather than a serious remediation program followed by aggressive efforts to remove non-improving staff, his approach was a low-key "teach by example." He frequently would visit classrooms to demonstrate model lessons, hoping that teachers would adopt his techniques. When no changes occurred, however, he dropped the initiative. No one could make sense of such leadership behavior. Dr. Newman's seeming willingness to tolerate both incompetence and a lack of commitment within the faculty undermined his relational trust with parents, community leaders, and his own teachers.

Although Dr. Newman was "a nice man" who demonstrated respect and personal regard toward teachers and LSC members, ultimately he failed to place the needs of his students above all other concerns. While extending regard toward other adults is central to developing and sustaining relational trust, alone it is not sufficient. Dr. Newman undoubtedly was caring in his encounters with staff and parents. This personal regard surely would have deepened the quality of social exchanges in the school had the other elements of relational trust also been in place. But this was not the case. Dr. Newman's lack of integrity—saying one thing but doing another—created distrust of his leadership. By failing to fulfill others' perceptions of his role obligations, Dr. Newman heightened their feelings of vulnerability. For teachers, his lack of follow-through raised anxieties about what the LSC might try to do next and how that might affect them. For parents, although they had substantial governance authority and sought aggressively to use it, Newman's behavior only reinforced their long-standing sense of powerlessness to affect the adverse conditions influencing their children's lives.

The conflict at Ridgeway was grounded in a pervasive distrust of the intentions of others. This distrust constrained all parties from looking beyond narrow self-concerns to the broader interests of children. Individual affronts were perceived first and then used to justify personal reactions. Taken as a whole, role expectations among adults in this school community were wildly misaligned. Reforming such a context makes complex demands on school leadership. Leaders need to articulate and enliven principles that privilege the best interests of children. Simultaneously, they must also reach out emphatically to others in order to build a following around this work. Not every view in the school community can or should be supported. Some surely will disagree with particular steps taken and may choose to leave instead. Still others might be encouraged to do so.[4] Despite Dr. Newman's strengths, which were considerable, such transformative leadership appeared beyond his grasp.

= Chapter 4 =

Thomas Elementary School: Cultural Diversity as an Obstacle to Trust

THOMAS Elementary School is located in a neighborhood that has been a port of entry for Mexican immigrants for the past thirty years. Beginning in the 1980s, immigrants came increasingly from more rural and impoverished areas of Mexico. Most of these families spoke only Spanish and had little formal education. Typically, the adults immediately looked for work, and once they succeeded in obtaining jobs with steady incomes, they left the neighborhood for areas with better housing and services. As a result, Thomas Elementary School had one of the highest student mobility rates in the city, with new immigrants continually replacing more assimilated and English-proficient students.

The staff at Thomas faced a difficult task in seeking to forge a meaningful partnership between school and home. Communication could be problematic, since many parents were not English proficient, and some lacked reading and writing skills even in their native tongue. In response, the faculty and administration worked hard to create a friendly and supportive atmosphere at the school. Parents were encouraged to visit classrooms and to drop in on the principal at any time. A Parent Center was established to expand home-school ties by involving parents as classroom aides and in community outreach efforts.

Prior to the 1988 Chicago School Reform Act, teachers were assigned to schools according to seniority rights negotiated in collective bargaining agreements. The Central Office paid only modest attention to the special needs of particular communities. As the enrollment of Mexican immigrants grew at Thomas, a bilingual program supported by federal funds was added. In accordance with federal guidelines, this program had its own budget, hired its own teachers, and selected its students based on their proficiency in English. Over time, two essentially separate schools emerged at Thomas with different levels of fiscal support, philosophical orientations, curricula, and staff. When a new principal was hired at the onset of Chicago's decentralization reform, his first goal was to build a more cohesive school environment. The reform's focus on making schools more responsive to the needs of the community, coupled with the demographics of the neighborhood, led to a seemingly inevitable conclusion: Thomas should be a fully bilingual school.

Examining Role Relations

Principal Gonzalez: Child Psychologist

Raul Gonzalez left a position in the Central Office in 1988 to take his first principalship at Thomas Elementary School. Dr. Gonzalez is South American, not Mexican. He came from an upper-class family and earned a Ph.D. in child psychology before immigrating to the United States. He brought to Thomas a child-centered vision of schooling. He talked about how district policies prior to reform often worked against the best interests of children. His response in such situations focused on how best to serve students. "As I said, in many cases, I don't break the law. I interpret the law. The spirit of the law. I interpret it to the benefit of the children" (Gonzalez, 1: 15).

Dr. Gonzalez believes that the school staff has an active responsibility to work with parents to create a consistent, supportive environment for their children's development. He spoke passionately about the importance of strengthening ties between home and school.

> I would say that Chicago School Reform provides the opportunity for society to define a specific school that fits some kind of common values—a place that will be called the neighborhood school in which the values of the home and school are going to be similar. It is amazing to me how much discontinuity exists between the school values and the home values. Especially in the inner-city schools, you definitely find that there is a tremendous gap. For me, that is one of the basic reasons for school failure, the tremendous gap that exists between the school and parents. (Gonzalez, 1: 3)

Dr. Gonzalez saw bridging this gap as central to his role as principal. He understood personally the vulnerability experienced by immigrant parents in his school community. Dr. Gonzalez worked tirelessly as an advocate for parents, constantly pursuing ways to enable their engagement with their children's school. He also knew that most of these parents had neither the academic background nor the political skills to be expert members of a local school council. Many might even feel uncomfortable with the responsibility of voting for someone else to take on this role. One of Dr. Gonzalez's first initiatives as principal was to encourage parent participation in the first LSC elections in 1989.[1] He went door to door throughout the neighborhood introducing himself and talking with parents and community members about the upcoming elections and the importance of their participation.

At his first meeting with the full faculty of Thomas, Dr. Gonzalez articulated a vision for the school as "becoming fully bilingual." He argued that if the school was to work for the children in this community, it had to connect better to parents and their culture. His arguments were forceful, his analysis compelling.

Advancing this goal of a truly bilingual school, however, would prove more difficult than Dr. Gonzalez initially imagined. He quickly learned that his announced plans had provoked considerable upset among the faculty. "I have six teachers that may be very much overreacting in terms of my being a bilingual principal who is going to change this to a bilingual school. And I say, 'Sure, if the community needs a bilingual school, I'm going to [create a] bilingual school.' And that created a lot of anxiety" (Gonzalez, 1: 18). The faculty at the school was predominately monolingual English. These teachers had rights, assured through collective bargaining, which, they believed, entitled them to maintain their positions at the school.

Advancing his bilingual objective for Thomas also conflicted with a second priority: strengthening literacy instruction. Specifically, Dr. Gonzalez felt that the school's curriculum needed a more *whole language* focus. (Whole language instruction combines reading and writing throughout the curriculum and emphasizes students' acquisition of language skills through rich literary experience. Whole language was widely viewed as a key instructional reform initiative in the early 1990s in Chicago.) Most of Thomas's whole language teachers, however, were monolingual. If Dr. Gonzalez actively pursued the idea of creating a totally bilingual school, he might lose some of his strongest teachers and thereby diminish the school's capacity to advance his primary instructional improvement initiative. This created a genuine dilemma. Dr. Gonzalez strongly believed that whole language was a good fit for Thomas's uneducated immigrant population: it offered students a natural exposure to English reading and writing, and it provided a more child-centered atmosphere for young students whose language skills were just beginning to form. How could he advance both whole language instruction and his bilingual school priority at the same time?

Nurturing Teacher Leadership: Dr. Gonzalez's Views of the Faculty

Just prior to Dr. Gonzalez's appointment as principal, Thomas had been designated as a Project CANAL (Creating a New Approach to Learning) school. This program, supported by federal funds, was designed to develop faculty leadership and promote shared governance among professional staff. Project CANAL required a Core Planning Team, composed of faculty at each school, to develop and direct its efforts. This planning team was similar to the Professional Personnel Advisory Committee (PPAC) subsequently written into the 1988 Chicago School Reform Act. The PPAC advised the LSC on curriculum and instruction matters. The CANAL Core Planning Team had decision-making authority over use of CANAL program resources at the school. Faculty membership on these two committees overlapped at Thomas, with many of the same teachers involved in both.

Dr. Gonzalez supported the shared governance philosophy undergirding CANAL and the PPAC. He encouraged teachers to get involved in both groups. Only a modest portion of the teachers, however, actually responded to these invitations. Dr. Gonzalez worried that these "overcommitted" individuals were "taking on too much" responsibility; he wanted more faculty to get involved (Gonzalez, 1: 14).

Dr. Gonzalez viewed his less active teachers as not fulfilling their professional obligations. "Although they have been given opportunities, they don't want to take them. They are seen around the school as individuals who are not committed. They don't want to do the work. They don't want to come. They don't want to be cooperative" (Gonzalez, 1: 14).

Dr. Gonzalez strategized about how he might draw these "noncommitted teachers into a more collective vision of the school" (Gonzalez, 1: 14). He created common planning time so that they could work together on a regular basis with their more active colleagues.

> So what I will do, eventually, is restructure the schedule, trying to give the teachers the opportunity to have at least one prep period a week together, grade level teachers together. And I'm still trying to figure out how I can give them a block [of larger time to work together]. If I can accomplish that, then I can start demanding from my teachers, planning production. . . . These people were given the responsibility to be team

players when they don't know how to be team players. So it has to be very difficult for them. (Gonzalez, 1: 18)

Dr. Gonzalez believed that by providing time for teachers to work together and making available professional development resources, he could both foster individual teacher learning and promote greater collective ownership around his vision for the school community.

Dr. Gonzalez used a variety of positive reinforcements to signal his support for the whole language and bilingual initiatives. He set aside resources to support teacher training in these areas. He provided release time for teachers and showered attention on those who pursued these efforts. He also withheld personal support from teachers whose classroom practice was weak and who resisted change, arguing that "In order to accomplish the goals of an institution, you must have all the pieces working together. But [teachers who are] not even meeting the minimum standards . . . [still want you to say] 'Oh, you're doing a wonderful job!' and I just don't believe in doing this" (Gonzalez, 1: 31).

Although Dr. Gonzalez spoke extensively with us about his concerns over weak and resistant teachers at Thomas, he, like Dr. Newman at Ridgeway, sent few direct messages to these teachers that they must improve. He believed that it was too early in the change process to take an aggressive stance. He acknowledged, however, some uncertainty about his strategy of emphasizing rewards for participation but providing no obvious consequences for those who refused to do so. "I may have to become a little more flexible in living with their reality and supporting them somehow. A last resort would be to say, 'I'm sorry but you have to leave.' At that point [I would] not be afraid to say it. If there is anything that I cannot stand, it is mediocrity" (Gonzalez, 1: 32). While he said the words, one could also sense his reluctance to pursue such a tough stance.

Promoting Community Growth: Dr. Gonzalez's Approach to Parents

Dr. Gonzalez wanted parents to take a larger part in their children's schooling. He believed that schools traditionally had consigned parents to a relatively meaningless role.

Parents were used. The only collaborative role that they had was bringing cakes and coffee to the school. Cooking lunch, basically. . . . That was the only partnership that we had. So definitely this has to be, in terms of restructuring, rethinking the schools, reforming the schools . . .

a group partnership, an equal beginning. You need everybody. (Gonzalez, 1: 3)

Dr. Gonzalez sought to use Chicago's decentralization reform as an opportunity to expand parental participation, including an active role for parents in shaping the school's vision and values.

Dr. Gonzalez's advocacy for parents included his taking personal responsibility for leading them through the intricacies of Chicago's school reform. "Let's rethink [this]. Everybody has the right to begin at the same line, as equal. Parents, students, teachers, unions. [But] who is going to take the lead?" (Gonzalez, 1: 3). His answer was direct. Assuring a meaningful voice for parents and local community members in school reform was his role. Dr. Gonzalez was a soft-spoken man, not taken to strident declarations. Yet on this point he was adamant: the Thomas community should be able to articulate its distinctive needs and see that they were addressed.

Dr. Gonzalez also recognized the supportive function that parent outreach could play in his efforts to transform the Thomas School. "The thing that actually brought them together and kept them together is that they have faith, and they have trust . . . in the principal. Parents have a lot of trust in me. We have some disagreements. Not everything is perfect, but I do perceive that there is a lot of trust between parents and myself" (Gonzalez, 1: 17). Regardless of whatever specific issues might arise, parents saw Dr. Gonzalez as consistently acting in the best interests of their children. They came to trust him, even though they may not have understood or necessarily agreed with every decision he made.

Playing Favorites: Teachers' Views of Dr. Gonzalez

Many teachers at Thomas recognized and appreciated Dr. Gonzalez's efforts to afford them an expanded role in school governance. A teacher who actively participated in the CANAL Core Planning Team and PPAC acknowledged,

> Well, I take a great deal of pride in Thomas. I really do. Because I think we've done very well with some of the changes. I guess I have to compliment Dr. Gonzalez as well, because certainly I think a lot of things are not happening in other schools . . . because administrators feel much too threatened in their positions and really won't allow teachers and parents and students to take on some of the roles that were outlined for them in reform. (Teacher 1, 1: 11–12)

Despite their appreciation, teachers still criticized Dr. Gonzalez for what they perceived as his "rewarding favorites." Teachers who felt left out expressed dissatisfaction for his not providing more personal attention and resources for their classrooms. These teachers described the group committed to school reform as "an elite group who receives all the benefits" (Teacher 2, 1: 6–7). A first-grade bilingual teacher talked of her reaction.

> If I . . . only single out five [teachers] all the time and these are my favorites . . . the other [teachers] will become affected emotionally. Not that I am saying that I am so sensitive and I am going to feel bad. But you can see that it undermines the other ones. (Teacher 2, 1: 6–7)

Interestingly, even some of the teachers in Dr. Gonzalez's "elite" group felt uneasy about the rewards he extended to them. One fifth-grade teacher commented,

> I think there's an attitude from the administration, even statements that are made that I feel uncomfortable witnessing. For example, myself, I have gone to two conferences this year on whole language [that] nobody else was invited to go to. He just decided, "You're going to go." For no reason other than that he knows that I'm trying to do [whole language in my classroom] and that I probably would benefit from it. But . . . it could have been more fair as to who would go. (Teacher 3, 1: 69–70)

This favoritism appeared reserved for teachers who shared Dr. Gonzalez's vision for the school. Teachers who used whole language instruction (or who were open to learning it) were one set of recipients. Teachers active in local school governance and some bilingual teachers also were part of the elite group.

While whole language instruction, bilingualism, and shared governance activities clearly were the principal's priorities, teachers who did not participate in any of these initiatives remained uncertain about where they stood. A whole language monolingual teacher commented, "Right now, not everyone here buys into whole language, and I don't think that they ever totally will. Nonetheless, I don't think Dr. Gonzalez is ever going to say to us, 'This is a whole language school'" (Teacher 4, 1: 7). Much the same could be said about Dr. Gonzalez's support for making Thomas a truly bilingual school. When his first speech on this topic precipitated some negative faculty reactions, Dr. Gonzalez backed away from actively pushing for this change. Absent a clear and consistently articulated message about the direction for the school, however, many teachers fell into a confused state of limbo. They recognized that their efforts were not necessarily consistent with their principal's views, but was this truly a problem? Absent overt pressure to change, Dr. Gonzalez appeared to be signaling that teachers' personal priorities would be accorded deference, as they had been under prior school leadership. This perception extended to teachers' lack of involvement in various school governance committees. They had not been involved in school governance before; moreover, the union contract did not require such participation as a term of employment. Why should they be afforded less esteem if they chose to just follow the old rules?

Another point of contention for some teachers at Thomas revolved around Dr. Gonzalez's approach to disciplining students. One teacher claimed that a student had been suspended for chronic tardiness while nothing happened to another student who swore at a teacher and threw things in her class. Other teachers lamented that students did not fear being sent to the principal's office. They saw their principal often joking with students rather than acting as a stern disciplinarian. These teachers felt that Dr. Gonzalez's child-centered approach was too lenient and ultimately undermined their authority. In addition, they complained that he was often not in the office and immediately available to discipline students. They worried that children would come to view being sent to the principal as just a good opportunity to skip class.

Student conduct and discipline was another area in which Dr. Gonzalez maintained a strong reform agenda—in this case, moving Thomas toward a more personalistic environment where adults knew students well and understood better the family and community conditions that affected their students' lives. Yet here too Dr. Gonzalez's expectations were not clearly communicated to his staff. Dr. Gonzalez was attempting to establish new norms governing adult-student relations at Thomas School. Teachers, however, now felt unsure about what actions they should take and how their behavior—as well as that of their students—would ultimately be judged. This added just a bit more to teachers' overall sense of vulnerability about their work.

A Respectful and Caring Leader: Parents' Views of Dr. Gonzalez

Day in and day out, parents at Thomas witnessed Dr. Gonzalez's genuine regard for their children. He played soccer with them on the playground. He knew them all by name. He was a constant presence out in the neighborhood, demonstrating his interest and concern for youth activities in the community. One parent commented that "if every principal was as for the children and for the school as he is, there would be no problems, city-wide" (Parent 1, 1: 22–23).

Parents also talked about how Dr. Gonzalez listened to them and valued their input. One parent, who first worked at Thomas as a teacher's aide before taking a seat on the LSC, described the principal's interactions with parents.

> He is a person who respects the opinions of others. And he is good with this. When something can't be done, he says why it can't be done. But he explains and he is a person I think that does respect. And he does ask for opinions. . . . He is a person who listens with patience. He doesn't say what he thinks until he already has heard the other person. (Parent 2, 1: 122–24)

Unlike the teachers, then, parents did not share a sense of uncertainty and vulnerability vis-à-vis their school principal. Indeed, the opposite was true. Dr. Gonzalez moved in a very aggressive and consistent fashion to open the school up to its local community. He was personally involved with students and their parents, and his concern for their well-being was palpable. With regard to this role relation, Dr. Gonzalez was a highly effective school leader.

Communicating Across Divides: Teachers' Views of Teachers

The faculty at Thomas had historically consisted of two separate groups made up of bilingual and monolingual teachers, respectively. The whole language instruction initiative introduced a compounding fault line, distinguishing progressive teachers from their more traditional colleagues. Shared local governance activities, however, partially ameliorated these divisions by creating opportunities for cooperative teacher work across these various divides.

The Bilingual-Monolingual Split   When Principal Gonzalez declared that Thomas should be a fully bilingual school, he fueled some already existing controversies between the bilingual and monolingual teachers on his faculty. Scrutiny of how Thomas was implementing the transition of bilingual students into monolingual classes suddenly intensified. Normally, these transitions occurred around the third grade, but with some occurring as late as sixth grade. A monolingual teacher stated, however, that fewer students were now being transitioned at grade three. She questioned whether instructional policy governing bilingual programs suddenly had changed. "[Y]ou're supposed to be teaching x minutes of English a day versus Spanish. I don't know. I hope that those teachers do it right. I hope that they give them the right amount of language each day." Nonetheless, even this teacher went on to acknowledge that such a policy change might well be in students' best interests. "I do know that research is showing that they do better if they stay in it until sixth grade, if they stay in their own language. And they transition out better at sixth grade versus third grade" (Teacher 4, 1: 19–20).

At base, this teacher, like most others at Thomas, saw the bilingual-monolingual split as "a real sticky issue. It is real political. It affects my job" (Teacher 4, 1: 19–20). That is, if the bilingual program expanded, monolingual teaching positions would have to be reduced, and some teachers who had been at the school for many years might be displaced. Thomas teachers understood that "being a truly bilingual school" was not just another innovative practice that could be acquired through in-service training. The rise and fall of this initiative might have direct implications for their jobs.

Although it occurred largely by accident, the initial composition of faculty leaders in Thomas's local school governance also split along bilingual-monolingual lines. Both the CANAL Core Planning Team and PPAC were composed primarily of monolingual teachers. A bilingual teacher who was on the Core Planning Team talked of her concerns about the lack of bilingual teacher participation.

> I was upset about that because the bilingual teachers are the ones that speak Spanish and probably have a little bit more—maybe not more—but a different kind of communication with the parents. Should the Core Planning Team meetings be translated into Spanish? There were three sessions on that. One person even resigned because of it. And so that bothered me. And because all these crucial issues are decided there, it's just like this hot potato. (Teacher 4, 1: 71–72)

A similar issue arose with regard to the LSC. Both teachers elected to the first council came from the monolingual program. The head of the Parent Center noted,

> [T]here was some concern as to the ability of the two [monolingual] people that won—their ability to communicate because we are a Hispanic school and many of the parents are not English-fluent and would need translation. [Moreover,] there's more to communicating than just translating, and so that was a concern. But, at that point, it was too late. (Teacher 5, 1: 94)

While little could be done immediately, efforts were made over time at Thomas to reshape teacher representation to achieve a better balance of monolingual and bilingual faculty. The initial imbalance was unfortunate, however, because it created another factor amplifying the unease among the faculty at a critical juncture in the school's history. Dr. Gonzalez had just become principal, and the local school governance arrangements under Chicago's decentralization were just being instituted. This added another layer of uncertainty to the mix: major changes seemed likely at Thomas, but would all interests have equal voice in how these played out?

One area where common agreement did emerge was around shared teacher concerns about how the bilingual-monolingual program split affected students at Thomas. Monolingual program students often taunted their bilingual program peers for not fitting into the mainstream English-dominant culture. Tensions between the two groups had on occasion resulted in fistfights. A bilingual teacher explained that "the kids are pressured into being cool, and with cool, you're speaking English not Spanish. So if you're still in the bilingual program, you're considered an outsider, although you are of the same cultural background of all the kids that are in the regular program" (Teacher 3, 1: 73–74). Monolingual students also tended to regard bilingual schoolmates as slow learners because they had not transitioned out yet. Teachers across the school worried that the message that English is cool and Spanish is not was causing problems for students' self-esteem and cultural identity.

The Whole Language Split   Both the CANAL Core Planning Team and the PPAC actively supported whole language instruction for the school. These teachers felt that all classrooms should use this approach. As a fourth-grade teacher explained, students encountered problems when they moved between whole language and traditional classrooms.

> If I was a child and I moved from one setting where I'm allowed to go to the bathroom when I want to and I can work in my journals or work in my science or whatever, and then the next year I'm pulled into being told what to do, I'd have this problem. I feel guilty because [some of the kids I had last year] come and say, "You know, you didn't prepare us for this." (Teacher 6, 1: 24)

As was the case with the bilingual initiative, the status of whole language reform also remained unclear at the school. A CANAL member noted that "the words [whole language] weren't there in the school improvement plan, but [they were] certainly visible in the things written about staff development by the staff development design team" (Teacher 4, 1: 7). As noted earlier, Dr. Gonzalez clearly preferred whole language for Thomas and rewarded individual teachers who were willing to work at it. Yet the absence of whole language as a formal priority in the annual School Improvement Plan was curious. This document guided each school's local improvement efforts under Chicago's decentralization reform, and especially to the point, it was the principal's responsibility to develop this document. The unspoken question in these teachers' minds was, "Gonzalez had verbalized whole language as a priority, then why wasn't it written down in the School Improvement Plan?"

Such contradictions signaled much about the overall uncertainty at Thomas regarding its future direction. Clearly, a major transformation would be needed if the school were to more effectively engage its students and the local community. A sensible vision had been articulated (that is, fully bilingual whole language instruction, shared governance with faculty, and active engagement of parents and local community), but the commitment to advance all of its elements remained uncertain. Some teachers were willing to take the lead on the whole language initiative, but they did not sense the full support from Dr. Gonzalez that they needed. More to the point, they saw little effort on his part to win over their more resistant colleagues to this approach. Since teachers have no formal authority to compel instructional changes, and can even feel uncomfortable making suggestions about changes in someone else's practice, Dr. Gonzalez's reluctance to press for whole language undermined the budding instructional leadership displayed by these teachers. As for the more traditional teachers, they knew that their classroom practices were being questioned and clearly felt little esteem or personal support from their principal.

Such tensions among a faculty are natural as schools initiate change. Working through these tensions is an important step in moving toward meaningful reform. Unfortunately, the latter never happened at Thomas. Many teachers remained uncertain about their status in the school and felt vulnerable, albeit for different reasons. Absent efforts by Dr. Gonzalez to acknowledge this vulnerability, teachers' unease continued to simmer, leaving unsettled relations among faculty colleagues.

Integrating Across the Divides Despite the concerns raised earlier about the initial imbalance in committee memberships, the introduction of local school governance at Thomas did create opportunities for at least some teachers from various factions across the school to work cooperatively together on important local problems. As one teacher leader commented,

I think it's given us [that is, teachers from both monolingual and bilingual programs] an opportunity to sit and make decisions together, decisions that at one time, like I mentioned, were made only by administration, and we really didn't have anything to do with that. In fact, we were waiting for someone to tell us what to do. The teachers really didn't feel that they needed to think about those things, and are [now] thinking about those things and find that they are doing very well in thinking about those things . . . I think it's opened up what you'd call new vistas, you know. We might not have explored certain restructuring techniques if we hadn't been involved in CANAL and reform, and we talked about the need to really do some things specifically and especially for our children who are unique in certain ways. Those are things that we didn't consider when we had mandates coming down from the board saying that children at this level should be taught this thing and that thing. We never really thought about where these children live and these kinds of children coming from this type of influence at home. . . . [Y]ou know, it just allowed us to feel OK about looking a little more personally and interpersonally at the children. (Teacher 1, 1: 17)

The character of social exchanges among teachers was gradually changing at the school, and teachers attributed this to their participation in the new shared governance arrangements. For example, a fifth grade teacher said,

We even resolved that [the sharing of resources] a little bit through the PPAC. . . . Those classrooms that are not in a special program [for example, bilingual] would get a little bit of extra money to spend. And then also by having this little more of a friendship type of thing. Like if you are a bilingual teacher and I know you have an overhead [projector], then I feel comfortable to say, "Can I borrow your overhead this morning?" Whereas before it was kind of like nobody told what they had. (Teacher 7, 2: 103)

In sum, teacher leaders, like their school principal, had to confront complex organizational realities in moving reform forward at Thomas. The long history of an essentially separate bilingual program at the school had produced a sharp cleavage in the faculty. The whole language initiative further amplified this split, since the whole language leaders were primarily from the monolingual program. Further compounding this were ethnic differences across the two groups: the bilingual program was heavily Latino and the monolingual program was predominately European American. Given this structure, teachers might have few opportunities for meaningful social exchanges across their core organizational divide. As a result, a situation ripe for teacher distrust had formed.

Teachers' involvement in local school governance, however, ameliorated this to some degree. Their participation on various committees created opportunities for respectful social exchanges to occur among faculty who might otherwise have little in common. Teachers now had a chance to get to know each other better and develop personal regard. Perhaps most important, this work offered occasions for teachers to reaffirm together their shared concerns about the education and welfare of the children in the Thomas community. In short, the social exchanges around shared local governance created multiple opportunities for trust building within the faculty.

Synchrony: Parents Respect Teachers and Teachers Seek to Reduce Parent Vulnerability

Parents at Thomas generally viewed education as the school's job, and typically deferred to school professionals on most matters. As one parent commented,

> The parents think, for example, that the teachers, that they can do everything. That they are going to decide everything. I think that if they realized that for parents to work with teachers is much better, this would change. But I think that they think that the teachers are the professionals and that they are sufficient. (Parent 2, 1: 119)

In an immigrant community such as Thomas, there are deep cultural roots to such beliefs, and parental deference toward school professionals is quite understandable.[2]

Regardless, Thomas faculty initiated numerous programs to alter this pattern. Through a variety of school committees and local school community activities, parents could take on new roles in their children's schooling, experiences that proved transformative for some. As a parent representative on the LSC commented,

> A lot of people, and I was one of them, tend to put a lot of people up on pedestals because they have a title, and it doesn't have to be that way. I think what this is, you need to spend time with these people to realize that they're just people. (Parent 4, 1: 10)

In general, parents described Thomas as a very open and welcoming school. One parent, who served as the first LSC chair, noted, "All of the teachers are very courteous to parents. It's an open door policy where anyone at anytime can just go into the office. They don't have to knock and sit and wait for an appointment. Or they don't have to call ahead. It's very comfortable, it's a comfortable feeling" (Parent 1,

1: 35–36). Another parent spoke of how one teacher conducted workshops for the parents to demonstrate her instructional techniques and help parents become better educators of their own children. "She made me feel welcome since my daughter started school. We were in there for workshops and it was fascinating to know how, just opening up a book and reading to your kid may not be enough for the kid. She motivates them" (Parent 3, 1: 93).

Parents also recognized that Thomas's teachers worked hard to advance their children's education. A parent who volunteered at the school spoke of one teacher's dedication.

> I noticed that my son's teacher likes to work because she stays there when you don't have to stay there. Because it is sure that she'll stay there until six. And other days she stays and does things, and she says, "What do you think?" and "How do you see this? What will the parents say? Do you think they will like it?" She likes her work. (Parent 2, 1: 137)

This willingness of teachers at Thomas to reach out to parents, to listen to their concerns, and to go the extra mile for their children was much appreciated by parents, and they reciprocated by extending strong support to teachers.

The teachers at Thomas in turn felt that parents valued education and respected the teacher's role in the classroom. A third-grade bilingual teacher linked the parents' regard for education to their native culture.

> Just in general, I believe, and I am sure most teachers believe, that the Mexican community still respects education. Most of the parents that are here, the families that are here, have come from hard times. They found hard times here, but they are hoping that their kids will be better [off]. (Teacher 8, 1: 72)

Teachers at Thomas saw reaching out to parents as a key part of their job. As a fourth-grade monolingual teacher explained,

> I think that both teachers and parents must work together. That's my belief. I'm on the phone or I'm writing a letter almost every day. And not only to let the parents know how badly or how well the kids are doing. Sometimes as a teacher you wonder why certain kids are disruptive in school, you want to find out, is this [true] at home also, and what the parent and teacher can do about it. (Teacher 6, 1: 26)

This teacher also understood that such interactions with the school could feel intimidating to Thomas's immigrant parents. "A student told me, 'My mom doesn't want to come to school and help.' And I asked, 'Why?' 'Because she thinks she would sound stupid'" (Teacher 6, 1: 27–28).

Teachers at Thomas recognized parents' sense of vulnerability and actively sought to make them feel more comfortable. How best to accomplish this, however, remained uncertain. The head of the Parent Center explained that child care and coffee were made available at parent activities to promote attendance. Teachers conducted raffles at parent meetings as another strategy in this regard. The school put forth extra efforts to notify and remind parents of activities. "Most of the time we send out a flyer—we send it out twice, one week in advance and then right before. Depending on how urgent the meeting is, sometimes we sit and make phone calls to people" (Teacher 5, 1: 89–90). Nonetheless, teachers still felt that the school could and should do more.

Overall, a high level of mutual respect characterized the parent-teacher relationship at Thomas. Parents afforded school professionals wide discretion on education matters. In return, teachers actively sought parental input, looked for ways to increase parent involvement in the school and support parenting efforts at home. With this social foundation in place, parents and teachers were able to address productively most any problem that might arise. For example, with the introduction of whole language instruction at the school, some concerns about order and discipline in the classroom were raised. A bilingual teacher who used whole language explained, "The parents don't see things as we teachers or professionals do in the educational field. [Parents ask:] 'Why are the kids talking so much? Why aren't they in rows, and the teacher up in the front?' You know, questions like this. They've criticized a lot of us for that" (Teacher 3, 1: 83). Most parents at Thomas expected traditional teacher-directed classroom instruction. They worried that the freedom that came with whole language instruction might lead to behavior problems for their children.

We saw in chapter 3 how similar parental questions about teachers' classroom activities at Ridgeway School promoted suspicion and distrust. In contrast, at Thomas, teachers were open to parental inquiries and willing to discuss such teaching issues. Several teachers at Thomas, for example, scheduled after-school meetings with parents to help them better understand the rationale for whole language instruction. One teacher responded to the parents' concerns by holding a series of workshops in which she demonstrated whole language techniques. Another teacher explained how she used her position on a school governance committee to create a schoolwide forum for a discussion on discipline.

That was one of the reasons I changed design teams, because I was able to work more closely with parents. It gave me the opportunity to explain things to parents from a different perspective. For example, we gave out the teacher survey and one of the questions had to do with discipline. It was like 85 percent of the teachers felt that the school was well-disciplined, so when we took this all back and discussed the results, and parents were saying they wanted more discipline, I was saying, "I understand that, but you're asking people who already feel that there is enough discipline, for more discipline. You've got to understand why their reaction is this way." So, I think it was a little bit easier for them to see, not just based on one teacher here or there, or two teachers, you know. It was a whole group responding. (Teacher 5, 1: 102)

Structural Complexity and Personal Vulnerability

The change efforts at Thomas in the early 1990s were strongly influenced by the school's distinctive history. As reform began, Thomas operated as two schools within one building: one bilingual, the other English dominant. These schools had separate curricula, followed different time schedules, and benefited from varying levels of fiscal support. Significant philosophical differences further amplified these structural divisions. Most of the bilingual faculty was committed to a traditional instructional program taught primarily in Spanish. Many of the monolingual faculty, in contrast, were experimenting with more progressive teaching strategies.

Not surprisingly, the social ties between these two faculties were weak. The bilingual teachers worried about the fact that their monolingual colleagues could not communicate easily with many of the school's parents and some of its students. Many of the monolingual teachers in turn believed that they were the ones most willing to innovate in their classrooms to improve student learning, and they wondered about the instructional design of the bilingual program. Why did so many students still need additional help with reading and numeracy skills after transitioning out of bilingual education?

Strong principal leadership was needed to bring this faculty together. Dr. Gonzalez came to Thomas school as reform began. He articulated a vision for Thomas as a responsive institution to its local community. He sought to strengthen the role of parents in the education of their own children and demonstrated his personal regard for them through his day-to-day efforts at the school and around the neighborhood. He also recognized the importance of building a professional community among his teachers, and dedicated resources for their professional development (which was relatively uncommon in the early 1990s in Chicago). In many ways, Dr. Gonzalez offered a very appealing vision for both teachers and parents at Thomas School. Nonetheless, reform never really came together at Thomas during our three years of fieldwork there.

Dr. Gonzalez's early action—advocating that Thomas should become a fully bilingual school—provoked considerable controversy. Many monolingual teachers worried that if this policy went forward, they could lose their jobs. Although bilingual teachers supported this aspect of Dr. Gonzalez's plan, they felt vulnerable on other accounts. Specifically, they were unsure whether their traditional classroom practices would still have a place in this school, given Dr. Gonzalez's embrace of whole language. Taken together, the reforms proposed by Dr. Gonzalez around instruction were very ambitious. His vision called for the integration of progressive instructional practices within a dual language program. Each of these reforms is demanding. Undertaking both at the same time could be overwhelming. The likelihood of failure here, and the risk associated with this, was high.

Uncomfortable with the faculty tensions that his vision for Thomas School had precipitated, Dr. Gonzalez responded by taking a low-key approach. His reform rhetoric abated, and in its stead he sought more subtle ways to advance his objectives. He created opportunities for teachers to work together, hoping that his stronger staff would inspire his more reticent ones. Thomas's strong teachers, however, felt uncomfortable in this reformer role because they did not perceive consistent public support from their principal for their initiatives.

Dr. Gonzalez also sought to use positive incentives to advance his reforms by rewarding participating teachers with various professional perquisites. In contrast, he gave little feedback, either positive or negative, to other teachers who continued their past practices. Ironically, Dr. Gonzalez's behavior made both the rewarded and the ignored feel vulnerable. In general, a norm of fair treatment for all pervades school faculties. Differentiated rewards within a school typically are suspect, and considerable efforts are needed to legitimize their use. Absent such efforts at Thomas, it is not surprising that some teachers interpreted Dr. Gonzalez's action as favoritism. His demonstrated lack of personal regard for them diminished their trust in him. Since discernments about favoritism also tend to pit teachers against one teacher, the allocation of differential teacher rewards worked to undermine teacher-teacher trust here as well.

During our four-year presence at Thomas school, teachers remained unsure about what really was expected of them. While Dr. Gonzalez had articulated a strong vision for the school, much of his subsequent behavior became less clear for teachers to interpret. Thus, Dr. Gonzalez came up somewhat short from an integrity perspective as well in his relations with teachers.

On balance, Dr. Gonzalez confronted a genuine dilemma. The school needed fundamental change were it to become more responsive to its local community and more effective in educating children. Such fundamental change is likely to create conflict within an organization. One might expect relations to fray and trust to weaken a bit, at least temporarily, as the school seeks to realign around a new direction. Had Dr. Gonzalez moved more aggressively, he undoubtedly would have increased tensions even further.

Embedded here is an important general lesson. As we also saw in the Ridgeway case, principals must be prepared to engage conflict in order to advance reform. Yet they also need social support and trust from a solid core of the faculty if reform is to have a chance of succeeding. The actions that principals take on the first course may weaken teacher trust in them and diminish their capacity to lead. Action taken on the second course, however, may assuage teacher concerns by eviscerating any meaningful reform. The dilemma of leadership often entails navigating a narrow course.

Switching role sets, whatever difficulties Dr. Gonzalez faced with his faculty did not carry over to his relationships with parents. Parents saw Dr. Gonzalez as a committed educator who was knowledgeable about instruction and placed primacy on the interests and welfare of students, parents, and the community. He reached out, he listened, and he cared. In short, from every angle—respect, personal regard, competence, and integrity—Dr. Gonzalez merited parents' trust.

Similarly, most teachers had good relations with parents. Parents respected teachers and supported teachers' work at school and at home. Teachers in turn respected parents, listened to their concerns, and went the extra mile for their children. A genuine synchrony in reciprocal obligations and expectations was achieved in this role set relation, and trust was high here as well.

Thomas proved a difficult case of local school reform to analyze. The school had much going for it, including a principal and many parents and teachers who were genuinely committed to improving opportunities afforded their children. Nonetheless, the pattern of social relations that developed here was complex and impeded somewhat the pace of local reform. Our theory of relational trust shows how uncertainties within the staff about their own role obligations and expectations for others contributed to tensions among the professionals at the school. The theory also helps to identify some specific leadership behaviors that undermine trust relations among teachers and with their principal, and aspects of the school's local governance arrangements that work to ameliorate some of these tensions. On a clearly positive note, this case also points out some key dynamics where principals and teachers effectively build trust with parents—a theme we consider further in the next chapter.

Chapter 5

Holiday Elementary School: Dedicated to the Welfare of the Children

I N A well-known book, *There Are No Children Here*, Alex Kotlowitz chronicled the experiences of two brothers, their family, and friends who lived in a public housing project on Chicago's west side.[1] A poignant episode describes the family's turmoil when the Department of Public Aid threatened to cut off benefits because the father occasionally stayed with the family. Four agency workers laid out the evidence of fraud in a fifteen-minute administrative hearing and asked the welfare mother to disprove their findings. The caseworkers made no effort to establish rapport with the mother and had not even introduced themselves. The mother, caught by surprise, was neither afforded counsel nor given time to prepare. Accused and worried about her future, she fled the room without offering a defense.

As this account vividly portrays, public bureaucracies created to help the disadvantaged often exacerbate their problems. Given large caseloads and the overwhelming needs of the populations they serve, public employees often harden themselves against their clients' troubles and easily can lose sight of the individuals they seek to assist. Ironically, those whom we have charged with helping the poor sometimes contribute to their impoverishment.

Holiday Elementary School sits in the neighborhood described by Kotlowitz. Unlike many other similarly situated schools and public service agencies, Holiday is an energized and engaging environment that provides individual attention and care for its 550 kindergarten through eighth grade students. The school draws two-thirds of its student body from the public housing complex across the street. Many of the students' parents are unemployed, on welfare, or are single heads of households. For most of these children, the presence of drugs, crime, and violence is never far away. Despite this troubled context, Holiday maintains a safe and orderly environment. According to the school's principal, Holiday eighth-graders are "heavily recruited" by high schools across the city due to their reputation for good behavior (Goldman, 1: 10).

Examining Role Relations

Dr. Goldman: The Team Manager

Holiday's principal, Dr. Morty Goldman, is an anomaly. In a school system where communities have taken control over the hiring and firing of principals, local school councils have typically found it important to "hire one of their own."[2] Dr. Goldman is one of the few remaining white male principals in a Chicago school serving a 100 percent African American population. "I have a pretty good following around here, and it amazes me that most of the time (knock on wood), racial politics don't play a line," Dr. Goldman commented.

> I look at all the other schools that serve Chicago housing projects, and there aren't too many white, male principals left, and everyone that was removed was certainly replaced with a minority, so that's just something right there. And even when [minority principals] are there, the strange thing is that it appears that they're having more difficulty than me, and I can't figure it out. I just really work on my rapport with the community. All those stories about what you shouldn't do, I don't do. Like, I don't ignore someone coming into the building, or I don't talk to someone the way I wouldn't want to be talked to. . . . And I specifically think that one of the keys is, most people want attention. So I give them the attention. I mean, I'm not going to ignore someone, so I speak to everyone, and just develop a rapport and a relationship. (Goldman, 1: 6)

Dr. Goldman attributed his long tenure at the school to the fact that he really listens to parents, teachers, and community members. In addition, Holiday parents had many opportunities over the years to observe Dr. Goldman enliven his words with personal action.

Dr. Goldman compared his school to a highly motivated sports team: parents and community constitute the fans, the teachers are the players, and the Board of Education and outside consultants serve as the coaching staff.

> So when I see a team that goes out there and plays selflessly, who have a community of purpose, who really come on as professionals, and who are dedicated and caring, you are going to have a winning season. And

a winning season is that the teachers are productive and satisfied, the children are gaining a positive self image, they have the best education possible given to them. The parents feel that the money was well spent. (Goldman, 1: 35)

Dr. Goldman strove to strengthen his team by hiring teachers who cared about students and their parents, had the necessary subject matter knowledge and pedagogic expertise, and shared his vision of education for the Holiday School.

Dr. Goldman inspired a community of purpose in his teachers around advancing the education and welfare of children. Children are the focus of his work and primary source of his job satisfaction. He sees the school as developing "lifelong learners, children that appreciate the opportunity to gain understanding and authentic achievement and real skills that would enable them to become happy and successful adults" (Goldman, 1: 16). Moreover, this mission extended for Dr. Goldman beyond his formal role responsibilities; it was for him a crusade. "I feel a moral responsibility to a child who is innocent and vulnerable in this society to try—at least in my little neck of the woods—to give them a good taste of America. And I certainly will. I certainly have that determination" (Goldman, 1: 19).

While he acknowledged the challenges faced by the school, Dr. Goldman expressed a commitment to overcoming them.

Yeah, we're very cognizant of the fact that here we are in a sense, as you look across the country, in one of the most economically depressed areas. . . . I mean, there aren't too many other places that could say, "Well, look, we're worse off." . . . [But] we don't use it as an excuse; we use it as a motivator. (Goldman, 1: 21)

The Players: Dr. Goldman's View of Teachers

Teachers played a key role in Dr. Goldman's game plan. "I think that given persons with the professionally right attitude, commitment, dedication, expertise, and know-how, there's no issue with money or reform or what's needed, because it gets done where the rubber meets the road" (Goldman, 1: 17). Dr. Goldman's initial school improvement efforts centered around strengthening his faculty to advance the learning of all children in the community. He spoke at length about this topic in our first interview. "That's what I look for in my teachers—crusaders. . . . They're people who have a passion for what they're doing" (Goldman, 1: 18). He believed that Holiday School teachers must have a moral commitment to *these* children and *their* community. They also must have the professional skill to tailor instruction to the needs of each child.

> I think we've got enough resources. I think the key is the people who use the tools—the teachers. I think the whole concept is, if you're given appropriate instruction, all children can learn. You've got to have the right person giving the instruction. So I have enough money now. I don't have the right kind of teachers though. (Goldman, 1: 16)

As reform began, Dr. Goldman inherited a number of teachers who were accustomed to leaving school with students at the 2:30 P.M. closing bells, and who displayed little interest in changing their classroom practices.

Ideally, Dr. Goldman would have the authority simply to remove those teachers who did not share his vision for the school and refused to embrace his reform efforts. As he put it, "I basically want to magically be able to let go of some of these people—those teachers, those perceptions, those experiences [and] be able to create a new camaraderie and collegiality of people who are committed and have the expertise . . ." (Goldman, 1: 18). Given bureaucratic realities, however, Dr. Goldman had to create incentives to encourage faculty members who did not embrace his standards to either retire or leave on their own. This process of "counseling out" staff was time-consuming and sometimes demanded great creativity, but it was key nonetheless to the faculty reshaping that Dr. Goldman had in mind.[3] Although it took almost three years, Dr. Goldman eventually was able to replace most of these individuals with new teachers who quickly came to share his commitment to strengthening the Holiday school community.

As Dr. Goldman built his new faculty team, he also embraced a more collaborative stance toward decision making. "[M]ore people are involved in the decision-making process now. Therefore more of the success and failure is shared. And other than certain day-to-day decision-making requirements, most of the decision making is more of a group collaborative effort" (Goldman, 2: 19). Dr. Goldman enjoyed the collective brainstorming that comes with shared decision making. "Hey, twenty heads are better than one. I like that" (Goldman, 2: 19). He also saw shared decision making as key to expanding the social resources at Holiday. Dr. Goldman believed that collaboration promotes increased buy-in to policy decisions and helps to ensure their successful implementation.

Dr. Goldman recognized that encouraging a meaningful participation of staff in policy decisions requires a special effort on the part of a principal. "I want to stay a little distant from them. I don't want to even subconsciously influence them. I want them to feel that they can recommend whatever their group really wants to do, and if it's in the best interest of the school and the students, it will always be accepted" (Goldman, 2: 26). In a school system that historically had been very autocratic, asking faculty to voice their opinions can feel very dangerous to teachers. In the past, speaking up often got people in trouble. A principal's efforts to reduce this sense of vulnerability is key to making shared governance come alive.

A Dedicated and Resourceful Urban School Leader: Teachers' Views of Dr. Goldman

Dr. Goldman's actions authenticated his vision for the school. His commitment to the children was manifest for all to see. As one teacher noted during the LSC's evaluation of the principal for his contract renewal, "We all know that he is concerned about the children, the welfare of the children, and we are just very positive" (Teacher 1, 1: 19). The teachers at Holiday reported consistently that Dr. Goldman's behavior enacted the principles he espoused: we must do whatever is needed to advance the welfare of the children.

Teachers also viewed Dr. Goldman as an effective manager, someone who gets things done. "If he can deal with it, it will be dealt with immediately" (Teacher 2, 1: 12). He managed well the school's resources, such as building maintenance, time schedules, and the stocking and distribution of classroom supplies.

Similarly, teachers confirmed Dr. Goldman's support for shared decision making. The Holiday School staff continually mentioned Dr. Goldman's open-door policy toward the faculty. Teachers talked about having real input through various committees on staff development activities, curriculum and textbook selection, and the spending of discretionary funds. More generally, they perceived his willingness to listen to and act on teachers' suggestions. "The administration does a wonderful job. Our principal's open to anything you want to try. You just let him know, and if it sounds good, he'll say go ahead and try it, you know. He's very open to that" (Teacher 2, 1: 4). The Holiday faculty also valued the easy access that they had for informal one-on-one conversations with their principal. Each such occasion created an opportunity for Dr. Goldman to demonstrate that "he really cared" about his teachers and their success.

In sum, teachers at Holiday viewed Dr. Goldman as a principled leader who enacted his beliefs. Their support for his leadership appeared quite natural, since most of the faculty (as it eventually was transformed) embraced these same beliefs. In addition, he was a competent school manager: he recognized what needed to be done and made it happen. Teachers especially appreciated that Dr. Goldman gave them a voice in school decision making and encouraged them to expand their roles beyond traditional classroom concerns.

Delimited Involvement: Dr. Goldman's View of Parents

Holiday School parents endured the numerous disadvantages that plague residents in poor urban neighborhoods. Many had left high school without graduating, became teenage parents, and were now unemployed. Few had ever held "real jobs" for any extended period. Coupled with the racial and economic isolation of their homes and communities, these young parents had been denied access to the "American Dream."

Dr. Goldman believed that this lack of experience and accompanying isolation limited parents' capacity to meaningfully engage in school decision making. Few of Holiday's parents knew much about good teaching, since few had ever experienced it themselves. Even fewer knew much about administering the complex operational dynamics of an urban public school like Holiday. In thinking about his engagement with parents in his school community, Dr. Goldman made a sharp distinction between parent involvement and parent input. In his view, direct involvement was more like interference, while input, in the form of recommendations or suggestions, was appropriate and desirable. "You tell me what you want and you let me do it, now hold me accountable. . . . [B]ut you don't need to be right over my shoulder when I do it" (Goldman, 1: 15). Extending Dr. Goldman's sports team analogy, fans should be fans. Their place was in the stands, not on the playing field.

This view placed Dr. Goldman somewhat at odds with the visionary rhetoric of Chicago's decentralization reformers. They believed that resources existed in every school community, which if unleashed, could generate productive local change.[4] To be sure, there were resources in the Holiday community, but far less so than in most other neighborhoods.[5] Moreover, these community leaders and institutions were stretched thin, given the immense needs of their neighborhood. In response, the Holiday school figured out how to make Chicago's local school governance reform work their own way.[6]

Parents' lack of education and professional experience at Holiday took on special salience in the context of the work of its local school council. In particular, the council chair at Holiday recalled what a "scary process" it was when it came time for them to evaluate Dr.

Goldman and make a determination about his contract renewal. She felt that the parents and community members on the board, including herself, were not capable of judging the principal's competence. "[Somebody] should have taught us before we got up there to vote [on the principal's contract]. A lot of us didn't even know why we were there. A lot of council members cannot read, but they [are] running somebody's business" (Parent 1, 1: 14).

Not surprisingly, Dr. Goldman preferred his informal personal relations with parents to the more formal processes that governed interactions at LSC meetings. While walking through the school hallways, he called parents by name, joked with them, inquired about their families and lives outside of school. He commented,

> In most schools, you don't have to rely on the principal for anything other than being an instructional leader with regard to academic-type strategies, curriculum. But in a school like this, they rely on me to create a climate, [to be] a manager of people. . . . And many times, the demand is for me to be a listener and to be a soother and empathizer to everyone else's ills. (Goldman, 1: 11)

Through these frequent social interactions, Dr. Goldman demonstrated his respect for parents and their community. By acknowledging the difficulties they faced, he communicated genuine personal concern.

About the Business of Educating Children: Parents' Views of Dr. Goldman

Parents at Holiday said that Dr. Goldman made them feel comfortable at the school and encouraged them to get involved in their children's schooling.

> He's an exciting person to me. He has excitement for the children to learn. When he sees you, I mean, you could have just seen Dr. Goldman today and you go back and you see him again later and it's like he didn't see you at all, "Hello, and how are you!" . . . He's funny, great sense of humor, but he's about the business of educating the children, too, so I like that. I really admire Dr. Goldman. (Parent 2, 1: 14)

Virtually every Holiday parent with whom we spoke confirmed Dr. Goldman's respect for parents and his personal regard for their children. They consistently commented on his communicative style.

> Okay, he keeps the school up, talks to the teachers like they are teachers, then he talks to them like they're humans. He treats every-

body in this school as equal. I don't care if you're black, white, Puerto Rican, he don't treat you different. That's what makes this school and this community what it is. He don't have no racial nothing about him. He don't come up to you where he's scared to touch you. Seriously, this is the way I feel. And, you know, a whole lot of other people coming, you know, from other schools say, "Boy, your principal is really something else. I'm going to transfer my kids here." And, they do those things because of his ways. That's just how he is. . . . Anything that has to do with coming in between those kids and his staff, he stands up for them, and I agree with it. (Parent 1, 1: 1)

Another parent added that Dr. Goldman is like a "big brother that you can really talk to." Also echoing the teachers at the school, this parent said, "If you ask him something, he'll try his best to do it" (Parent 3, 1: 66).

The Holiday School parents witnessed Dr. Goldman's principles in action when the alderman endorsed a proposal for a halfway house for released prisoners to be located next to the school. Dr. Goldman mobilized the parents, teachers, and other concerned residents to protest the placement with the zoning board. He argued that placing convicted criminals so close to the school might put the children in jeopardy. Although their efforts failed, the parents recognized and appreciated Dr. Goldman's willingness to take a stand with them. Fighting the alderman certainly wasn't in his job description, and it could have even gotten him into trouble, but he did it anyway because it was for the children.

A Shared Personal Regard for Children: Teachers' Views of Teachers

Teachers at Holiday School displayed the same tone of respect and personal regard modeled by their principal. Demonstrating personal concern for the children was a core professional role obligation for these teachers. Holiday teachers frequently used family metaphors to describe their relationships with students. They spoke in terms of expectations and aspirations that a parent would have for his or her child.

Professional means giving to others the best you can. I've raised two daughters of my own, and I'm trying to give [to Holiday's children] what I hope that some teachers did for my children. So I think being a professional is being as open and positive, interesting, having as active a classroom, a participating classroom, as you can possibly make it. (Teacher 2, 1: 8)

Another teacher, in discussing school discipline issues, made a direct connection between his role as a teacher and his life as a parent. "If I have to administer discipline, I will, and I will administer it to him the same way I would have my son's teacher administer it to him" (Teacher 3, 1: 4).

A willingness to go the extra mile for the children constituted the key yardstick that teachers used in judging one another's work. They did not see their responsibilities as limited to what they could accomplish in the 9 A.M. to 2:30 P.M. school schedule. Rather, they spoke about giving all they had to help their students learn. One said,

> When I leave here, I'm tired. And tonight I go to class, and then from there I go to the college, and I might not get in until one o'clock, so my day and night are already spoken for, and I'm still able to get up at four o'clock and get here the next morning, to provide preparation time, because I care. It's how you feel about it; if you don't want to give anything back to these kids, I don't think that you should be a teacher. (Teacher 3, 1: 10)

Going the extra mile also was evident in teachers' commitments to the larger school community. In describing the teacher elections for the local school council, a teacher commented on her colleagues' dedication.

> I remember the courageousness of one of the individuals that ran, and that she would be willing to make whatever sacrifices were needed in order to help our students achieve. . . . I think that the majority of the teachers would do the same. They would give the maximum effort. Perhaps it was the intensity of the speech which she gave that really electrified me. But I think most of the staff would probably give the maximum. (Teacher 4, 1: 95–96)

As noted in chapter 2, teacher-teacher trust is predicated on a confidence that one's colleagues will act in a professionally responsible manner. This norm of acting professional at Holiday School was anchored in a commitment to put forth extra effort for the students rather than in some externally defined professional practice standards. Interestingly, classroom observations at Holiday showed that while teachers generally maintained a tone of warmth and respect in their classrooms and worked hard to engage their students in learning, their actual subject matter instruction was not especially strong. To be sure, Holiday faculty viewed manifest discipline problems in the classroom and gross student learning deficiencies as evidence of poor teaching. In this regard, there was a clear agreement among the faculty about the base qualities required to be a teacher in good standing. Beyond these minimum pedagogical competencies, teachers judged each other primarily in terms of their commitment of effort toward the children. The willingness to extend one's time beyond any contractual role obligations operated as the critical evaluation standpoint for teachers' discernment about the integrity of their colleagues. In the minds of Holiday's teachers, this is what you are supposed to do if you are really about helping the children of this community.

The establishment of this norm at Holiday undergirded a strong base of teacher trust. As conflicts arose among the faculty, this trust in turn created a safe atmosphere for critical discussions about the best way to move forward.

> I think that at times issues are raised, and if there are varying opinions, then they're aired. . . . Even though we tend to disagree on some issues, as a whole, I think that we realize that . . . we are [all] fighting for the good of the school. And we can kind of lay those [differences] aside. (Teacher 4, 1: 97)

Agreement on Goals and Expectations: Parents and Teachers

The crushing poverty and limited education of parents at Holiday created a severe imbalance in their power relationship with teachers. Even though parents held a majority representation on the local school council, they had little capacity either individually or as a group to affect directly what the school did about their children's education. In this regard, parents remained largely dependent on the good intentions of school staff. The Holiday School faculty acknowledged this parental vulnerability and acted vigorously to relieve it. Teachers reciprocated parents' trust by welcoming them into the school and proactively engaging them in their children's education.

In interviews, Holiday teachers consistently spoke about the importance of respecting parents, regardless of their background or education attainment. "I have a great deal of respect for parents, in that learning isn't solely done in a classroom, it's done at home too," noted one teacher leader (Teacher 4, 1: 102). Although many students came from troubled homes, teachers did not attempt to distance themselves from their students and their families. Rather, they understood the importance of working constructively with all parents. "As a teacher, your helpmate is your parent. I mean, between the parent and you, you can approach a child. You must have them. You always needed the parent, you always have, and you always will" (Teacher 2, 1: 17).

These deliberate efforts by teachers to establish rapport with parents were recognized and acknowledged. As one parent who was active in the school described it,

> The teachers can relate to me. They may not like me personally. I might not like them personally. In here we relate to one another. We talk. If they have a problem with my child or somebody else's child, they figure I know. They'll come to talk to me [to see] if I have any suggestions to make. They'll listen to what I have to say. It's not like they look down on me or something like that. (Parent 3, 1: 6)

As is common with most teachers, the faculty at Holiday expected children to respect them as important adults in their lives, and they expected parents to support the school's efforts at home. Moreover, teachers indeed generally felt that parents and students made serious efforts to respond to these expectations. As one teacher stated, "For the most part, they seem to be well-disciplined children. Every parent, without qualification, really believes in education and tries as best they can to support this" (Teacher 2, 1: 19). This synchrony of teachers' expectations and parent obligations did not, however, occur by chance. Rather, Holiday teachers knew that they had to make a concerted effort to help parents understand what they needed to do for their children to progress in school. "I talk to my parents. I let them know what I really expect from them and their kids, and that kind of thing, and what I will be doing" (Teacher 5, 1: 38). In addition, the Holiday staff encouraged parent visits to their classrooms and sought to use these visits as opportunities to model how parents could better support their children's learning.

> Basically, the more we involve parents, the more they understand what our job is, the easier our job will become. When parents come and they truly understand exactly what's going on, when they feel comfortable to come in this building, come and sit in a classroom, come see their children, I think when they understand just what we're talking about, our job will get easier. (Teacher 4, 1: 7)

For their part, parents took special notice of the care that teachers demonstrated toward children. As one parent stated,

> There's one teacher down here . . . he acts like he's those kids' father. I mean, he talks to them like he's their father; he talks to them like he's their big brother. Then, he's their teacher. I really like that, you know. Sometimes I just stand there and listen to the way he talks to his class. You know, they're not mean and hollering at you. They try to see what's wrong with you. I mean, this is one thing I know they stress a lot. They

try to find out what's wrong with you first, before you can learn. They try to figure out the problem because, you know, for years they've been trying to find out if something happens in between the time you left that day, and come back the next day. If they can find out what the problem is before they start, then they can clear it up before they start whatever it is that morning. (Parent 1, 1: 2)

Several other parents offered similar responses.

I think I can connect to a lot of what I see at Holiday School to when I was in school, and I don't see that in a whole lot of other places. That's a part of why I want my daughter here, because I do see something here that I usually don't see—they're generally concerned about the children. They're not concerned about just a part of the child, they're concerned about the holistic well-being of the children, and I see that as connecting me to a part of my elementary school. They care. They push you and they work with you. (Parent 2, 1: 2)

In many ways, Holiday was an unusual school community. Compared to other Chicago schools in similar neighborhoods, the social interactions at Holiday were much more constructive.[7] The large, social class differences between parents and school staff easily could have created strife between home and school. Yet teachers' active encouragement of parents, coupled with their demonstrated personal regard for the children, opened up possibilities for teachers and parents to negotiate complementary roles in the children's education. What might well have been a problem in other school contexts turned out to be a social resource for improvement at Holiday.

A Unifying School Priority to Place the Interests of Students First

The message at Holiday School of children first was explicitly articulated and visibly enacted in innumerable ways. It started with the leadership of the principal, Dr. Goldman, and was extended through daily interactions within the school's professional community, which viewed going the extra the mile for the children as the key test of a colleague's integrity.

In contrast to the principals at Ridgeway and Thomas, Dr. Goldman engendered broad support from his staff, the students, and the school's parent community. Early on in reform, Dr. Goldman established a tone in his building of genuine respect and personal regard. Parents felt that he truly cared about their children, was open to them, and treated them with respect. Similarly, teachers felt they could raise problems with him, and he would listen to what they had to say. Dr. Goldman valued an esprit de corps among his teachers, and saw their development as school leaders as essential to Holiday's improvement efforts. To be sure, he did not necessarily agree with every expressed opinion, and when he didn't, he let people know it. The key to working through such disagreements at Holiday, however, was always the same: How can we work together to better advance the learning of our children?

This tone of respect carried over into teachers' interactions with students and parents as well. For teachers it started in the classroom, where screaming at students and using demeaning forms of discipline were viewed as unprofessional. Similarly, teachers took extra steps to help parents understand what the school expected of them and the role they needed to play in their children's education. These expectations were communicated directly, but not condescendingly— and, most importantly, with genuine concern about "what can we do together that is best for your child."

Parents in poor urban communities such as Holiday are especially vulnerable. Dr. Goldman recognized this and acted consistently to ameliorate it. On balance, as a white male principal in a very disadvantaged African American community, Dr. Goldman too was vulnerable. To continue his work, he needed parental support, and he knew that such support hinged on parents' views of his commitment to their children. Parents judged him in this regard as a man of great integrity. Thus, a genuine synchrony was attained. Dr. Goldman respected parents and held them in high personal regard. Parents in turn valued his commitment to the children, and they would do almost anything he asked to support the school staff's efforts in their children's behalf.

In short, advancing the interests of children created a unifying value for Holiday School. To be sure, the personal concerns of adults were considered, but the priority on what is best for children was very clear. Dr. Goldman believed that the teachers had an obligation to go the extra mile for the students, and stated flatly that staff members who did not share this view did not belong at Holiday. Over time, he managed to "counsel out" several teachers who preferred to work in a less demanding environment. The end result, as we concluded our fieldwork during the fourth year of reform, was the formation of a cohesive school community organized around a genuine regard for the children.

Holiday School had achieved high trust in every role set relation. Its social resources were quite different than at Thomas, where the school's historic cleavages, coupled with hesitant principal leadership, continued to undermine collective faculty action. They were even more different from Ridgeway, where contested community politics, coupled with an appeasement-oriented leadership and manifest teacher incompetence, left the school with very limited social resources to initiate change. As we exited Holiday School, we felt optimistic about its enlarged capacity to undertake serious improvement work. A faculty community—willing to take risks and commit extra effort to improve—had formed. They trusted their principal and enjoyed widespread parental support. Thus, key organizational conditions were now in place for this school to accelerate its improvement initiatives and, especially, to take on the complex and often conflict-laden decision making associated with broad-based instructional change.

= Part III =

Effects and Implications

We concluded from our field-based study of school change in Chicago that the relational dynamics in each school community significantly influenced whether meaningful improvement efforts emerged. The cases presented in part II analyze how these dynamics actually played out in three different Chicago communities. Taken together with the discussion of relevant theory in chapter 2, they offer a deep and detailed account of the nature of relational trust and how it operates in very disadvantaged urban school communities.

We now turn to our last analytic concern: examining the link between the development of relational trust in school communities and the likelihood of organizational improvements that culminate in increased student learning. Examining this question is difficult. The processes of organizational restructuring are complex; they can be quite varied across different school communities and can take many years to develop fully. While our detailed field analyses, based on the first three years of Chicago school reform, suggest that developing relational trust is an important factor in school change, the ultimate proof is whether relational trust actually contributes to improvements in how much students learn. Fortunately, we had access to a seven-year survey and test score database on more than four hundred elementary schools to help us evaluate these claims.[1] Part III presents our analyses of these data and the implications of these results for promoting wide-scale school improvement.

═ Chapter 6 ═

Relational Trust and Improving Academic Achievement

K EY TO evaluating a claim about the importance of relational trust for school improvement is the ability to reliably measure differences in this organizational property across school communities and over time. Developing measures of this sort entails a complex interplay of theory (as articulated in chapter 2), firsthand field observations (as presented in chapters 3 through 5), and empirical results from pilot research. We began our first work on this task in 1993 as our field study was concluding. Although the in-depth analysis of the field data had yet to begin, we were already convinced that the quality of social relationships in school communities were key to understanding the early successes and failures at school improvement. This led us to pilot a set of survey items on respect, trust, and caring in different role relationships (teachers with principals, teachers with parents, and teachers with other teachers).[1] The success of this initial pilot work in a small number of schools convinced us of the utility of assessing these organizational features in a citywide teacher survey in 1994.[2] This survey provided our first major source of data on relational trust in elementary school communities.[3]

Measuring Relational Trust

Specifically, teachers were asked to assess whether they felt mutual respect in their relationships with parents. We inquired whether they received parental support and if the staff worked hard to build trust with parents. The survey items composing the 1994 teacher-parent scale mainly tapped aspects of respect and personal regard in participants' discernments of each other. A high score on this measure indicated strong relational trust among teachers and parents.

The teacher-teacher trust scale in 1994 was similar; it contained

Figure 6.1   1994 Survey Reports on Relational Trust in Three Case Study Schools, Compared to School System Average

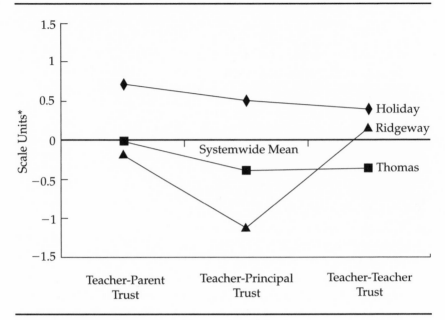

Source: Authors' configuration.
*All of the Consortium survey measures are based on Rasch Rating Scale Analyses that have been transferred into a 0–10 point scale. The mean differences presented here are in the 10-point scale metric.

some general questions about whether teachers trusted, respected, and had personal regard for each other. Teachers were also asked whether faculty in the school respected teachers who led school improvement efforts. The latter item offers some perspective on teachers' discernments about their colleagues' integrity.

The teacher-principal trust measure focused on the extent to which teachers felt their principal respected and supported them. Teachers were asked if their principal looked out for the welfare of the teachers, had confidence in their expertise, and if they trusted the principal's word. Represented here are a mix of probes about respect, competence, and personal regard. A high score on this measure means that teachers perceived their principal as trustworthy.

Figure 6.1 presents the 1994 survey results for our three case study schools in comparison to citywide averages. Holiday performed well above the school system mean on teacher-parent trust, teacher-principal trust, and teacher-teacher trust. The shared commitment, described in our case study, to advancing the best interests of the children solidified trust across all the adult role relations in this school community. Ridgeway, however, recorded results below the mean for teacher-principal trust and teacher-parent trust, results that reflect the deep conflicts that pervaded the school. As our case analysis suggested, Dr. Newman's lack of leadership allowed problems between teachers and parents to fester and grow. These same leadership issues also eroded the teachers' trust in Dr. Newman.

Not surprisingly, our middle case study school, Thomas, presented mixed results on the trust measures. The reports on teacher-principal trust were about a half point below the citywide mean, but still almost one point and a half above that of Ridgeway. Teacher-teacher trust at Thomas also was below the mean. None of this is surprising given the history of Thomas as essentially two separate schools with different missions, different resources, and most salient, two faculties with quite different personal and cultural backgrounds. The strongest trust reports for Thomas were for the teacher-parent role set. This too is expected given our field observations. In general, the 1994 survey results supported our case analyses, and provided additional field-based evidence that surveys could reliably measure relational trust in school communities.

Based on continued analysis of the field data, psychometric studies of the 1994 measures, and our theory review, we were able to further refine the trust measures for a 1997 follow-up survey of CPS teachers.[4] The revised measures contain virtually all of the items asked in 1994, with additional questions written to deepen our focus on the competence and integrity dimensions of relational trust. Specifically, we asked teachers whether or not the principal is an effective manager and whether teachers respect their colleagues who are experts at their craft. We also asked teachers whether the principal places the needs of the children ahead of his or her personal and political interests and whether teachers believe that parents do their best to help their children learn. (Appendix B provides further detail about both the 1994 and 1997 measures and their technical properties.)

Does Relational Trust Vary Among Schools?

Since we view trust as an organizational property, a first key test is whether our trust measures vary substantially across a large sample of schools. If they do not, it would be impossible for them to explain much of the between-school variability in academic improvement. In fact, we found that substantial variability does exist among schools on these measures.[5] To illustrate these results, we compare teacher survey responses in high and low scoring schools on each of the three

Figure 6.2   Comparing Responses in Top and Bottom Quartile Schools on Teacher-Teacher Trust (1997 Survey)

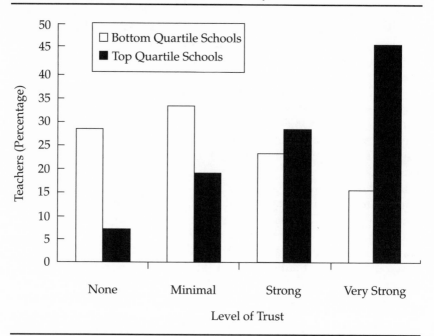

Source: Authors' configuration.

different relational trust measures (teacher-parent, teacher-principal, and teacher-teacher). For this purpose, teachers' responses are grouped into one of four categories that range from reports about no or minimal trust to reports of strong or very strong trust across their school community. The development of these categories is based on a statistical procedure called Rasch Rating Scale Analysis.[6] A nice feature of rating scale analysis is that associated with each scale score is a modal pattern of teacher responses to all the items that comprise the scale. For example, each relational trust measure was placed on a 10-point scale. A teacher with a value of 2.0 on this scale typically disagrees or strongly disagrees with virtually all of our probes about whether respect and trust characterizes a particular role relationship. In contrast, a teacher with a score of 9.0 would be strongly agreeing with virtually every item. (For a detailed description of the categories for each measure see appendix B.)

Figures 6.2 to 6.4 present teacher responses from the top and bottom quartile schools in Chicago on each measure from the 1997 surveys. High levels of teacher-teacher trust are dominant in the top

Figure 6.3   Comparing Responses in Top and Bottom Quartile Schools on Teacher-Principal Trust (1997 Survey)

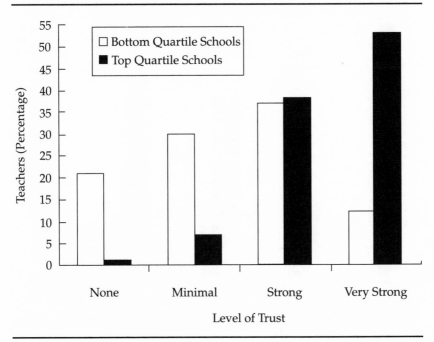

Source: Authors' configuration.

quartile schools. About three-quarters of teachers in these schools report either strong or very strong trust relations with colleagues. These teachers typically describe an atmosphere of general respect among colleagues. They value others who are expert at their craft and who take leadership roles in school improvement. Teachers in these schools also typically report that they trust, confide in, and care about one another. The bottom quartile schools are quite different. The majority of teachers in these schools describe no or minimal levels of trust among teachers. These teachers typically experience little or no respect from their colleagues. They explicitly report that teachers do not confide in, trust, or care about one another.

The responses for teacher-principal trust show a similar pattern. Over half of the teachers in the top quartile schools offer very strong reports about their principal. Virtually all teachers in these schools feel very good about this relationship. These teachers typically describe their principal as an effective manager who supports their professional development. They perceive that the principal looks out for their welfare and also places the needs of students first. In the bottom

Figure 6.4   Comparing Responses in Top and Bottom Quartile Schools on Teacher-Parent Trust (1997 Survey)

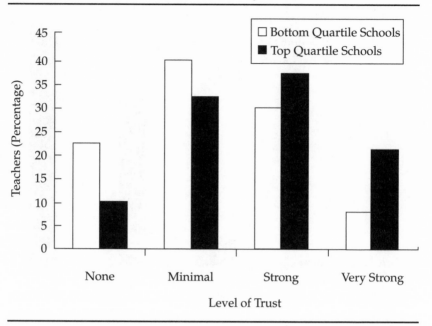

Source: Authors' configuration.

quartile schools, however, a majority of the teachers report minimal or no trust in their principal. Teachers in these schools typically do not feel respected by their principal, and they do not respect the principal as an educator. Teachers explicitly state that they do not trust their principal and do not feel comfortable confiding in him or her.

The pattern of reports for teacher-parent trust is somewhat less differentiated between high and low trust schools. In general, the reports from the top quartile schools are not as positive for this role relation as for the previous two. This is not surprising given the highly disadvantaged clientele served by most Chicago public schools. Even in the highest rated schools, only about 20 percent of teachers characterize the trust among teachers and parents as very strong, with another 37 percent rating the trust level as strong. Teachers in these schools generally agree (but not strongly) that they feel parental support, and that talking with parents helps to improve their teaching. Parents and teachers in these schools show mutual respect, and teachers report little conflict between themselves and parents. Trust reports between teachers and parents are much lower, however, in the bottom quartile schools. We characterize over 60 percent of the reports from teachers in this group as signaling no or minimal trust.

Teachers in these schools typically sense little respect from parents and offer little or no respect for parents in return. They perceive only weak support from parents for their teaching efforts, and teachers make no efforts to engage parents as partners in the schooling enterprise.

Taken together, these results indicate substantive differences in trust levels across Chicago schools. Again, in broad terms, the survey reports are quite consistent with our field observations. The differences between top and bottom quartile schools are highly visible in day-to-day social exchanges, and this can readily be discerned even in relatively brief visits to such schools.

What Kinds of Schools Have Strong Relational Trust?

Given the substantial variability across schools in relational trust, we next sought to examine the kinds of school communities where this organizational attribute was most prevalent. We undertook a number of analyses to consider how aspects of school structure and social composition might affect the development and maintenance of trust. Prior research suggested that small school size might be an important facilitating factor, since it is easier to maintain frequent communication and informal relations in small schools. In contrast, in larger social networks, misunderstandings can more readily occur. They also can be harder to correct, and their persistence undermines trust. More generally, a substantial body of research now documents the positive impact of small school size on the social engagement of teachers and students and the effectiveness of school change efforts.[7]

Trust relations are easier to maintain between parents and teachers in schools with more stable student populations. As noted in chapter 2, social trust is built up over time through sustained social interactions. Although the reputations of individual school leaders can help to maintain trust in unstable social networks, social instability will tend to tax the overall level of trust and may ultimately undermine it.

Trust between parents and teachers should also be much easier to sustain in schools with demonstrated effectiveness. Parental trust of professionals should be higher in schools where a body of evidence shows that students are learning. Thus, the past achievement level of a school is another factor influencing the maintenance and growth of trust.

Finally, the absence of racial and ethnic tensions in the school community makes it easier to maintain social trust. In the context of a persistent urban segregation, racial divisions remain prevalent in some schools. Under these circumstances, to interpret any misunder-

Table 6.1   School Context Effects on 1997 Relational Trust Measures

School-Level Variables	Teacher-Parent Trust	Teacher-Principal Trust	Teacher-Teacher Trust
Racial conflict among teachers	−1.1100***	−1.8842***	−2.3065***
Prior school achievement, 1989	0.0027*	0.0061**	0.0021
Low income (percentage)	−0.0021	0.0077	0.0033
Small school size	0.1232	0.2930	0.3115*
Stability of student body	0.1829*	0.0527	0.2443**
Racial-ethnic composition			
Predominantly African American	−0.3665***	−0.7036***	−0.3776***
Predominantly Hispanic	0.1649	−0.4505*	−0.0633
Predominantly minority	−0.1117	−0.1094	0.0324
Racially mixed	−0.1622	−0.5154*	−0.2430*

Source: Authors' compilation.
Note: All of the school composition characteristics used in this analysis are from the 1993 to 1994 school year. The data on racial conflict come from the Consortium's 1997 teacher survey.
*$p < 0.05$.
**$p < 0.01$.
***$p < 0.001$.

standing and miscommunication along racial lines is natural. Maintaining a broad base of trust is not likely in such situations.[8]

Table 6.1 presents the results of our final analysis.[9] We found that the stability in a school's student population significantly predicts both teacher-parent and teacher-teacher trust but not teacher-principal trust. The stability of a student population conditions the nature of the relationships that teachers can have with parents. With a stable student body, teachers have more opportunities to develop and sustain meaningful interactions with the parents of their students. It would not be unusual, for example, for someone who has taught in a stable school community to have been the classroom teacher for several children from the same family. These stability effects appear to carry over into higher teacher-teacher trust levels as well.

Interestingly, the rate of turnover in the student body does not appear to affect teacher-principal trust. We suspect that this is primarily influenced by the direct exchanges among teachers with their principal. Given the strong asymmetry in these relations (as discussed in chapter 2), we would expect teacher-principal trust to be primarily explained by the principal's actions to develop supportive ties that relieve teachers' sense of vulnerability. Our data suggests that this can be accomplished even in settings where high student turnover occurs.

As predicted, a history of positive academic achievement at the school is related to teacher-parent and teacher-principal trust. Our composite measure of student achievement prior to reform offers an objective indicator that is readily accessible to external groups such as parents. This measure affords parents one basis for making judgments about how much to trust their child's school, absent direct experiences to the contrary. In addition, a history of strong prior achievement at a school also suggests an established organizational effectiveness. From this perspective, the positive effects reported in table 6.1 may well indicate a carryover effect of relational trust that existed prior to reform in higher-achieving schools.

Also as predicted, the presence of racial-ethnic tensions among the faculty clearly identified schools with low levels of relational trust. In previous analyses of these data, racial conflicts were found to be more prevalent in schools that enrolled several different racial-ethnic groups and where no one group dominated.[10] In such contexts, multiple cleavages along racial-ethnic lines easily can develop, each of which has the potential for fomenting social distrust. This also is consistent with results in table 6.1, where we see that racially mixed schools report lower trust levels.

Negative trust relations also were reported in schools with predominately African American student bodies. This is consistent with other case study accounts of the difficulties of initiating meaningful school change in some of these contexts.[11] We also know more generally that these schools were less likely to show major improvements in student learning in Chicago between 1990 and 1996.[12]

We also found, as expected, somewhat better reports for teacher-teacher and teacher-principal trust in small schools with enrollments of less than 350 students.

Measuring Schools' Contributions to Student Learning

The variability among schools in relational trust documented herein is important to us only to the extent that an actual link exists between it and improvements in student learning. To investigate this issue, we drew on results from the annual standardized tests administered by the Chicago Public Schools. During our study period from 1990 to 1996, virtually all students in grades 3 through 8, and most students in grades 1 and 2, took the Iowa Tests of Basic Skills (ITBS) in reading and mathematics. Different forms of the ITBS were administered each year, however, which makes a comparison of results over time a bit more complex. Fortunately, the Consortium on Chicago School Research undertook a study to equate these different test forms. This allowed a rescaling of the seven years of test data into a common metric, which affords a better basis for judging the actual improvements in student learning. We used this rescaled metric in the analyses described here.[13]

We note that some concerns have been raised about the validity of standardized test data from public schools. These issues appear especially salient in the context of high stakes accountability initiatives where, for example, individual students may be retained in grade and where teachers and principals may receive bonuses or alternatively lose their jobs based on published test scores. Under such circumstances, strong incentives exist to "get better numbers," and reported test score data become more suspect. Legitimate questions can be raised: Are schools really making significant improvements in overall effectiveness, or just focusing efforts on test preparation and other short-term initiatives (for example, changing the criteria to exclude weaker students from the testing program) aimed primarily at making the numbers look better?

Fortunately for our research purposes, the Chicago Public Schools did not operate under a test-driven high-stakes reform during the period of our inquiry. Although the School Reform Act of 1988 aimed to raise student achievement, no explicit rewards or sanctions were applied based on the annual ITBS score reports. Rather, the reform encouraged a broad-based restructuring of school operations and organization, which admittedly might take several years to effect. Under such low-stakes circumstances, we maintain that standardized test score trends do in fact provide a reliable signal about any significant changes in overall organizational effectiveness. That is, if a school truly improves its productivity, we should see at least some signs of it in these data.

It would be tempting to form a simple test score trend based on yearly mean achievement in each school and use this as a basis for judging school improvement. Such a trend indicator is problematic, however, especially in urban contexts with high rates of student mobility. A school may be adding a lot to student learning, but if the school has a continuous influx of new weakly prepared students, annual test score reports may miss these positive effects.[14] On the other side of the ledger, if a school begins to attract better students as a result of neighborhood gentrification, for example, its achievement scores are likely to improve, but this may not signal any real change in organizational productivity. Indeed, getting better students is probably the easiest way to get better test scores.

Concerns of this sort lead to the following basic principle for judging school improvement. In order to make a valid inference about changes in the performance of a school (that is, whether it is improving over time), we need to answer two questions: How much are children learning while they are enrolled at that school, and are these learning gains improving over time?

The Academic Productivity Profile

This perspective focuses attention on assessing trends in student learning gains. That is, if genuine productivity improvements are occurring, the school's contribution to students' learning should be increasing over time. To be clear, improving school productivity does not necessarily mean high test scores. If a school enrolls a large proportion of weakly prepared students, the school may contribute a great deal to their learning (that is, high productivity), but overall test scores may still be rather low because of the prior academic background that these students brought to the school.

To implement this idea of measuring a school's contribution to student learning, we developed a *school academic productivity profile*. The school profile actually consists of a set of profiles, one for each grade in the school for which end-of-year and prior-year test scores are available. Figure 6.5 illustrates the idea of a grade productivity profile using data from sixth grade at the Prairie School.[15]

The grade productivity profile is built up out of two basic pieces of information for each year under consideration: the *input status* for the grade and the *learning gain* recorded for that grade. The input status captures the background knowledge and skills that students bring to their next grade of instruction. To estimate this input status, we first identify all of the students who received instruction for a full academic year in each grade in each school, and then retrieve their test scores from the previous spring. (Students who move into or out of a school during the academic year do not count in the productivity profile for that year.) For our illustrative case, we retrieved the end of grade 5 test scores for students who spent grade 6 at the Prairie School. The average of these students' previous year's test scores is the input status for that school grade. This input status is what the

Figure 6.5   Constructing a Sixth-Grade Productivity Profile for Prairie School, 1991 to 1996

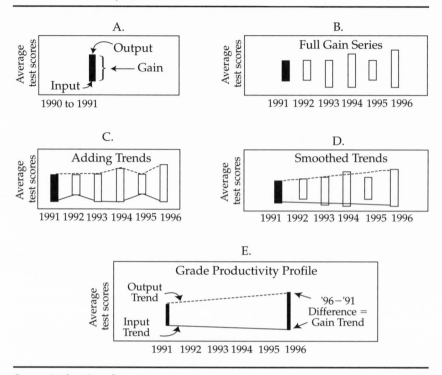

Source: Authors' configuration.

grade 6 teachers at Prairie School had to build on in seeking to advance their students' learning over the course of the next academic year.

As for the learning gain for each school grade, this is simply how much the end-of-year results improved over the input status for this same group of students. By adding the learning gain to the input status, we recover the third piece of information: the *output status*. This tells us about the knowledge and skill levels of the students in each school-grade as they end another year of instruction.

Panel A in figure 6.5 displays the input status, learning gain, and output status for grade 6 at Prairie School in the base year of 1990 to 1991. We then add to this in panel B the data for years after 1991. The panel now contains all of the basic data for examining changes in the academic productivity in grade 6 at Prairie School. We are interested specifically in the time trends reflected in these data. A visual scan of panel B suggests that the inputs to grade 6 at Prairie School may be declining over time. Countering this, the learning gains appear to be increasing and, with this, the outputs also appear to be increasing. To make this clearer, panel C adds an *input trend* and an *output trend* to the profile. Even so, notice that considerable noise remains, which tends to obscure the overall patterns in the data. To highlight this better we compute smoothed trends that involve estimating the best summary line that fits these data, presented in panel D. To make the trends clearer, panel E presents the trend lines with the basic data removed.

Indeed, the inputs to grade 6 have declined. We also see more clearly now that the input and output trend lines have spread apart. (Also notice how the right-hand side of the trapezoid is larger than the side on the left.) This indicates an improving gain trend; that is, the learning gains in grade 6 at Prairie School at the end of the study (the 1995 to 1996 academic year) were greater than at the beginning (the 1990 to 1991 academic year). In addition, notice that the output trend also is rising. This means that the end-of-year test results for grade 6 also are tending up as well.

Key to making such judgments is the estimation of smoothed trend lines through the use of a statistical model.[16] The fitting of such a model also serves another important function: it allows us to adjust the trend estimates for other factors besides school effectiveness that might be changing over time. In seeking to develop the best possible estimates of school productivity, we considered a range of factors, including changes in a school's ethnic composition, percentage of low-income students, retention rates, percentage of students enrolled who are old for their grade, and proportion of bilingual students. Generally, the time-trend effects associated with these factors were not large. As a result, the final adjusted trends used in the analysis were quite similar to the unadjusted estimates.

An Overall Index of a School's Productivity Trend

The school productivity profile contains all of the necessary information for judging changes over time in a school's contribution to student learning. In order to relate these data about trends in school productivity to other organizational characteristics—in particular, our measures of relational trust—we need to summarize the graphic information presented in figure 6.5 in an overall index. Since preliminary analyses suggested that whether a school grade showed an improving gain trend depends to some extent on the initial input status

(1990), the initial gain (1991), and the input trend over time, we decided to compute a summary indicator that adjusted for or held these other three components constant. In essence, we are comparing the gain trend for a particular grade in a given school to all other school grades that are just like it—that is, that started with the same achievement level, had the same amount of achievement gain the first year, and had similar input trends over time. An improving school by this criterion has a gain trend much better than others that started in the same place and experienced similar input trends. Formally, we computed this adjusted gain trend for each grade in each school and then averaged them to form an overall composite indicator of each school's productivity trend.[17]

Productivity Differences Between Improving and Nonimproving Schools

Figures 6.6 through 6.9 illustrate the end results of this process. We identified the top and bottom one hundred schools in the CPS based on this overall indicator of school productivity. We refer to these two groups as improving and nonimproving schools. The separate grade profiles from each school within these two groups were aggregated together grade by grade to produce these composite pictures. Excluded from our analyses are approximately 15 percent of Chicago elementary schools that were initially high achieving (that is, at or above national norms in 1989). This excluded sample consisted primarily of magnet schools, which were under little pressure to improve in the early 1990s and benefited from selective recruitment of their student body.

The output trends for improving schools (figures 6.6 and 6.8 for reading and mathematics, respectively) are quite different from those found in nonimproving schools (compare with figures 6.7 and 6.9, respectively). The output trends in both reading and mathematics are significantly up in virtually every grade in improving schools. In nonimproving schools, however, the output trends are generally flat and in some grades even negative.

More significant are the trends in learning gains over time. These trends signal the extent to which students in 1996 were learning more than their counterparts did in 1991. The percentages appearing in each grade productivity trapezoid are the extent to which the test gains at the end of our study, 1996, exceed (or in some cases are less than) what they were during the base period of 1991. A simple average of these percentages across grades 2 through 8 shows that student

Figure 6.6   Consistently Improving Schools: ITBS Reading Productivity Profile, 1991 to 1996

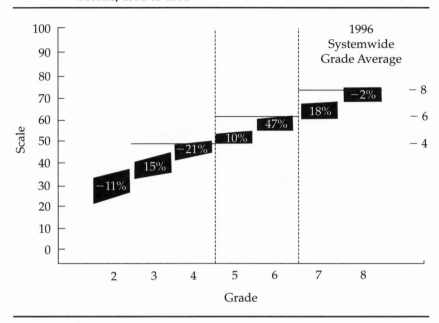

Source: Authors' configuration.
Note: The numbers presented in each grade productivity profile calculate the percentage change in learning gains over the period 1991 to 1996. Positive numbers indicate a positive gain trend. Negative numbers mean a productivity decline in the particular school grade.

learning gains in improving schools at the end of the study were about 8 percent larger in reading than in the base period. For improving schools in mathematics the learning gains in 1996 were almost 20 percent larger than in the base period. Nonimproving schools, however, actually lost ground in reading (gains in 1996 were about 5 percent smaller than in 1991) and stayed about the same in mathematics (gains in 1996 were 3 percent larger than in 1991).

Clearly, our school productivity trend indicator has identified two very different groups of schools. The top 100 schools show marked improvements in academic productivity. The bottom 100 schools, in contrast, show no improvement in mathematics and some signs of decline in reading. These results offer some assurance as we proceed to use this indicator as our key outcome in the analyses to be presented.

**Figure 6.7   Consistently Nonimproving Schools: ITBS Reading
Productivity Profile, 1991 to 1996**

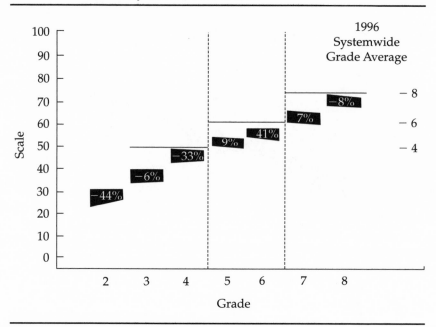

Source: Authors' configuration.
Note: The numbers presented in each grade productivity profile calculate the percentage change in learning gains over the period 1991 to 1996. Positive numbers indicate a
positive gain trend. Negative numbers mean a productivity decline in the particular
school grade.

Linking the Development of Relational
Trust to Improvements in
School Productivity

We are now ready to evaluate the central proposition of this book. We
have posited that relational trust across a school community is a key
resource for improvement. In theory, the base level of trust at any
given point conditions a school's capacity to undertake new reform
initiatives. This effect should be especially strong for complex reforms
that require mutual support and coordinated work among school professionals and sometimes parents as well. Our theory also suggests
that the underlying social processes of school change entail a recur-
sive dynamic. Small wins at school improvement help expand relational trust, thereby creating an enlarged capacity to undertake more
complex changes in the future.[18] Assuming these subsequent efforts

Figure 6.8   Consistently Improving Schools: ITBS Mathematics Productivity Profile, 1991 to 1996

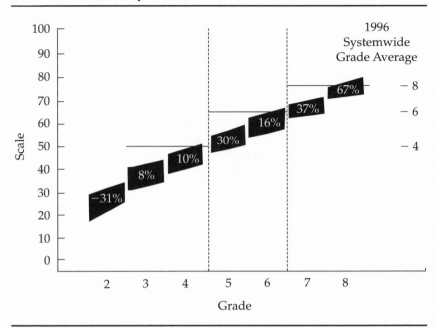

Source: Authors' configuration.
Note: The numbers presented in each grade productivity profile calculate the percentage change in learning gains over the period 1991 to 1996. Positive numbers indicate a positive gain trend. Negative numbers mean a productivity decline in the particular school grade.

also are successful, such efforts should further enlarge the social resources of the school community for subsequent rounds of work. In short, school improvement and social resource development are processes that occur over extended periods and in a real sense, feed each other.

To fully test such a model linking relational trust and improvements in student learning would require frequent, reliable time series information on both school productivity and relational trust. Unfortunately, the data available were somewhat more limited. Nonetheless, our theoretical perspective still suggested a basic analytic approach to pursue. If relational trust operates as a resource for school improvement, we expect that in school communities where relational trust develops over time, achievement trends also should improve. This observation directs us toward examining the linkages, if any, between *changes* in relational trust and *improvements* in student learning.

Figure 6.9   Consistently Nonimproving Schools: ITBS Mathematics Productivity Profile, 1991 to 1996

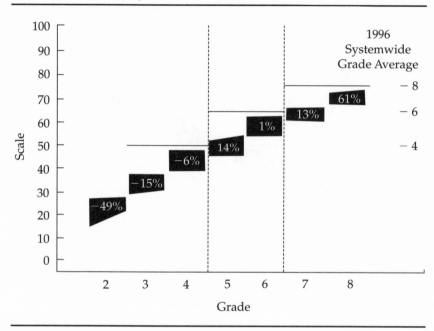

Source: Authors' configuration.
Note: The numbers presented in each grade productivity profile calculate the percentage change in learning gains over the period 1991 to 1996. Positive numbers indicate a positive gain trend. Negative numbers mean a productivity decline in the particular school grade.

Some Simple Descriptive Results

We analyzed the relationship between the school productivity trend indicator, developed in the previous section, and the periodic survey reports that we collected on the quality of social relations in school communities from 1991, 1994, and 1997. Figures 6.10 and 6.11 display the trust report data from 1994 and 1997 for schools that clearly improved academic productivity during the early 1990s and for those that did not. To simplify the display, we averaged the three separate role-relational trust measures for each school into a composite measure for 1994 and 1997, respectively. We also were able to identify a set of items on the 1991 teacher survey about the quality of adult relationships in school communities. Although the 1991 survey was not explicitly designed to measure relational trust in each role set, by clustering a number of different items together we were able to derive a good overall indicator of the state of adult relations during the base

Figure 6.10   Trends in Relational Trust for Improving and Nonimproving Schools in Reading

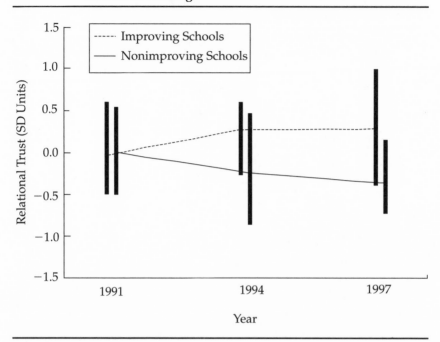

Source: Authors' configuration.
Note: The lines in the figure connect the mean levels of trust on the composite indicator across the three years for each group. The lengths of the bars reflect the interquartile range. The middle 50 percent of the schools are captured here. The top 25 percent offer reports above the top of the bar; the lowest 25 percent fall below the bottom of the bar. All results are in standard deviation (SD) units for the composite trust indicator.

year of our study, 1990 to 1991. These results also are included in figures 6.10 and 6.11.

The patterns of effects are similar for both reading and mathematics. As reform began in the 1990 to 1991 school year, the base quality of social relations in schools that would eventually be identified as "improving" was slightly higher than in those eventually categorized as nonimproving. The modest size of these initial differences is not surprising. The Chicago School Reform Act sought fundamental structural change in the organization and operation of Chicago's public schools. As the Consortium was collecting teacher survey data in the spring of 1991, over 40 percent of the schools had either just taken on a new principal that year or were in the process of making a decision to replace their current leader. In a third of the schools, over 20 per-

Figure 6.11   Trends in Relational Trust for Improving and Nonimproving Schools in Mathematics

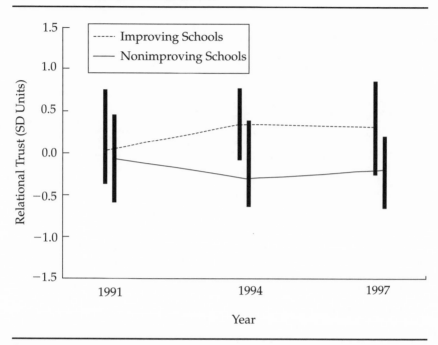

Source: Authors' configuration.
Note: The lines in the figure connect the mean levels of trust on the composite indicator across the three years for each group. The lengths of the bars reflect the interquartile range. The middle 50 percent of the schools are captured here. The top 25 percent offer reports above the top of the bar; the lowest 25 percent fall below the bottom of the bar. All results are in standard deviation (SD) units for the composite trust indicator.

cent of the faculty had been hired in just the last two years.[19] Local school councils, composed primarily of parents and community members, were also just beginning to exercise fully their legally sanctioned authority over local school matters. New and different social processes were emerging in various school communities that would shape the progress of their reform efforts over the next five years.

Much more significant for our purposes is what happened next. By 1994, much higher levels of trust, on average, were reported in schools that eventually would be categorized as academically improving than for those eventually categorized in the nonimproving group.[20] These differences persist through 1997, with almost three-quarters of the nonimproving schools, in both reading and mathematics, offering negative reports on the composite indicator of trust.

In general, the composite trust measure is highly predictive of school productivity trends. Schools reporting strong positive trust levels in 1994 were three times more likely to be categorized eventually as improving in reading and mathematics than those with very weak trust reports.[21] By 1997, schools with strong positive trust reports had a one in two chance of being in the improving group. In contrast, the likelihood of improving for schools with very weak trust reports was only one in seven. Perhaps most telling of all, schools with weak trust reports in both 1994 and 1997 had virtually no chance of showing improvement in either reading or mathematics.[22]

These data provide our first evidence directly linking the development of relational trust in a school community and long-term improvements in academic productivity. Although schools eventually identified as improving and nonimproving offered only slightly different reports about the quality of social relations as reform began in 1991, by 1997 these two groups of schools represent very different social contexts. Many academically improving schools were now in the top quartile on relational trust (see figures 6.2 through 6.4 for a summary of teachers' survey responses from such schools). Similarly, many of the nonimproving schools reported trust levels in 1997 among the bottom quartile of schools in the system.

More Refined Analyses

While these descriptive results strongly suggest that relational trust is a key resource for school improvement, we must acknowledge that other explanatory factors also could be at work here. We have already shown, for example, that the social context and student composition of high- and low-trust schools are somewhat different. Perhaps these factors are contributing to the results observed in figures 6.10 and 6.11. It also is possible that improving schools simply recruited better teachers who were more effective in engaging student learning. This too could account for the simultaneous improvements in achievement and relational trust.

In order to assess more formally the effects of changes in relational trust on improvements in academic productivity, net of these other possible explanations, we undertook a series of Hierarchical Multivariate Linear Model (HMLM) analyses using the overall school productivity indicators in reading and mathematics as the outcomes. We included as predictors a set of school-level factors such as racial composition of the student body, stability of student enrollment, prior achievement history at the school, school size, percentage of low-income students, and concentration of poverty in the school neighbor-

Table 6.2   Effects of Changing Levels of Relational Trust on Improvements in Reading Productivity, 1991 to 1996

Teacher educational background, 1997	-0.0029	-0.0011
Teacher professional background, 1997	-0.0032	0.0009
New teachers hired in first three years of reform (percentage)	0.0001	0.0001
Average years teaching in school, 1997	0.0062	-0.0028
Small school size	0.0416	0.0392
Racial-ethnic composition		
Predominantly African American	-0.0838***	-0.0682**
Predominantly Hispanic	-0.0493	-0.0267
Predominantly minority	-0.0856**	-0.0816**
Racially mixed	-0.0374	-0.0227
Concentration of poverty	-0.0221*	-0.0209*
Low-income students (percentage)	0.0007	0.0008
Stability of student body	0.0173	0.0123
Prior school achievement, 1989	-0.0004	-0.0004
Trust, 1991		-0.0887***
Trust, 1994		0.0971***
Change in trust, 1994 to 1997		0.0366

Source: Authors' compilation.
*$p < 0.05$.
**$p < 0.01$.
***$p < 0.001$.

hood. This allowed us to examine how various student composition and school context factors might link to changing productivity. We also added school-level measures on the percentage of new teachers hired in the first three years of reform, and on teachers' professional background and the average number of years teachers had been at the school in 1997. Taken together, this set of variables provides a test of the hypothesis that differences in teacher personnel were the key distinguishing factor between improving and nonimproving schools. If this were the primary explanation, we should find strong effects associated with each of these variables.[23] Lastly, we introduced our composite measures of relational trust from 1994 and 1997 and our composite indicator of social trust from the base year of 1991. We used the 1991 trust indicator as a control for the overall quality of a school's social relations as reform began. We included the 1994 trust composite and the change in the trust composite from 1994 to 1997 to assess the growth of trust over the next six years.[24] If relational trust is a resource for improving academic productivity, we should find posi-

Table 6.3   Effects of Changing Levels of Relational Trust on Improvements in Mathematics Productivity, 1990 to 1996

Teacher educational background, 1997	0.0433*	0.0465**
Teacher professional background, 1997	0.0025	0.0056
New teachers hired in first three years of reform (percentage)	0.0008	0.0012
Average years teaching in school, 1997	0.0128	0.0045
Small school size	0.1002***	0.0981**
Racial-ethnic composition		
Predominantly African American	−0.1260***	−0.1073***
Predominantly Hispanic	−0.1360***	−0.1175**
Predominantly minority	−0.1814***	−0.1758***
Racially mixed	−0.1252***	−0.1118**
Concentration of poverty	−0.0402**	−0.0353**
Low-income students (percentage)	0.0007	0.0008
Stability of student body	0.0131	0.0033
Prior school achievement, 1989	−0.0008	−0.0009*
Trust, 1991		−0.0849*
Trust, 1994		0.1030***
Change in trust, 1994 to 1997		0.0752**

Source: Authors' compilation.
*p < 0.05.
**p < 0.01.
***p < 0.001.

tive effects for both of these variables (for further details on these analyses see appendix C).

Tables 6.2 and 6.3 display the final results for reading and mathematics, respectively.[25] Improvements in academic productivity were less likely in racially isolated, predominantly minority and racially mixed schools as compared to integrated schools with at least 30 percent white children. The same was true for schools located in communities with a high concentration of poverty. Improvements, especially in mathematics, however, were more likely in small schools. This result is consistent with previous Consortium studies, which found that Chicago's decentralization reform was more likely to be implemented well in such schools.[26] The teacher background variables contributed only modestly to explaining changes in school productivity.[27]

Most important for our purposes, there is no indication that any of these factors explains away the observed connection between developing relational trust and improving academic productivity. That is, even after controlling for differences among schools in various aspects of school context, student composition, and teacher background, we still find strong effects linking changes in relational trust to improvements in academic productivity. The relational trust reports from teachers in 1994 strongly differentiate between schools eventually classified as improving and nonimproving. Moreover, since the analyses control for the base quality of adult relations in schools in 1991, these are in essence change effects. That is, schools that strengthened relations from 1991 to 1994 were more likely to show academic productivity improvements. Similarly, the analysis includes a direct measure of changes in relational trust from 1994 to 1997. Although the estimated effect is weaker in reading than in mathematics, we find here too that developing relational trust is linked to improving productivity. Interestingly, the base level of trust in 1991 is now negatively related to the productivity trend. This means that some schools with initially weak social resources substantially improved their academic productivity over the next six years. For this to happen, however, their relational trust most likely also strengthened over time.[28]

We can demonstrate the substantive importance of these statistical findings by using them to examine some possible, school change scenarios. Suppose, for example, a school was average in all respects in 1991 but was among the bottom quartile of Chicago Public Schools on the trust composite. Also assume that role relations at the school remained basically unchanged for the next six years, and the school continued to report relational trust levels among the bottom quartile for the school system. Our analyses indicate that the overall productivity index for such a school would rank it around the fortieth percentile for reading and the forty-fourth percentile for mathematics as compared to the productivity results for all schools in the system over this period (see figure 6.12).[29] Thus, even though the school was average in terms of student composition and teacher background, its productivity performance would be significantly worse than average. Suppose, however, that a similar school in 1991 began a major restructuring effort and moved to the median of Chicago Public Schools on relational trust by 1994 and into the top quartile of CPS on relational trust by 1997. Our analyses predict that substantial improvements in reading and mathematics productivity would be realized in this case. Concomitant with the change in trust from the bottom to the top quartile, this school would have moved up to the seventy-second percentile among CPS on reading productivity and to the seventy-third percentile in mathematics.

Moreover, we might reasonably expect at least some additional improvements in academic productivity over the next few years, post-

Figure 6.12   Impact of Improving Relational Trust on Trends in Academic Productivity

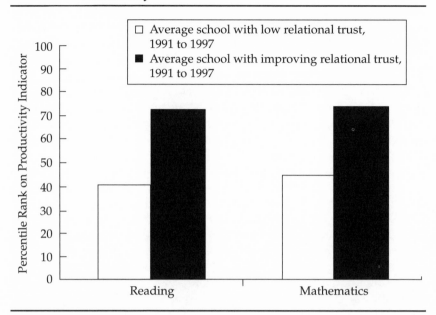

Source: Authors' configuration.

1997. As a social resource for school improvement, relational trust facilitates the development of beliefs, values, organizational routines, and individual behaviors that instrumentally affect students' engagement and learning. As a result, we would expect some time lag between changes in relational trust and subsequent improvements in these student outcomes. Although admittedly speculative on our part, three years seems like a short time frame in this regard. If a school substantially improved its relational trust over a three-year period, the lag effects on learning might continue to grow for a few more years.

Key Organizational Conditions Affected by Relational Trust

The analyses presented here offer strong statistical evidence linking relational trust to improvements in student learning. These results are based on a measure of academic productivity that estimates each school's actual contribution to student learning, and whether this added value has improved over time. We have taken into account the base state of each school as reform began, in terms of average achievement and initial learning gains, and whether there were any changes over time in student background characteristics and prior achievement. Moreover, our analyses document a strong statistical link between *improvements in relational trust and gains in academic productivity*. The latter represents much more compelling evidence than simply documenting through one-time cross-sectional analyses that good schools have strong relational trust. Short of a large-scale social experiment with specific interventions aimed at building relational trust in schools, it is hard to envision a stronger evidence base documenting the significance of relational trust as a resource for school improvement.

We can, however, apply one additional set of tests. As discussed in chapter 2, relational trust does not directly affect student learning. Rather, trust fosters a set of organizational conditions, some structural and others social-psychological, that make it more conducive for individuals to initiate and sustain the kinds of activities necessary to affect productivity improvements. This occurs through four broad mechanisms.

First, relational trust reduces the sense of vulnerability that school professionals experience as they are asked to take on the new and uncertain tasks associated with reform. In this regard, trust acts as a catalyst for change processes that instrumentally connect to improving academic productivity. Specifically in the context of urban school reform, relational trust should facilitate teachers' efforts both to innovate in their classroom in order to develop more effective instruction and to reach out to parents in order to deepen their support around students' engagement in learning. Both of these processes are key to improving academic achievement. Research on school improvement has documented that teachers' orientation toward innovation is an important precondition for instructional improvement.[30] Unless teachers internalize responsibility for improving student learning, better achievement remains unlikely.[31] Similarly, that urban schools must also foster greater parental involvement is well documented.[32] Without such involvement, students' engagement with the school remains weak, and efforts to improve academic achievement will likely be frustrated, regardless of the actual quality of classroom teaching.

Second, relational trust facilitates public problem-solving within an organization. The presence of relational trust among a faculty allows it to coalesce as a professional community where teachers can undertake genuine collective work together.[33] This is important because critical aspects of instructional improvement (such as curriculum alignment across classrooms and maintaining internal accountability among professional staff to ensure that all students learn) require joint problem-solving among teachers and therefore make significant demands on the social resources of a school's faculty.[34]

Third, relational trust also undergirds the highly efficient system of social control found in a school-based professional community. When professional standards are clearly understood and widely shared, the resultant organizational norms strongly order day-to-day work, yet teachers still sense considerable autonomy and mutual support for their individual efforts.[35] This normative aspect of a school-based professional community is especially important as teachers aim for more ambitious classroom instruction.[36] Such instruction entails new, complex teaching practices that demand continuous teacher learning. In a school-based professional community, teachers sense a press to engage in such work and genuinely support each other's learning through the many cycles of trial and error that are involved. In the absence of relational trust, teachers are more likely to withdraw to the privacy of their own classrooms and repeat past practices, even if they clearly do not work.[37]

Fourth, relational trust creates a moral resource for school improvement. School reform is a long-term process that demands sustained adult effort. Extant social-psychological research documents that the level of trust within an organization influences the development of strong personal attachments to the organization and beliefs in its mission.[38] When school participants hold such commitments, they are more willing to give extra effort, even when the work is hard. This is another key to instructional improvement.

Measures of Core Organizational Conditions

Taken together, these arguments suggest that we investigate the extent to which developing relational trust across a school community supports teachers to engage in new practices both in the classroom and in their interactions with parents; how such trust promotes the emergence and maintenance of a school-based professional community; and the degree to which it nurtures teachers' affective commitments to the school and its mission. We used four additional measures, created by the Consortium from the teacher surveys in 1994 and 1997, for this purpose (see appendix B for further details).

Orientation to Innovation   This measure indicates whether teachers are continually learning and seeking new ideas, have a "can do" attitude, and have internalized responsibility to change their practices in order to advance student achievement.

Outreach to Parents   This measure consists of a series of questions to teachers about the school's initiatives to engage parents around the education of their children.[39] Items ask about teachers' efforts to work with parents on meeting individual student needs, to encourage parents to visit classrooms, and to provide opportunities for parents and community members to voice concerns about the school.

Professional Community   Our measure of professional community is actually a composite of four separate measures that assess both the collaborative work practices of teachers and the normative controls guiding this work.[40] Two measures focus on work processes: assessing the extent to which shared work (for example, designing new instructional programs) occurs among faculty, and the prevalence of teachers' conversations with one another about instruction and student learning. Complementing these behavior reports are two measures that tap the nature of professional norms in the school. One measure assesses the extent to which teachers share a commitment to improve both their personal teaching and general school operations. The second measure examines the degree of faculty focus on student learning—considering, for example, whether teachers hold well-defined learning expectations and set high standards for academic performance. We averaged these four separate measures together to create an overall composite indicator of the extent of school-based professional community.[41]

Commitment to the School Community   This measure includes items that ask whether teachers looked forward to working in the school, feel loyal to the school, and would recommend the school to other parents.

Analyses and Results

We have argued that relational trust operates as a social resource for school improvement. If this is the case, then we should find that as trust across a school community improves over time, teachers should offer increasingly positive reports about each of these four factors as well. To evaluate this claim, we examined the link between the *base level of trust in 1994* and changes from 1994 to 1997 in teachers' orientation to innovation, outreach to parents, the degree of professional community, and school commitment. We also examined the relationship between *changes in trust from 1994 to 1997* with changes over the same period in all four outcomes. Again, we controlled for various aspects of school composition. We also controlled for the school's prior reports in 1994 on each respective condition. In this way, we are reasonably confident that we are assessing the effects of the base level of relational trust in 1994 and the growth of relational trust from 1994 to 1997 on the subsequent development of core organizational conditions instrumentally linked to improving academic productivity. (See appendix C for full statistical details about these analyses, including final results.)[42]

In general, the pattern of results proved highly consistent across all four organizational outcomes. Typically, the base level in 1994 on each of the organizational measures was negatively related to changes on that same measure over the period from 1994 to 1997. This means that schools that were initially low on teachers' orientation to innovation, outreach to parents, degree of professional community, and school commitment were somewhat more likely to report improvements in each of these areas over the next three years. Of key significance, the base level of social trust in 1994 was positively related to the size of these improvements. That is, organizational conditions were more likely to improve between 1994 and 1997 if the school had a strong base of relational trust in 1994. This is exactly what we would expect if relational trust functions as a social resource for school improvement. Schools with a strong base of social ties are better positioned to improve their organizational effectiveness. Those lacking such social resources find the task more difficult.

In addition, the changes in relational trust from 1994 to 1997 also were significantly related to positive changes over this period in orientation toward innovation, outreach to parents, professional community, and school commitment. This indicates that schools where relational trust was deepening between 1994 and 1997 also were more likely to report collateral changes in each of these important organizational conditions. So, even if a school started in 1994 with weak relational ties, their organizational effectiveness could improve over the next three years if relational trust grew over this period.

In order to assess the substantive significance of these statistical findings, again we can use our analysis results to simulate the effects of some possible change scenarios. Suppose that we had a school in 1994 that was average in all respects and remained so through 1997. In contrast, suppose that in a similar school, a major restructuring effort was initiated in 1994 and that relational trust improved, so that by 1997 this school resembled one of the top one hundred schools in the CPS on this measure. How much change would we actually witness in teacher reports about orientation to innovation, outreach to parents, professional community, and school commitment? Figure 6.13 presents these results.[43]

Our status quo school would have ranked around the fiftieth percentile among Chicago public elementary schools on each organizational condition. In contrast, our restructuring school would have

Figure 6.13   Impact of Improving Relational Trust (1994 to 1997) on Core Organizational Conditions Over Same Period

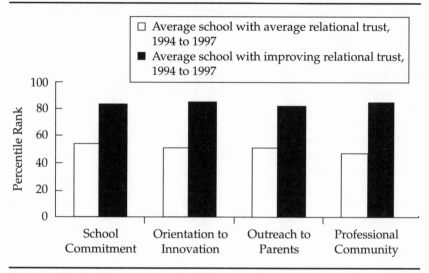

Source: Authors' configuration.
Note: The four measures of core organizational conditions were created by the Consortium on Chicago School Research from teacher surveys in 1994 and 1997.

moved by 1997 into the top quartile on all four measures. Such developments signal a major change over three years in the organizational life of a school. The likelihood of a major improvement in student learning over the next several years in such a school is very high.[44]

Conclusion

The results presented in this chapter are the culmination of a long and complex analytic journey. We have described how the interplay of theoretical understandings and fieldwork findings from parts I and II guided us toward more precise measurement of our core concept— relational trust in school communities. Similarly, we have detailed the logic behind a long progression of statistical analyses aimed at measuring individual school productivity and its changing character over time. Without satisfactorily resolving this latter issue, we could not be sure that our findings were actually detailing an important school change phenomenon rather than an unrelated statistical artifact.

We have focused on recounting the defining moments in this analytic journey, relegating to notes and appendices the technical details of most interest to social science colleagues. Nonetheless, the ideas presented here remain complex both conceptually and empirically. This is because, at base, the problem we seek to understand—improving the academic productivity of very disadvantaged urban schools—is itself complex. Even under good conditions, meaningful school improvement takes years to unfold and entails collateral changes along multiple dimensions at the same time.[45] The primary task of this chapter has been to demonstrate how a core phenomenon—the growth of relational trust in a school community—fuels these multiple strands in the school change process and thereby contributes to improved student learning. Clearly, relational trust matters as a resource for school improvement.

= Chapter 7 =

Analytic and Policy Implications for School Reform

THROUGHOUT this book we have probed the nature of relational trust in urban elementary school communities. We have described how trust is rooted in the microdynamics of day-to-day social interactions among teachers, principals, and parents and the discernments that various participants make about these interactions. In this regard, our work is quite different from other research that describes good schools in diffuse cultural terms as having a distinctive climate or ethos. We have focused instead on detailing the specific behaviors that ground relational trust and the interpretative frameworks that school participants use to judge such behavior.

We have also shown, through both case studies and survey analyses, how the myriad social exchanges that make up daily life in a school community fuse into distinct social patterns that generate (or fail to generate) organization-wide resources. These resources manifest themselves in several ways. First, collective decision making with broad teacher buy-in occurs more readily in schools with strong relational trust. This feature is especially significant in times that call for major structural change, as was the case in Chicago schools throughout the 1990s. The absence of relational trust, however, as vividly demonstrated at Ridgeway school (chapter 3), provoked sustained controversy around resolving even relatively simple organizational concerns.

Second, when relational trust is strong, reform initiatives are more likely to be deeply engaged by school participants and to diffuse broadly across the organization. This situation is different from the superficial implementation or even outright resistance to change observed at both Thomas and Ridgeway schools. Key in this regard is that relational trust reduces the risk associated with change. When school professionals trust each other and feel supported by parents, it feels safe to experiment with new practices. Equally important, relational trust also lubricates the necessary social exchanges among school professionals as they engage together, learning from each other in the trial and error of implementing new practices. To be able to talk honestly with colleagues about "what's working, what's not" means exposing one's ignorance and making oneself vulnerable. Absent trust, genuine conversations of this sort remain unlikely.

Interestingly, the ideas just mentioned about the organization of teachers' work—shared control with internal accountability, where support exists for social learning—are core functional elements in a school-based professional community. Recognizing this is important because a growing body of research during the 1990s indicates that the formation of strong school-based professional communities is necessary to support more ambitious classroom instruction.[1] Thus, the connection of relational trust to the operations of a school-based professional community is highly salient. In essence, trust functions as the social glue necessary for this form of work to coalesce and be maintained.

Third, relational trust foments a moral imperative to take on the hard work of school improvement. Teachers had a full-time job prior to reform. Most worked hard at their teaching, doing the best they could for as many students as they could. In addition to taking risks with new classroom practices, reform also requires teachers to take on extra work: for example, engaging with colleagues in planning, implementing, and evaluating school improvement initiatives. Similarly, reform asks teachers to confront conflict, as this commonly occurs in organizational change processes. From a purely self-interested viewpoint, it would seem quite reasonable for teachers to ask, Why should we do this? A context characterized by high relational trust provides an answer. In the end, reform is simply the right thing to do.

Our analysis of Holiday School (chapter 5) provides strong testimony in this regard. Both professionals and parents at Holiday shared a commitment to go the extra mile for the children. Virtually every person whom we interviewed spoke about the school community in these terms. Strong evidence on this point emerged in our survey analyses as well. In schools with improving relational trust, teachers increasingly characterized their colleagues as committed and loyal to *this school* and more eager to engage in new practices that might help students learn better.

Not surprisingly then, we found that elementary school communities characterized by high relational trust were much more likely to demonstrate marked improvements in academic productivity across the early to mid 1990s in Chicago. Our final composite measure of

Figure 7.1   Relational Trust as a Social Resource for School Improvement

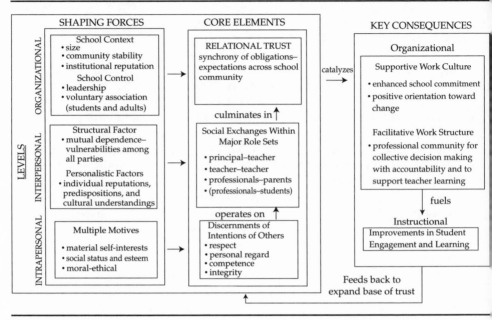

Source: Authors' configuration.

relational trust, based on about two dozen items concerning teachers' discernments regarding their colleagues, principals, and parents, proved a powerful discriminator between schools showing improved academic productivity and those that did not. A school with a low score on relational trust at the end of our study had only a one in seven chance of demonstrating improved student learning between 1991 and 1996. In contrast, half of the schools scoring high on relational trust were in the improved group.[2] Perhaps most significant, schools with chronically weak trust reports over this period had virtually no chance of improving in either reading or mathematics.

We proceed now to revisit key features of relational trust operating in disadvantaged urban schools, to discuss some of the forces that shape the development and maintenance of this trust, and to offer some policy implications that flow from this research. Figure 7.1 provides a summary of this empirically grounded theory.

A Grounded Theory of Relational Trust

Embedded within all of the social exchanges in school communities is an interrelated set of mutual dependencies. This observation is key to understanding the significant function served by relational trust. Regardless of how much formal power attaches to any given role in a school community, all participants remain dependent on others to achieve desired outcomes and feel efficacious about their efforts. These structural dependencies create a sense of mutual vulnerability for all individuals involved. Consequently, deliberate actions taken by any one party to reduce this sense of vulnerability in others can go a long way toward building trust within the community.

Our research has focused on the nature of the social exchanges occurring in each of the major adult role sets found in a school community—the school principal and teachers, teachers with each other, and school professionals with parents. Each party in these role sets maintains an understanding of their personal obligations and holds some expectations about the obligations of the other. These understandings form the basis for judging the actual behavior transacted within each role set.

Effective practice requires a synchrony between parties, both in terms of general understandings about each other's expectations and obligations and in terms of the interpretations made about the specific behavior occurring. For a school community to work well, synchrony must characterize all of the role sets. A major weakness in any one role relation could seriously delimit the school's overall capacity for change.

A Core Intrapersonal Process: Discerning the Intentions of Others

As individuals go about their daily lives in schools, they are constantly engaged in a process of discerning the intentions embedded in the actions of others. These discernments take into account the history of previous interactions that have occurred between the parties. In the absence of prior interpersonal contact, participants may initially rely on the general reputation of the other party and also on ascriptive similarities—for example, commonalities in terms of race, gender, age, religion, or upbringing.

The actual processes of making trust discernments fuse a mix of considerations, including instrumental aims about achieving valued outcomes and the ability to influence the processes that directly affect these outcomes; psychic concerns about advancing one's sense of status, self-esteem, and efficacy; and ethical considerations about "doing right by children." Thus, our theory entails a complex perspective on individual motivation. Specifically, we view the advancement of self-interest–based objectives as interacting with participants' desires to take into account one's own feelings and those of others while also being concerned about enacting one's moral duty.

This theory of motivation in turn implies that four specific evaluative standpoints frame these discernment processes. At the most basic level, relational trust is grounded in social respect. A key practice in this regard is how discourse is structured within a role set relation and more generally across a school community. Respectful exchanges are marked by a genuine sense of listening to what each person has to say, and in some fashion, taking this into account in subsequent actions or conversations. Even when people disagree, individuals feel that the value of their opinions has been recognized. Such social exchanges foster a sense of connectedness among participants and promote affiliation with the larger institutional context.

Without interpersonal respect, social exchanges may literally cease as participants typically choose to exit demeaning situations, if they can. When this exit option is not available, sustained conflict may erupt instead. The interactions among parent leaders and professional staff at Ridgeway School are a prototypical case in this regard. It is ironic that one of the LSC's major initiatives at Ridgeway was a respect program toward students when little of this could be found in the social interactions among parent leaders and key school staff.

Personal regard represents a second, important criterion operating in trust discernments. The social encounters around schooling are more intimate and sustained than typically are found in most modern institutions. Powerful interpersonal bonds can form when school community members sense that others really care about them. A key practice in this regard is the willingness of participants to extend themselves beyond what is formally required by, say, a job definition or a union contract.

The actions of Holiday's principal, Morty Goldman, offer strong testimony to the importance of personal regard. Virtually every parent and teacher with whom we spoke commented effusively about Dr. Goldman's personal style, his openness and welcoming of others, and a genuine willingness to reach out to parents, teachers, and students alike. His efforts established a tone that permeated schoolwide and played a major role in the high level of interpersonal trust found in this, "the most unusual of places."

Third, discernments about role competence also operate as a critical concern. Each participant in a school community assesses the likelihood of attaining desired outcomes in their interactions with others. Parents are concerned about achieving important learning objectives for their children. Teachers seek supportive work conditions for their practice. School administrators value good community relations. In general, we found that individuals working within any given role may address their particular responsibilities in very different ways and yet still be judged in a positive light by others. No one best set of practices characterizes participants' evaluative standpoints in this regard. A consensus does seem to form quickly, however, around judgments about negligence and gross incompetence in the execution of someone's formal responsibilities. Such behavior, if allowed to persist, can be highly corrosive to relational trust. This was, for example, a major factor undermining parent-school relations at Ridgeway, where some clearly incompetent and uncaring teachers were nonetheless allowed to continue to practice.

Lastly, perceptions about personal integrity also shape trust discernments. At a very basic level, we ask whether others can be trusted to keep their word. Within the various role relations around schooling, participants expect consistency between what people say and what they actually do. Such judgments about personal reliability are essential to trusting another. At a more fundamental level, integrity demands that a moral-ethical perspective guides one's work. Conflicts frequently arise among competing individual interests within a school community. In the end, a commitment to the education and welfare of children must remain primary.

The principals at Holiday and Ridgeway offered compelling contrasts in this regard. Like Morty Goldman, Dr. Lionel Newman at Ridgeway was respectful and caring in his social encounters with both parents and teachers. No one was really sure, however, where Dr. Newman stood. He sought to assuage everyone, but rarely followed through on the promises he appeared to make. Even more troublesome, when concerns surfaced regarding some very problematic teachers at Ridgeway, he chose a course of least resistance rather than confrontation.

This aspect of the Ridgeway case also helps to illumine the systemic nature of trust discernments. Dr. Newman demonstrated both high personal regard and respect in his encounters with others. Although serious questions were raised about his approach to personnel management, he did competently execute most of his other basic managerial responsibilities. The school had established routines; extant resources were fairly distributed; and at least by urban standards, the school ran reasonably well. Hardly anyone criticized him on these accounts. Given this, one might have expected at least reasonably positive reports about Dr. Newman's leadership.

Unfortunately, Dr. Newman came up short on the fourth criteria, integrity. Neither teachers nor school community leaders felt that he could be trusted to keep his word. In addition, as Dr. Newman engaged the conflicting agendas at work in his school, hardly anyone interpreted his efforts as primarily directed toward advancing the welfare of children. Far too much of the conflict at Ridgeway was about the competing interests among adults. More so than most places, leadership needed to articulate and advance a program of improvement that placed the education of children first. Dr. Newman, however, never advanced such a program. Any opportunity to bring this school community together was lost.

In sum, individuals' discernments about the actions of others must join together in a coherent fashion. A serious deficiency in any one criterion can be sufficient to undermine relational trust. Fulfilling one's obligations requires competent actions that are undertaken in respectful and caring ways and for what are perceived to be the right reasons.

The Interpersonal Level: Power, Dependency, and Role Relations

Individuals' discernments about intentionality are influenced by the differential power associated with relative social status in an organization. Most relations in schools are asymmetrical with respect to power. Principals hold considerable authority over teachers, and local school professionals in turn hold status over parents. This power asymmetry can be especially extreme in large urban school districts, where poor parents, for example, have little individual recourse if school professionals fail to advance meaningful learning opportunities for their children.

Although important variations exist in the power distribution across roles in an urban school community, no one person exercises absolute power. Even principals—the single most influential actors in schools—remain dependent on both parents and teachers to achieve success in their work. Unfortunately, this structural interdependence among school community members often goes unrecognized as individuals focus instead on their relative status within the large, impersonal urban school district. As a result, their need to cooperate to secure mutually valued aims is given too little consideration.

Principles of Leading a School Community   Teachers are dependent in numerous ways on the actions of their principal, if they are to be successful and feel efficacious. Principals directly control major aspects of teachers' work lives through decisions about such matters as the students they assign to them, and the amount and kinds of instructional resources made available. Principals also indirectly influence teachers' work through the basic social norms that they help set for their schools. These expectations and associated organizational routines can either constrain or enhance how teachers interact with students, parents, and other teachers. At a more personal level, principals signal through day-to-day behavior their regard for individual teachers. Teachers in turn quickly discern whether they are valued and respected by their school leader.

Consequently, any actions taken by a principal that reduce teachers' sense of vulnerability can be highly salient. Establishing inclusive decision-making procedures that afford teachers real opportunities to raise issues is one key practice in this regard. The teachers at Holiday, for example, praised Dr. Goldman for his open-door policy and felt confident that any concern they might have would get a fair hearing. Teachers understood that they had a voice in important decisions affecting their work lives.

Our cases also illustrate how teachers' sense of vulnerability is especially heightened during clarion calls for reform. As public criticism focuses on schools' inadequacies, teachers need to know that their principal values their efforts and senses their good intentions. We witnessed how this concern played out in complex ways at the Thomas School. The principal, Raul Gonzalez, articulated a compelling vision for Thomas as a fully bilingual school and vitalized this vision with extensive outreach on his part to parents and the community. Unfortunately, his interactions with his faculty were much less coherent, leaving many teachers feeling uncertain and vulnerable about their place in his reform plans. Dr. Gonzalez largely ignored some teachers in an attempt to tacitly signal his disapproval. This use of silence had an unnerving impact on these individuals. They clearly did not sense Dr. Gonzalez's support, but they also remained uncertain as to what he really expected of them. Others, who were praised and rewarded, also felt uneasy, because the reasons they received these rewards were also never satisfactorily articulated.

In general, school faculties expect that all teachers should be treated similarly. Considerable effort is needed to legitimate differentiated rewards among teachers within the same school. Without compelling explanations, that some interpret Dr. Gonzalez's action as teacher favoritism is not surprising. Such discernments tend to pit teachers against teachers, and thus undermine not only teacher-principal trust but teacher-teacher trust as well.

Teachers Working with Teachers   U.S. teachers spend most of their time working alone in classrooms with groups of students. While a teacher might have one or more free periods each day, these typically are used for individual lesson planning or supplemental work with individual students. Very little time is available in most U.S. schools for professional collaboration. Since teachers largely work in isolation from colleagues, one might be tempted to conclude that teachers are not especially dependent on colleagues in the conduct of their work. Research, however, suggests that this is far from true.[3] Teachers in fact remain reliant on colleagues in complex ways to achieve personal success.

Teachers need each other's help to carry out the basic routines of schooling. As teachers plan instruction, for example, they depend on students having acquired certain knowledge, skills, and dispositions as they advance from grade to grade. A serious teaching deficiency in a prior grade can make a teacher's work more difficult and may even thwart her or his success. Similarly, teachers' classroom efforts are either enabled or constrained by a wide range of policies, typically developed by a school faculty, on such matters as student discipline, textbook use, and alignment of curricular objectives. Depending on the content of these decisions and the extent to which they are commonly adhered to, these too can either support or undermine teachers' work.

At a deeper level, relational trust within a faculty is grounded in common understandings about what students should learn, how instruction should be conducted, and how teachers and students should behave with one another. For teachers to sense integrity among colleagues, a faculty must not only share these views but also perceive that the actions taken by other teachers are consistent with them. We note in this regard that the moral-ethical dimensions of classroom life are prominent in teachers' thinking about their work.[4] Most individuals who enter the teaching profession tend to express strong sentiments about caring for children, and instances of flagrant disregard for children—even if only by a few teachers—can have profound effects. While faculty members may be reticent to directly confront their offending colleagues, teachers will eschew collaborative activities with others whom they regard as behaving unprofessionally. In short, teachers must work together to advance educational opportunities for children; but if teachers don't trust their colleagues (which often is the case in schools most in need of reform), the required collaborative efforts are unlikely to be initiated and sustained.

Professionals Engaging Parents   In the context of power asymmetry, the burden generally falls to the more powerful party to initiate actions that reduce the sense of vulnerability experienced by others. Given the significant power imbalance between poor parents and school professionals in most urban contexts, it is incumbent on school professionals to take the lead. During our field research, we observed a variety of initiatives aimed at this problem. These included starting a parent center at the school; designing instructional support activities that parents can do at home to assist student learning; and developing parent and family programs in response to local needs. Often accompanying these specific programs were more general efforts by school staff to welcome parents and demonstrate a personal interest in their children. While each program or activity might seek to address a specific problem, all of them also serve to enlarge the social resources within the school community. As parents perceive a wide range of behaviors intended to make them feel more comfortable, they come to understand that school staff hold genuine regard for them and really care about their children. Moreover, the consequences are especially salient for poor, immigrant school communities such as Thomas, where the local public school is truly a foreign institution.

The power dynamics within the parent-school professional role set were particularly interesting in our study, given the context of the 1988 Chicago School Reform Act. This legislation deliberately sought to redress the power imbalance between poor parents and school professionals by devolving genuine authority and resources to local school councils. The Holiday and Ridgeway cases offer especially interesting contrasts in how these provisions actually unfolded. Even though parents and community members in both sites held a supermajority (eight out of eleven slots) on their local school council, only limited human resources actually existed on the Holiday LSC to direct school improvements. Both parents and community representatives on the LSC recognized this and generally deferred to the judgments of professional staff about appropriate improvement plans. School staff, however, did encourage an active, parental presence in the school and regularly demonstrated genuine caring for students. In essence, teachers and parents at Holiday negotiated a complementary role relationship supporting the education of children. Given the large social class differences between parents and school staff, and the racial difference between the parents and principal, one might have expected at least some conflict at Holiday between home and school. Instead of posing a problem, though, these social relations turned out to be a resource for improvement.

In contrast, parent and community leaders on the LSC at Ridgeway believed they knew best what their children needed and what school staff should do to accommodate them. LSC leaders sought major changes in school curriculum and instructional organization. Although many of their proposals may have appeared reasonable to outside observers, LSC leaders made little effort to recruit teachers as collaborators in these reforms. Formally, the 1988 Reform Act gave the council authority to legislate the local changes that it did. Interestingly, a case of power role-reversal emerged in the enactment of this local control at Ridgeway. Now the staff was suddenly dependent on parental authority. As the LSC tried to use this authority, it became incumbent on them to acknowledge the staff's vulnerability and make a good-faith effort to include them in the change process. Without such overtures on the part of the LSC, relations remained negative and the envisioned reforms went nowhere. The fact that parent leaders now had and sought to use their considerable authority did not vitiate their continued dependence on school staff to effect desired improvements for their children.

In retrospect, Chicago's legislated reform was a bit shortsighted in this regard. Simply transferring formal authority to parents and community leaders did not solve the social misalignments (discussed in chapter 1) that exist in many urban schools between local professionals and the parents and communities they are supposed to serve. At base remains a deep-seated issue in professional-parent role relations. Teachers expect some recognition from parents of their professional expertise. The absence of this recognition in a poor community such as Ridgeway was particularly upsetting as teachers asked, Who are these poor people telling us how best to do our jobs? Yet we also observed a very similar dynamic in an integrated middle-class Chicago school that was also studied as part of our larger research project.[5]

In general, as parents and community leaders seek to use legal authority to change a school, they must recognize that the exercise of this authority is likely to provoke feelings of vulnerability among professional staff. Since parents and community leaders now hold the superordinate power position, their responsibility is to acknowledge teachers' vulnerability and actively seek to reduce it. Such leadership demands considerable social and political skill. Attention must focus on personal affirming of staff. At the same time, school leaders need to constantly communicate a vision for change and demonstrate integrity in advancing actions toward this vision. This complex of behaviors is relational trust building for school change.

Key Shaping Forces at the Organizational Level

We have articulated a three-level theory of relational trust as a resource for school improvement. Such trust takes root in the discernments that individuals make about the interpersonal social exchanges occurring within a school community. These social exchanges, and the discernments made about them, are in turn shaped by a number of key school community-level factors. We already alluded, for example, to the powerful influences that school leadership plays in this regard. Similarly, chapter 3 documents how Ridgeway School's reputation in the community as an unresponsive institution and how the reputation of community-based organizations as aggressive and politically self-interested conditioned the social exchanges between professionals and parent leaders toward distrust.

We also found in our statistical analyses in chapter 6 that two key structural aspects—school size and the stability of the student-parent group—affects a school's capacity to develop and maintain relational trust. As elaborated further in the next section, both of these factors significantly influence the nature of the social exchanges that occur within a school community.

Similarly, our case studies direct attention to how membership is formed in a school community. Other research on Chicago's reform has documented the importance of a school leader's ability to control the entry and exit of faculty as a lever for school change.[6] We saw how relational trust was promoted at Holiday by a principal's skillful use of his expanded authority under the 1988 Reform Act with regard to the hiring of new teachers. We also saw how the principal's inability to remove problematic teachers at Ridgeway undermined trust in that context.

Policy Implications

The results presented here demonstrate the powerful impact that the quality of social exchanges can have on a school's capacity to improve. A strong base of relational trust lubricates much of a school's day-to-day functioning and is a critical resource as local leaders embark on ambitious education reforms. These findings have important implications for the extensive efforts, now ongoing nationwide, to enhance student learning.

Connections to Contemporary Conversations About School Reform

Chapter 1 began with a brief overview of diverse efforts currently under way to reform U.S. schools. Many of these initiatives cluster around two major themes: governance reform and instructional improvement. The first perspective views the weaknesses in our public education system as linked to the large-scale democratic control of public education by school boards (both state and local) and their attendant public bureaucracies. It is argued that unless these institutional arrangements are fundamentally altered, little improvement is likely to occur. While this policy analysis is most closely linked to choice and charter and voucher initiatives, the authors of Chicago's democratic localism reform actually shared a similar view of the reform problem.[7]

Policy advocates in the second group, however, argue that reform must focus first and foremost on instruction and its improvement. Everything else is a distraction. They maintain that policy should aim at the immediate instruments most likely to improve instruction— such as standards, new curricula and assessments, teacher development, and instructional leadership. Policy also should attend to systemic sanctions and incentives that might catalyze changes in all of these instruments.

Our research intersects these disparate policy debates with a perspective on effective organizational change. Specifically, we have demonstrated that improving student learning requires a base of social resources in a school community. Without such resources, neither initiatives arising from within the school nor those developed externally are likely to deeply engage a school faculty or broadly diffuse across the organization.

When viewed in combination with other research findings on Chicago's decentralization reform, our results offer a concrete explanation as to how governance reform can make a difference.[8] Specifically, by reshaping the power relationships among principals, teachers, parents, and local community leaders, Chicago's 1988 reform pressed local actors to revisit their expectations of each other and to reconsider their own sense of obligations. When this structural change actually resulted in constructive new dialogue within school communities, it opened up possibilities for developing new social resources at the school-building level. To be sure, this did not happen in every Chicago school, as we saw at Ridgeway. Nonetheless, ample evidence now shows that this did happen in many of Chicago's elementary schools during the early to mid-1990s, and many of these schools substantially improved student learning.[9]

Our research on Chicago suggests that governance reforms matter to the extent that they catalyze a redress within school communities in the dysfunctional understandings that may now operate among adults about their mutual obligations for the education of children. We therefore expect that significant improvements in student learning might well follow from other governance reforms if the reshaping of the power distribution structured by these reforms actually foster a renewal of relational trust within school communities. Absent such relational trust building, improvements in the quality of schooling remain very unlikely.

Our results should also be read as a caution to instructional reform advocates. Clearly, teachers' interactions with students regarding subject matter must improve if major advances in learning are to occur. Such developments also appear very unlikely, however, so long as the social resource base remains dysfunctional in a school community. Regardless of the quality of professional development offerings, new instructional materials purchased, or technological resources provided, little of value is likely to accrue unless some collective capacity exists among adults to engage these external resources in meaningful ways.

In short, we view relational trust as creating the fertile social ground for core technical resources (such as standards, assessments and new curricula) to take root and develop into something of value. Without this, individual staff may excel at their work, certain school functions may be well executed, but the school as a social system will continue to fail many of its members.

Implications for Developing New Teachers   It is commonly argued in policy circles today that we need better teachers if more ambitious student learning is to occur. These arguments are typically followed by proposals to strengthen teacher education programs, introduce career ladders to make teaching more attractive to its senior members, and increase the fiscal incentives for more of our "best and brightest" to consider teaching as a career in the first place. In our view, all of these proposals have merit; all have a contribution to make in the overall reform of U.S. schools. Even so, our analyses also suggest that the basic observations on which these proposals rest can be turned on their head—that is, we may well need better schools as professional workplaces for adults if we are to have better teachers.

That much of teachers' professional practices are learned during their first few years of work in schools rather than in their college classrooms is well documented. What teachers learn or fail to learn on the job and the norms of practice that they develop will likely shape their work for a lifetime. In urban contexts such as Chicago, dedicated, energetic young teachers often encounter anomic school norms where teachers are alienated by basic work conditions. Many veteran teachers have come to view their students' needs as so overwhelming, and the larger school system as so resistant to change, that resignation becomes the only survival strategy. Such contexts create a revolving door for young teachers. Unable to establish supportive work relations that make sense to them, these individuals quickly spin out of urban public schools; unfortunately, they often exit the profession as well.

In short, to better prepare new teachers for urban schools, the workplace environment of these schools must be fundamentally different. Adult social relations must bind together around a shared sense of mission to educate urban children. Senior teachers must accept responsibility for developing new colleagues, seeing this not as an extra burden but rather as a central part of their role in the collective life of a school-based professional community. In such a context, new teachers are more likely to feel supported; they will know that it is safe to take risks, to try, fail, and then to try again at improving the educational opportunities afforded children.

The Processes of Building Relational Trust in a School Community   Relational trust is a complex concept that entails more than just making school staff feel good about their work and their colleagues. One could envision the latter occurring in some schools, for example, where resources are plentiful, teachers are offered extensive discretion over their work, and school leadership goes to some length to keep individual relations cordial. Consonant with high levels of teacher autonomy, norms of expressive individualism would moderate relations among the faculty. Ample space (both literally and figuratively) would exist for everyone to do his or her own thing. Missing from this school life description, however, is the unifying value that we have emphasized throughout: above all else, collective action focuses on advancing the best interests of children.

Resources remained scarce in the urban schools we studied. Critical decisions had to be made about what schools would and would not do. Fulfillment of basic adult needs—both instrumental and psychic—is important, but their fulfillment stands in a dynamic tension with responding to the multiple needs of children. School decision making must work for both adults and students alike. The key task for school leadership involves getting the balance right. This entails a constant moderation between demonstrating a personal regard for faculty while steadfastly advancing the primary mission of the school. When conflicts arise, organizational integrity must be preserved. Ultimately, adult behavior must be understood as directed toward the betterment of children.

Relational trust thus is not something that can be achieved simply through some workshop, retreat, or form of sensitivity training, although all of these can be helpful. Rather, relational trust is forged in daily social exchanges. Through their actions, school participants articulate their sense of obligations toward others, and others in turn come to discern the intentionality enacted here. Trust grows over time through exchanges where the expectations held for others are validated in action. Even successful simple interactions can enhance collective capacities for more complex subsequent actions; in this regard, increasing trust and deepening organizational change are reciprocal.

For relational trust to develop and be sustained, adults and students alike must be able to make sense of their work together in terms of what they understand as the primary purpose of the public school: Why are we really here? The answer, for the poor urban schools we studied, boils down to one core consideration: Can school practice be understood as aimed at affording disadvantaged youngsters a genuine bridge to the larger society?[10]

Centrality of Principal Leadership   Given the asymmetry of power in urban school communities, the actions that principals take play a key role in developing and sustaining relational trust. Principals establish both respect and personal regard when they acknowledge the vulnerabilities of others, actively listen to their concerns, and eschew arbitrary actions. If principals couple this with a compelling school vision, and if their behavior can be understood as advancing this vision, their integrity is affirmed. Then, assuming principals are competent in the management of day-to-day school affairs, an overall ethos conducive to trust is likely to emerge.

The actual dynamic of such leadership entails the constructive use of power to jump-start change. One does not build relational trust in a troubled school community simply by assuming its existence; indeed, to distinguish between the ends and means of reform is especially important. While the ends are clear—an environment of high relational trust rooted in professional colleagueship and mutual commitment—attaining this may require significant use of role authority. Key here are principals' efforts to reshape the composition of their school faculties.

The school-based teacher hiring provision of the 1988 reform offered Chicago principals a powerful assist on this point.[11] Leaders such as Morty Goldman aggressively used their newly acquired authority to recruit new staff who wanted to teach in their particular community and serve its children and parents. The shared sense of obligations established through this deliberate hiring process facilitated subsequent formation of relational trust.

Of similar importance is the principal's capacity to reshape the faculty by "counseling out" teachers who do not align with the renewed mission for the school. Although not especially enabled by Chicago's reform, principals such as Dr. Goldman nonetheless found creative ways to do this as well. As uncommitted teachers left Holiday, additional opportunities opened up to recruit new faculty more likely to embrace the emerging school vision. Other principals, however, such as Dr. Gonzalez at Thomas, simply accepted his staff as given. In fairness, most of Thomas's teachers were competent and dedicated. Even so, it was clear that this faculty had not been deliberately assembled to educate Thomas's children and to relate well to their parents. Dr. Gonzalez understood that a reshaping of the faculty was necessary if Thomas was to become more responsive to its local community. He was reticent to move aggressively on this, however, and reform offered no enabling policies to make accomplishing this onerous task any easier.

In sum, as principals seek to initiate change in their buildings, not everyone is necessarily affirmed, nor is everyone afforded a similar voice in shaping the vision of reform. Teachers who are unwilling to take on the hard work of change and align with colleagues around a common reform agenda must leave. Only when participants demonstrate their commitment to engage in such work and see others doing the same can a genuine professional community grounded in relational trust emerge. Principals must take the lead and extend themselves by reaching out to others. On occasion, principals may be called on to demonstrate trust in colleagues who may not fully reciprocate, at least initially. But they must also be prepared to use coercive power to reform a dysfunctional school community around professional norms. Interestingly, such authority may rarely need to be invoked thereafter once these new norms are firmly established.

Supporting Teachers to Reach Out to Parents   Parents in most urban school communities remain highly dependent on the good intentions of a school's faculty. Thus, it becomes incumbent on teachers to acknowledge these parental vulnerabilities and actively reach out to moderate them. Unfortunately, such responsibilities often are not acknowledged as a critical aspect of teachers' roles and may be addressed unevenly, if at all, in many schools. Moreover, the tendency in policy discussions today to emphasize the need for instructional improvement can work to silence discussions about addressing equally important relational needs. To be clear, this is not an either-or situation in our view. Instructional improvement is very much needed in urban school communities. Strengthening the social base for engaging students, teachers, and parents around more ambitious learning, however, also is essential.

While the need for school staff to initiate action here may be clear, how to effect more behavior of this sort is less obvious. Elementary school teachers spend the vast majority of their time engaged with children. Little in their professional socialization or formal training prepares them for working with parents and other adults in the community. Moreover, when we consider the class and race differences between school professionals and parents in urban contexts, it becomes readily apparent why conditions are ripe for misunderstanding and distrust.

Thus, our research suggests that effective urban schools need teachers that not only know their students well, but also have an empathetic understanding of their parents' situations and have the interpersonal skills needed to engage these adults effectively. Such capacities should be formally acknowledged in teachers' role responsibilities and included in annual personnel evaluation procedures. Professional development supports need to be provided as well through both preservice and continuing education programs so that teachers can acquire the necessary skills and dispositions. In our view, these needs are too important and too central for school improvement to be left to chance.

Systemic Reform and Trust Relations with Key District and State Actors   From a research point of view, Chicago's democratic localism created a natural experiment for studying the functioning of relational trust in school communities. As noted in chapter 1, this reform deliberately weakened the control of district actors over school-based decision making. Had these external influences been stronger, it would have made our study much more complex, perhaps even confounding our ability to understand well the social exchanges among school community members.

Increasingly, many districts (including Chicago) are engaged in reforms that have been centrally developed and driven by external agents that include staff developers, school reviewers, instructional coaches, and principal mentors. These external actors have taken on important roles in schools' social networks, and the development of relational trust across these new role sets also becomes important. Although we did not directly study this, we nonetheless expect that the basic logic of relational trust would apply here as well.

Specifically, individuals both internal and external to a school community maintain understandings of their role obligations and hold some expectations about the role obligations of others. Likewise, individuals inside and outside a school community will make discernments about each other using the same four criteria of respect, personal regard, competence, and integrity. A mutual dependence for success now exists across this expanded social network of internal and external actors. Since power relations typically will be structured with asymmetry favoring district and state agents, it becomes incumbent on these external agents to acknowledge the vulnerability sensed by school-based actors.[12] Any actions taken by external agents to reduce this vulnerability should go a long way toward building trust across this expanded social network.

Structural Facilitators

Our research on relational trust has focused attention on the nature of social relations within a school community and the local cultural and other contextual factors that condition these interactions. From an organizational theory perspective, our work is rooted primarily in an interpersonal analysis frame. Nonetheless, our research also indicates that select structural features of a school community come into play in important ways as well. Functionally, these structural elements are best conceived as facilitating factors. While their existence does not assure relational trust, the presence of these conditions makes it easier for school leaders to build and sustain trust when there is an active intention to do so.

Benefits of Small School Size   We reported in chapter 6 that relational trust among teachers is more likely in small elementary schools with student enrollments of 350 or less. This finding is consistent with basic organizational theory about the functioning of social networks. As organizations expand in size, subgroup structures form to coordinate work. Concomitantly, informal social networks also arise, frequently based around common workgroup assignments. As a result, face-to-face interactions across the organization may become limited and these relations more bureaucratic. Individuals' primary affiliations are likely to be defined in terms of a workgroup or social network, and ties to the larger organization may be weak or nonexistent. Sustaining good communication across the organization can become difficult under such circumstances. Not surprisingly then, to sustain high levels of relational trust is also harder.

In contrast, the work structures of a small school are less complex and its social networks typically fewer in number. Relational trust therefore is likely to form and be sustained more easily. To be sure, a dysfunctional small school can be just as anomic an environment as a large one; changing the latter, however, is a more difficult problem.

The Benefits of a Stable School Community   Similarly, we found in chapter 6 that the stability of the student body directly affects teacher-parent trust. In general, the building and maintenance of trust depends on repeated social exchanges. It is harder for school staff to develop and sustain direct positive engagement with all parents when student membership changes frequently. Moreover, the normal communication among parents that teachers are trustworthy, based on reputations that teachers build up through working with other parents, also occurs less readily. In such circumstances, it is not unreasonable to expect that parents who are new to a school will fall back on predispositions to distrust, especially if most of their other social encounters outside of the school tend to reinforce this worldview.

In a related vein, the presence of student instability also heightens the salience of both teacher-teacher and teacher-principal trust in the functioning of disadvantaged urban schools. Random acts of disrespect and disregard directed at teachers may occur regularly in schools with high mobility, since many parents may never get to know the staff well, or know of or have reasons to trust their reputations. While school staff well may understand the social forces that contribute to this negative behavior, it also is quite reasonable for them to feel badly treated. A high level of trust among school professionals would seem especially important as a counterforce in such contexts.

High student mobility is an unfortunate fact of life in many urban schools as parents seek better housing, better jobs, and safer neighborhoods for raising their children. Evidence shows, however, that a substantial portion of school mobility is not precipitated by residential mobility—and, even when residential mobility does come into play, these families' changes of residence are often over very short distances.[13] In short, research studies indicate that at least some reduction in student mobility can be affected by school district policies.

Combining these findings from research on student mobility with our results suggests that efforts to promote greater student stability can lead to improvements in achievement for all students, not just those who frequently move. Specifically, reducing student mobility can enhance trust formation and maintenance, which affords valuable social resources for school improvement. Both the presence of these social resources and any resultant positive changes in school operations create good reasons for parents to go to some length to keep their children enrolled in such improving schools. The process recycles with subsequent reductions in school mobility leading to a further expansion of social resources within the school community. As an end result, the school is better positioned for even more ambitious reform efforts.

We also have some evidence that faculty stability affects the formation and maintenance of trust across a professional community. The base state of the organization, however, affects the way this factor actually plays out. We have documented, for example, how school leaders can use planned instability (that is, counseling out of weak teachers and careful recruitment of new teachers) to catalyze trust building from a dysfunctional base state. We suspect that the contrary is also true: unplanned instability, accompanying the loss of key school leadership and the transferring in of new faculty, can suddenly place a high-functioning school at risk for trust degradation.

The Power of Voluntary Association   Much of the literature on good schools focuses on a set of characteristics, common to these schools, that make them akin to intentional communities.[14] Staff in these schools know both their students and each other well. They share a commitment to a distinctive sense of school mission, and engage in a common round of professional practices that enliven this mission. Work in such schools can have powerful effects on all involved, both students and adults alike. Yet precisely because these schools are particular, distinctive, and different from others, not all students, parents, or teachers will necessarily find any single such school to their liking.

This observation suggests another potent factor facilitating development of relational trust in schools: the degree of voluntary association that binds participants together in a particular school community. Quite simply, relational trust is more likely to arise in schools when both faculty and students wish to be there. Reform in Chicago during the 1990s received unanticipated assistance in this regard in that the move toward democratic localism in 1988 was accompanied by considerable school choice. In brief, over 30 percent of Chicago's public elementary school students do not attend their neighborhood school; at the high school level, over 50 percent choose to go elsewhere. Similarly, the 1988 reform, which eliminated systemwide bumping rights and transferred hiring decisions to the school building level, created in essence a between-school labor market. Teachers in Chicago now have considerably more discretion over their school assignments, and many make deliberate choices to affiliate with specific schools and not others. This is the supply-side consequence of transferring teacher-hiring decisions to the school building level.[15]

In situations like this with at least a modicum of choice for both parents and staff, relations among all parties are preconditioned toward trust, since participants have deliberately chosen to affiliate with a particular school. Assuming subsequent actions reinforce the wisdom of this choice, relational trust is likely to deepen. In contrast, forced assignment of individuals to schools is more likely to precondition some initial uncertainty and suspicion about the motivations and commitments of others. These a priori beliefs can represent a formidable additional factor to overcome in promoting trust across a school community.

Capacity to Remove Incompetent Teachers   We have already noted how the selection of new staff can promote alignment around a shared sense of obligations and thereby foster conditions conducive to trust formation. Of similar importance is the capacity to remove incompetent teachers from a school. We witnessed firsthand the corrosive effect that teacher incompetence had on the social relations at Ridgeway School. No one could really understand why some teachers were allowed to continue in their jobs when they refused to devote more than a minimal effort to their teaching, held very low expectations for children, and interacted with children and their families in demeaning ways. That such behavior was allowed to persist maligned the integrity of the whole institution.

Thus, our analysis of the role of relational trust in school improvement sheds new light on an important but also nettlesome policy problem of removing weak teachers. Existing due-process safeguards are extensive, and teacher unions are well organized to protect their weaker members. The failure of schools and districts to act on problematic cases is sometimes justified on the grounds that only a small percentage of teachers need to be removed, and the costs associated with this can be very high. A common response is to attempt to hide these teachers in less visible schools and teaching roles. Our analysis, however, suggests that much more is at stake than just the subset of students who are directly affected by these teachers' poor practice. Rather, the persistence of such teachers in a school community undermines its social capacity for action. No one can make sense of such a place, and commitments to the school are likely to remain highly delimited.

Conclusion

We have sought in this final chapter to connect our findings to ongoing policy discussions about school improvement. Governance reformers, in viewing the problems of school productivity from the high ground of overall system design, recognize the need to break the stranglehold of a dysfunctional status quo and create new incentives and opportunities for change. In a complementary fashion, instructional reformers understand that change ultimately must happen in classrooms. Unless there are major improvements in teachers' knowledge and skills, the instructional materials they have to work with, and the professional supports for the continued improvements in their practice, major improvements in student learning remain unlikely.

While acknowledging merits in both of these perspectives, neither one alone nor even in combination strikes us as sufficient. It is at the individual school where institutional incentives must collectively engage participants around improvements in the technical core of teaching and learning. We have identified a missing ingredient in the reform recipes: the nature of social practice among adults in school communities and how this is mobilized for sustained school improvement.

We view the need to develop relational trust as an essential complement both to governance efforts that focus on bringing new incentives to bear on improving practice and to instructional reforms that seek to deepen the technical capacities of school professionals. Absent more supportive social relations among all adults who share responsibility for student development and who remain mutually dependent on each other to achieve success, new policy initiatives are unlikely to produce desired outcomes. Similarly, new technical resources, no matter how sophisticated in design or well supported in implementation, are not likely to be used well, if at all.

We worry that reformers will continue to be frustrated in their efforts unless they meld a stronger organizational view of schools to their otherwise well-conceived initiatives. Good schools are intrinsically social enterprises that depend heavily on cooperative endeavors among the varied participants who comprise the school community. Relational trust constitutes the connective tissue that binds these individuals together around advancing the education and welfare of children. Improving schools requires us to think harder about how best to organize the work of adults and students so that this connective tissue remains healthy and strong. From a policy perspective, we constantly need to ask whether any new initiative is likely to promote relational trust within school communities or undermine it. We have offered in this book an empirically grounded perspective aimed at deepening practical understandings about these matters.

Appendix A: Description of the Field Study

T HE THREE cases presented in this book were drawn from a larger field study involving intensive work in twelve elementary schools over a three-year period. The design consisted of interviews, school and classroom observations, focus groups, and document collection. Two- to three-person research teams were organized for each field site. Over the three years, these teams conducted more than 200 interviews, attended 150 school activities (including local school council and Professional Personnel Advisory Committee meetings), spent 24 days observing in classrooms in each school, and held 9 focus groups, 3 each with principals, teachers, and parents.

We anticipated that the implementation of the Chicago School Reform Act of 1988 would vary among the schools depending on a range of school and community factors. Consequently, we designed a multilevel sampling plan to assure variation in structural school characteristics (for example, school size and magnet versus neighborhood schools); student characteristics (race and ethnicity of the student population, family income, student mobility, achievement, and attendance); schools' access to formal knowledge and technical expertise about school improvement practices (for example, formal involvement in externally supported restructuring efforts); level of social and financial resources in the community; and intensity of political activity regarding school matters (for example, extent of community participation and voter turnout in LSC elections and involvement of community-based organizations in schools).

Selecting the Schools

The majority of Chicago students are low-income and attend racially isolated schools. We therefore selected several schools that were representative of this modal type. In addition, we desired some schools that were engaged in an externally supported restructuring effort. At the time of the initial site selection, the Center for School Improvement at the University of Chicago was involved in intervention work in four racially isolated, low-income African American schools. We selected three of these, and complemented them with two additional racially isolated schools (one African American and one Hispanic) involved in Project CANAL. (Project CANAL was a school-based management and shared-decision-making program initiated by Chicago Public Schools in sixty racially isolated Chicago elementary schools, supported by federal desegregation funds.) The Holiday School was a member of this group.

Next, we considered the economic composition of the student body. As a sharp contrast to the low-income sites, we included two schools with a middle- to upper-middle-class composition similar to those found in nearby suburbs. Unlike the schools affiliated with the Center for School Improvement or Project CANAL, we hypothesized that such schools should have greater resources in their parent groups and communities for supporting school change. Of particular interest were schools with a substantial African American middle-class population. One of the major changes in the CPS in the last several decades has been the gradual decline in the number of such schools. As a consequence of magnet school enrollment policies, African American middle-class children tend to be dispersed throughout the system (and attend private and parochial schools) rather than being concentrated in neighborhood public schools. We eventually selected two middle-class schools, one integrated and the other predominantly African American. Had we chosen to write a fourth case for this book, it would have focused on one of these two schools.

Community Characteristics

We also paid close attention to community characteristics. First, we wanted to look at two types of magnet schools: those that predominantly enroll students from neighboring communities, and those that draw their students from throughout the city. We suspected that there might be differences in the political involvement between LSC members living in the neighborhood and those having only weak community ties. Consequently, we were interested in having one magnet school that had a substantial representation from the local community and one that did not.

Second, in order to look more closely at the relationship between political activity in the community and improvement efforts in the school, we included schools in neighborhoods where political activity was known to be particularly intensive. We focused attention on several Hispanic neighborhoods where substantial community organization around school reform was occurring. We selected two such schools with 100 percent Hispanic enrollment. The inclusion of these schools was further warranted by the fact that Hispanics constitute the second largest student group in Chicago and are the fastest growing population in the city. The Thomas School was part of this subset.

We also were interested in schools that were located in neighborhoods undergoing major ethnic transitions—generally from white to minority—or extensive gentrification. We chose two of these, one of which is the Ridgeway case presented herein.

In general, the selection of schools and communities for the larger study sought diversity in terms of the social resources available to support improvement efforts. We hypothesized that at sites where school staff and parents coalesce as a functional school community, a bond of trust forms that supports the work of both educators and parents. This perspective implies a different view of school community: rather than a place defined only by a geographical area, the school is a network of social ties that can bind children and families to each other, support families in the common task of parenting, and support teachers' efforts as well.

In making our final site selections, we developed profiles of eighteen schools that included information on school location, including community housing development status (for example, neighborhoods undergoing gentrification or targeted for redlining), grade levels, and school size. Student characteristics included racial and ethnic composition of the student body; percentage of students with limited English proficiency; percentage of students eligible for the federal free lunch program; percentage of students who enrolled in or transferred out after October 1; average daily attendance; percentage not promoted; and percentage at or above grade level. We also examined test scores in reading and mathematics from both the city and state testing programs, and the schools' academic rankings within their respective subdistricts and the city. Based on these data, we selected a final set of twelve schools that maximized variation on each of the aforementioned criteria.

The entry process to schools was complicated by the fact that, with the new reform legislation, it was unclear whose permission was actually required for us to undertake this work. Since we knew that we were interested in the activities of the principal, LSC, PPAC, and other active parent and teacher participants, we designed an extensive process of consultation with school stakeholders about the proposed study. Securing access to some sites took almost two months. Eventually we received permission to work in all twelve of the selected schools.

Year 1 Fieldwork

The general fieldwork plan for year 1 involved three rounds of data collection that began with in-depth interviews (one and one-half to two hours each) with the principal, and the LSC and PPAC chairs. Two additional parents and two teachers were interviewed in the second round, based on nominations by the principal and chairs of the LSC and PPAC. (We specifically asked for nominations of school leaders who might not share the principal's or the LSC and PPAC chairs' views of school reform.) In the third round, we interviewed three additional individuals who emerged during our field observations as centrally involved in school operations. This group was quite diverse and included a school engineer, a school clerk, two aldermen, a school-based union leader, and several community activists. For each school, we maintained a target of at least three teacher interviews in addition to the PPAC chair. The minimum number of interviews conducted for each of the twelve schools during the first year of the study was ten.

A separate protocol was prepared for each type of interview focusing on the particular role each individual was playing in school reform. In addition, we developed a core set of questions to probe respondents' views of school governance, leadership, local politics, and normative understandings of a good school, principal, and teacher. This set was incorporated in all of the interview schedules regardless of a respondent's role.

The fieldwork plan for year 1 also involved observations of LSC and PPAC meetings and special school events. A standardized format was developed to record these activities. Each set of notes contained a detailed description of the discussion and events, as well as a set of naturalistic observations about the nature of the social interaction among participants. We also asked field staff to offer an interpretative summary of the conceptions of a good school, good leadership, good governance, and the nature of democratic localism being enacted at each school site.

During these observations, we attempted to record as much of the actual dialogue as possible, using the natural language of the participants. As a result, the field notes read something like a play script.

Fieldworkers tracked the amount of time spent on each topic or activity. A time notation was entered whenever the discussion shifted or a new activity began. The running log of the meeting also was marked off in fifteen-minute intervals. In addition, fieldworkers collected copies of any materials distributed at the meeting such as notices, prior LSC meeting notes, and so on.

The naturalistic observations focused on three main ideas. First, we observed the exercise of leadership (that is, who was exercising power, control, and inviting or hindering participatory governance), and the specific content of discussions. The second area considered evidence of democratic localism. Here we focused on how individuals saw their roles and their relationships to each other, the local school, the community, and the larger school system. We attended to the boundaries of authority and control at the school, and the presence of any tension and conflict among local stakeholders and with the central administration. Finally, we recorded impressions of the normative understandings at work in these schools about what constitutes good leadership, good governance, and a good school. We eventually coded these LSC, PPAC meetings and special events around the same main themes as the interviews.

We also assembled an extensive library on Chicago school reform. We collected various CPS documents and guides, including budget books, *School Improvement Planning* guides, *Report on the School Improvement Plans of 1990*, *Lump Sum Budget* workbooks, school report cards, test scores, and selected school characteristics. We retrieved from each site school improvement plans and action plans, lump sum and program budgets, CANAL plans and budgets (if applicable), and curricular materials. We also gathered documents from various advocacy organizations and other groups that supported the implementation of reform in the CPS. These documents included the Chicago Panel on Public School Finance's data books on school characteristics and the Lawyers School Reform Project's *Guidelines for Principals*.

To help us refine our fieldwork plan, case debriefings for each of the twelve schools were held during the late winter and spring of 1991. Each school team systematically reviewed all interviews and observations to date; created a description of each school community, including political context, school history, school organization and instructional programs, student and staff characteristics, LSC, PPAC, and other school committees; and formulated some initial observations about leadership and governance in the school. From these discussions, we determined a plan for additional interviews and other information for year 2 that would be necessary to gain a more complete understanding of each school.

Year 2 Fieldwork

Year 2 fieldwork included further interviews and observations of meetings and other activities at each site. Two new initiatives were added: focus groups for principals, teachers, and parents; and observations in a sample of classrooms. These latter included reading and mathematics lessons at grades 1 and 3 and mathematics and social studies lessons at grades 6 and 8. We followed up each classroom observation with a teacher interview.

Two additional rounds of general interviews were conducted in year 2. In the fall, we met with individual members of the PPAC and with new LSC members who had been elected the previous fall. For the spring, we reinterviewed the principal and other selected school participants, as needed, to fill out our "story" of each school. Several new areas of interest emerged in the year 2 interviews regarding issues of teacher professionalism, school order and discipline, school politics, and stakeholders' perceptions of the strategic planning that was needed to create and sustain a good school. Specific questions on these topics were added to the protocols.

The greatest proportion of staff time in year 2 was directed at school and classroom observations. In terms of school observations, we observed the LSC Candidates' Forum (which every school was obligated to have prior to the LSC elections), school-specific special events, and the principal's first meeting with the faculty. Classroom observations were designed to learn about instructional improvements. In addition to observing one reading and mathematics lesson in grades 1 and 3 and one mathematics and social studies lesson in grades 6 and 8, we also observed any instructional initiative that was directly tied to the school improvement plan. In sampling teachers, we paid attention to possible structural divisions within the school— for example, bilingual versus regular programs and magnet versus standard programs. Two-person teams visited each school for two days to conduct these observations. We spent about one and a half to two hours observing a specific classroom lesson and then conducted a forty-five-minute interview with the teacher. These interviews focused on the details of the lessons observed, any efforts occurring within the school to improve instruction, and a few more general questions about school improvement and reform.

The focus of the observations was on the teacher and his or her interactions with the students. Consequently, each observer kept a detailed record of all teacher activities and language. Every fifteen minutes, the observer made an assessment of the percentage of students on task. The general physical environment of each classroom was also described.

The observations focused on both the academic and social development of students. On the academic side, we attended to:

(a) the structure of the lesson;
(b) books, dittos, and other instructional materials being used;
(c) teachers' mode of instruction (for example, whole class, subgroup, individual);
(d) instructional style (for example, didactic, Socratic, lecture, coaching);
(e) teachers' style of questioning (for example, evidence that students were asked to predict, summarize, and extend applications);
(f) nature of students' tasks (for example, academic segments, project oriented, learning facts versus higher-order thinking).

For social development, we examined the following:

(a) teachers' expectations for their students;
(b) evidence that the teacher promoted self concept, working cooperatively, and supporting each other's work;
(c) importance given to competition;
(d) attention given to issues of democracy, fairness, and equity;
(e) structures and routines used for maintaining order and discipline in the classroom.

For both academic and social development, we were especially interested in identifying the following:

(a) language and rituals used by the teacher to maintain control, and to enhance student self-esteem and ethnic and racial identity;
(b) evidence of moral homilies used to influence students' ethical development and interest in learning.

Each observer also was asked his or her personal assessment of the class in terms of the "authenticity of academic work" that he or she observed, and whether classroom life was oriented toward developing an "ethos of caring."

Our final research activity of year 2 involved separate focus group discussions for principals, teachers, and parent–community members. Each group met at least four times. The purpose of the focus groups was to provide a forum where individuals sharing similar roles could discuss the problems and insights they had gained under school reform. Each focus session was organized around a particular theme that was pertinent to each group. For example, in the principal focus group, we tackled the problems of working with a local school council, trying to implement instructional change, and pressures of accountability.

Year 3 Fieldwork

The University of Wisconsin Center on School Organization and Restructuring provided us with supplemental funding to continue our fieldwork in year 3 to obtain more comprehensive information on six of the twelve schools. (The first two years of the study were supported by a grant from the Spencer Foundation.) We conducted additional interviews with principals, teachers, parents, and community members. Additional observations were conducted at LSC and PPAC meetings and various school activities. The focus in year 3 was to deepen our understanding of how the various role sets interacted with one another with respect to school politics, issues of classroom instruction, and professional development more broadly. This supplemental database greatly facilitated the drafting of the cases presented here.

We selected the final three cases used in our analysis of relational trust from this subset of six schools. Each of these schools had a wealth of information on the quality of the relationships among the various role sets in the school and appeared to have wide variations in levels of trust.

Analytic Strategy

The original design of the field study focused on the micropolitics in Chicago elementary school communities. Our intention was to understand more fully the range of political behavior that occurs in school communities as they attempted to implement structural reform. Consequently, over the course of our investigations into the twelve field sites, we developed a theory of micropolitics that specifically examined the power relations within a school community (see Bryk, Sebring et al. 1998, ch. 2; Rollow 1998). This framework directed our attention to important distinctions among three sites of power within each school (the principal, the faculty as a collectivity, and the LSC); it also led us to create questions that examined how changes in practice and understandings occurred as these stakeholders learned to act and to internalize their new roles under reform. Thus, from the onset of our fieldwork we were explicitly concerned with how the values, attitudes, understandings, goals, and beliefs of various role sets played out in school change.

More specifically, we probed each informant regarding his or her views of the goals of schooling, expectations for a good school, good teaching, good leadership, how teachers should encourage their students to learn, what type of relationship teachers should have with their students' families, what responsibilities teachers have toward other teachers, how principals should lead their faculties toward change, and when the collective interests of the school should take precedent over self-interest. It became increasingly obvious that the quality of personal relationships among the various sites of power played a major role in reform implementation. Moreover, it appeared that the more relationships focused especially on the welfare of the children, the more likely individuals were to truly work with one another.

To bring greater analytic strength to our initial field observations, we undertook a series of systematic analyses of the field database. All of the interviews and observational records for the twelve schools were arrayed in data files. Using the NUDIST software program, we searched both for keywords such as *trust, caring,* and *respect,* and specific interview questions regarding individual perceptions of good schools, positive staff, parent, and teacher-student relationships, and components of school leadership. The NUDIST program generated hundreds of pages of text that we read and discussed. From these conversations, it became obvious that three of the schools, with extensive information from the year 3 data collection, offered the richest opportunity for developing an empirically grounded theory of relational trust. We then focused on just these three schools, thoroughly reading and rereading all of the field data records on them.

At this point, we also began a review of the trust literature. Our internal conversations regarding the three fieldwork sites were increasingly informed by these readings. Several ideas emerged from this combination of literature review and fieldwork analysis that we then proceeded to examine more systematically in each case. Key here was the importance of the discernments individuals were making about the intentionality of others. These discernments appeared to be shaped by the degree of vulnerability individuals felt toward others. A focus on principled behavior that we eventually came to term *integrity* became another key concern. In this regard, individuals pursuing their own self-interests and having little regard for the academic and personal welfare of the students were seen as not trustworthy. Relatively late in the process we focused attention on the competence dimension in individual discernments. This theme emerged more from our theory analysis than from our initial reading of the field notes. This in turn provoked us to explore in more depth why this might be the case in these schools. A final review and update of the literature by Kochanek (1999) helped us to finalize our conceptualization of relational trust.

In the end, the final drafts of the cases became quite analytic. They had moved a long way from simple descriptions of events and embedded issues. The cases gradually took their final form as expositions of the microdynamics of relational trust in the day-to-day life of urban school communities.

Appendix B: Measures and Other Variables Used

A LL OF the organizational measures used in our research were derived through Rasch Rating Scale Analysis (Wright and Masters 1982). This method involves an item response latent trait model. Survey items are used to define a measure based on the relative probability of a respondent choosing each category on each item. Individuals are then placed on this scale based on their particular responses to the items in the measure. The scale units—logits—constitute a linear measurement system and therefore are suitable for use in statistical procedures.

Three types of statistics are reported for each Rasch measure. The first is item difficulty, which estimates the likelihood that respondents will endorse the position, attitude, or behavior represented by each item within a scale. For example, common events, attitudes, and beliefs are "less difficult" to endorse; rarer ones are "more difficult." Second is item infit, which is the degree to which individuals respond to a particular item consistent with its placement in a hierarchically ordered scale. For a properly fitting item, individuals who endorse that item are more likely to endorse the easier, "less difficult" items below it in the scale, and are not as likely to endorse the items that are harder or "more difficult" and above it in the scale. Third is person reliability, which is a measure of the internal consistency of the scale items and is similar to Cronbach's Alpha.

Relational Trust

Since we use data collected in both 1994 and 1997 to assess relational trust, we were concerned about the interval stability of the measures over time. We performed separate, as well as linked, Rasch Rating Scale Analyses on each measure in 1994 and 1997. The relative ordering of item difficulties remained stable over time. In addition, using

155

Table B.1   Rasch Rating Scale of 1997 Teacher-Principal Trust

Teacher-Principal Trust Item	Measure Reliability: 0.92	
	Difficulty	Infit
It's OK in this school to discuss feelings, worries, and frustrations with the principal.[a,d]	0.79	0.91
The principal looks out for the personal welfare of the faculty members.[a,d]	0.33	0.84
I trust the principal at his or her word.[a,d]	0.21	0.84
The principal at this school is an effective manager who makes the school run smoothly.[a]	0.05	1.16
The principal places the needs of children ahead of her personal and political interests.[a]	−0.02	1.09
The principal has confidence in the expertise of the teachers.[a,d]	−0.17	1.14
The principal takes a personal interest in the professional development of teachers.[a,d]	−0.20	0.91
I really respect my principal as an educator.[a]	−0.27	0.85
To what extent do you feel respected by your principal?[c,d]	−0.73	1.22

[a]Four-point scale: strongly disagree, disagree, agree, strongly agree.
[b]Five-point scale: none, some, about half, most, nearly all.
[c]Four-point scale: not at all, a little, some, to a great extent.
[d]Item used in 1994 measure.

a hierarchical linear model (HLM), we were able to calculate correlations at the school level between the 1994 and 1997 measures disattenuated for measurement error. The two measures of teacher-parent trust (1994 and 1997) are correlated at 0.76. Teacher-teacher trust measures across these two time points correlate at 0.80, and teacher-principal trust measures correlate at 0.62. We therefore are reasonably confident that both measures capture the same phenomenon.

Tables B.1, B.2, and B.3 provide further detail on the difficulty and infit for the three measures of trust.

Category Definitions for Levels of Trust (1997)

All rating scale analysis measures were eventually placed on a zero to ten-point scale. The rating scale methodology allows us to introduce cutpoints on the scale at key thresholds when the pattern of respondents' answers appears to shift. This property of a rating scale analysis allows us to define modal patterns of responses for each

Table B.2   Rasch Rating Scale of 1997 Teacher-Teacher Trust

	Measure Reliability: 0.82	
Teacher-Teacher Trust Item	Difficulty	Infit
How many teachers in this school really care about each other?[b,d]	2.31	1.03
Teachers in this school trust each other.[a,d]	1.01	0.72
It's OK in this school to discuss feelings, worries, and frustrations with other teachers.[a,d]	0.34	1.00
Teachers respect other teachers who take the lead in school improvement efforts.[a,d]	−0.12	0.90
Teachers at this school respect those colleagues who are expert at their craft.[a]	−1.12	0.99
To what extent do you feel respected by other teachers?[c,d]	−2.42	1.32

Source: Authors' compilation.
Note: The 1994 measure also included "Most teachers in this school are cordial."
[a]Four-point scale: strongly disagree, disagree, agree, strongly agree.
[b]Five-point scale: none, some, about half, most, nearly all.
[c]Four-point scale: not at all, a little, some, to a great extent.
[d]Item used in 1994 measure.

measure category. The following describes the details for each measure.

Teacher-Teacher Trust

No Trust   Teachers in this category typically experience little or no respect from their colleagues. They report that teachers do not confide in, trust, or care about one another. Furthermore, they perceive that their colleagues do not respect those teachers who display expertise or take a role in school leadership.

Minimal Trust   Teachers in this category typically report some degree of respect between their colleagues. They perceive that other teachers respect those teachers who display expertise or take a role in school leadership. In general, they confide in their colleagues. Yet only some teachers trust and care about one another.

Strong Trust   Teachers here experience a great deal of respect among their colleagues and also for those who are experts at their craft or take leadership roles in school improvement. They typically report that they trust and confide in one another, but only about half of the teachers perceive that the teachers care about one another.

Very Strong Trust   Teachers in this category typically describe an atmosphere of respect among colleagues. They strongly agree that

Table B.3   Rasch Rating Scale of 1997 Teacher-Parent Trust

Teacher-Parent Trust Item	Measure Reliability: 0.78	
	Difficulty	Infit
How many of your students' parents do their best to help their children learn?[b]	1.83	1.12
How many teachers at this school feel good about parents' support for their work?[b,d]	1.59	1.03
How many teachers at this school really care about this local community?[b,d]	1.48	1.14
How many of your students' parents support your teaching efforts?[b]	0.90	1.05
Teachers and parents think of each other as partners in educating children.[a]	0.73	0.87
At this school, it is difficult to overcome the cultural barriers between teachers and parents.[a,e]	−0.02	1.36
Parents have confidence in the expertise of the teachers.[a,d]	−0.11	0.81
There is conflict between parents and teachers at this school.[a,e]	−0.21	1.05
Staff at this school work hard to build trusting relationships with parents.[a,d]	−0.41	0.81
Talking with parents helps me understand my students better.[a]	−1.23	1.20
To what extent do teachers in this school respect parents and community members of the local community?[c,d]	−1.39	0.84
To what extent do teachers in this school respect students' parents?[c,d]	−1.55	0.79
To what extent do you feel respected by the parents of your students?[c,d]	−1.61	0.85

Source: Authors' compilation.
[a]Four-point scale: strongly disagree, disagree, agree, strongly agree.
[b]Five-point scale: none, some, about half, most, nearly all.
[c]Four-point scale: not at all, a little, some, to a great extent.
[d]Item used in 1994 measure.
[e]Item was reversed for analysis purposes.

teachers respect those whom they consider experts and leaders in school improvement. They also report that teachers trust and confide in one another and that most or nearly all of the teachers care about one another.

Teacher-Principal Trust

No Trust   Teachers here typically do not feel respected by their principal. They report that the principal takes no interest in their professional development and lacks confidence in their teaching expertise.

They perceive the principal is an ineffective manager who places his or her own needs above those of the students. They neither respect nor trust their principal.

Minimal Trust While teachers in this category typically perceive a little respect from the principal, they do not respect the principal as an educator. They do not believe that the principal is an effective manager, looks out for their welfare, or has confidence in their teaching abilities. They do not trust their principal and do not feel comfortable confiding their worries in him or her.

Strong Trust Teachers in this group typically experience respect from their principal and express respect in return. They report that the principal takes an interest in their professional development, has confidence in their teaching, and looks out for their welfare. They also believe that the principal is an effective manager who places students' needs first. They trust and confide in this principal.

Very Strong Trust Teachers here report a great deal of respect between the teachers and principal. They strongly agree that the principal is an effective manager and supports the teachers' professional development. While they perceive the principal as looking out for their welfare, the teachers strongly agree that the principal puts the needs of the students first. They strongly trust and confide in their principal.

Teacher-Parent Trust

No Trust Teachers in this category typically receive very little or no respect from parents and believe that talking with parents helps them little or not at all in understanding students better. In addition, they perceive little or no support for their efforts from parents. The teachers perceive a great deal of conflict between parents and teachers, and they report a lack of caring about the school community among the faculty.

Minimal Trust Teachers here typically feel respected by and respect parents to some extent. They agree that talking with parents helps their teaching efforts, but perceive little support for their efforts at home. They report some conflict between parents and teachers, and only some of the teachers agree that the parents are partners in educating the children.

Strong Trust Teachers in this category report a great deal of respect between parents and teachers. They agree that talking with parents helps to improve their teaching efforts, but report that about half of parents support their teaching efforts at home. Teachers typically agree that no conflict exists between parents and teachers, but only about half of teachers care about the community and feel good about parental support.

Very Strong Trust   Teachers here feel respected by and respect for parents to a great extent. They report no conflict between parents and teachers and perceive parents as supportive of teachers' work at home. Teachers view parents as partners in the children's education and typically feel good about the amount of parental support they receive. Teachers perceive that nearly all the faculty care about the school community.

Measures of Organizational Conditions

Tables B.4 to B.11 provide technical details for three of the organizational measures used as outcomes in the final section of chapter 6 (orientation to innovation, teacher outreach, and teacher commitment). The fourth organizational outcome, professional community, is a composite of four separate measures. Details about the component measures of the professional communtiy composite appear in tables B.7 through B.10.

Table B.4   Rasch Rating Scale of 1997 Teacher Orientation to Innovation

	Measure Reliability: 0.89	
Orientation to Innovation Item	Difficulty	Infit
How many teachers in this school are willing to take risks to make this school better?[b,d]	0.49	0.97
How many teachers in this school are eager to try new ideas?[b,d]	0.31	0.89
In this school, teachers have a "can do" attitude.[a,d]	0.02	0.96
All the teachers are encouraged to "stretch and grow."[a,d]	−0.35	1.33
In this school, teachers are continually learning and seeking new ideas.[a,d]	−0.47	0.93
How many teachers in this school are really trying to improve their teaching?[b]	−0.68	1.14

Source: Authors' compilation.
[a]Four-point scale: strongly disagree, disagree, agree, strongly agree.
[b]Five-point scale: none, some, about half, most, nearly all.
[c]Four-point scale: not at all, a little, some, to a great extent.
[d]Item used in 1994 measure.

Table B.5   Rasch Rating Scale of 1997 Teacher Outreach to Parents

Outreach to Parents Item	Measure Reliability: 0.89	
	Difficulty	Infit
Teachers work closely with parents to meet students' needs.[a,d]	1.51	1.07
Parents are invited to visit classrooms to observe the instructional program.[a,d]	0.98	1.43
This school regularly communicates with parents about how they can help their children learn.[a]	0.15	0.93
We work at communicating to parents about support needed to advance the school mission.[a,d]	−0.05	0.91
We encourage feedback from parents and the community.[a,d]	−0.36	0.83
The principal pushes teachers to communicate regularly with parents.[a]	−0.51	1.30
Teachers really try to understand parents' problems and concerns.[a,d]	−0.67	1.03
Parents are greeted warmly when they call or visit the school.[a,d]	−0.69	0.97

Source: Authors' compilation.
[a]Four-point scale: strongly disagree, disagree, agree, strongly agree.
[b]Five-point scale: none, some, about half, most, nearly all.
[c]Four-point scale: not at all, a little, some, to a great extent.
[d]Item used in 1994 measure.

Table B.6   Rasch Rating Scale of 1997 Teacher Commitment to School Community

Commitment to School Community Item	Measure Reliability: 0.89	
	Difficulty	Infit
I wouldn't want to work in any other school.[a,d]	0.89	0.83
I would recommend this school to parents seeking a place for their child.[a,d]	0.31	1.08
I usually look forward to each working day at this school.[a,d]	−0.09	1.34
I feel loyal to this school.[a,d]	−1.10	0.88

Source: Authors' compilation.
[a]Four-point scale: strongly disagree, disagree, agree, strongly agree.
[b]Five-point scale: none, some, about half, most, nearly all.
[c]Four-point scale: not at all, a little, some, to a great extent.
[d]Item used in 1994 measure.

Table B.7   Rasch Rating Scale of 1997 Peer Collaboration

Peer Collaboration Item	Measure Reliability: 0.85	
	Difficulty	Infit
Teachers design instructional programs together.[a,d]	0.90	0.85
Teachers at this school make a conscious effort to co-ordinate their teaching with instruction at other grade levels.[a,d]	0.81	0.93
The principal, teachers, and staff collaborate to make this school run effectively.[a,d]	−0.23	1.17
Most teachers in this school are cordial.[a,d]	−1.48	1.55

Source: Authors' compilation.
[a]Four-point scale: strongly disagree, disagree, agree, strongly agree.
[b]Five-point scale: none, some, about half, most, nearly all.
[c]Four-point scale: not at all, a little, some, to a great extent.
[d]Item used in 1994 measure.

Table B.8   Rasch Rating Scale of 1997 Reflective Dialogue

Reflective Dialogue Item	Measure Reliability: 0.80	
	Difficulty	Infit
This school year, how often have you had conversations with colleagues about the goals of this school?[d,e]	0.85	0.78
This school year, how often have you had conversations with colleagues about development of new curriculum?[d,e]	0.84	0.76
This school year, how often have you had conversations with colleagues about managing classroom behavior?[d,e]	−0.04	1.12
This school year, how often have you had conversations with colleagues about what helps students learn best?[d,e]	−0.10	0.76
Teachers in this school regularly discuss assumptions about teaching and learning.[a,e]	−0.43	0.88
Teachers in this school share and discuss student work with other teachers.[a]	−1.03	0.90
Teachers talk about instruction in the teachers' lounge, faculty meetings, etc.[a,e]	−1.12	1.11

Source: Authors' compilation.
[a]Four-point scale: strongly disagree, disagree, agree, strongly agree.
[b]Five-point scale: none, some, about half, most, nearly all.
[c]Four-point scale: not at all, a little, some, to a great extent.
[d]Four-point scale: less than once a month, two or three times a month, once or twice a week, almost daily.
[e]Item used in 1994 measure.

Table B.9   Rasch Rating Scale of 1997 Collective Responsibility

Collective Responsibility Item	Measure Reliability: 0.92	
	Difficulty	Infit
How many teachers in this school feel responsible when students in this school fail?[b]	1.53	1.37
How many teachers in this school feel responsible to help each other do their best?[b,d]	0.83	0.90
How many teachers in this school help maintain discipline in the entire school, not just their classroom?[b,d]	0.73	1.26
How many teachers in this school take responsibility for improving the school?[b,d]	0.67	0.89
How many teachers in this school feel responsible for helping students develop self-control?[b,d]	−0.25	0.89
How many teachers in this school set high standards for themselves?[b,d]	−0.31	0.94
How many teachers in this school feel responsible that all students learn?[b,d]	−0.86	0.99

Source: Authors' compilation.
[a]Four-point scale: strongly disagree, disagree, agree, strongly agree.
[b]Five-point scale: none, some, about half, most, nearly all.
[c]Four-point scale: not at all, a little, some, to a great extent.
[d]Item used in 1994 measure.

Table B.10   Rasch Rating Scale of 1997 Focus on Student Learning

Focus on Student Learning Item	Measure Reliability: 0.88	
	Difficulty	Infit
This school really works at developing students' social skills.[a,d]	0.70	0.95
When making important decisions, the school always focuses on what's best for student learning.[a,d]	0.00	1.02
The school has well-defined learning expectations for all students.[a,d]	−0.04	0.78
The school sets high standards for academic performance.[a,d]	−0.11	0.80
The school day is organized to maximize instructional time.[a,d]	−0.55	1.09

Source: Authors' compilation.
[a]Four-point scale: strongly disagree, disagree, agree, strongly agree.
[b]Five-point scale: none, some, about half, most, nearly all.
[c]Four-point scale: not at all, a little, some, to a great extent.
[d]Item used in 1994 measure.

Table B.11   Rasch Rating Scale of 1997 Teacher Socialization

	Measure Reliability: 0.60	
Teacher Socialization Item	Difficulty	Infit
Experienced teachers invite new teachers into their rooms to observe, give feedback, etc.[a]	1.11	0.91
A conscious effort is made by faculty to make new teachers feel welcome here.[a]	−1.11	1.03

Source: Authors' compilation.
[a]Four-point scale: strongly disagree, disagree, agree, strongly agree.
[b]Five-point scale: none, some, about half, most, nearly all.
[c]Four-point scale: not at all, a little, some, to a great extent.

Professional Community Composite

The following four measures were combined to create the professional community composite measure in 1997. The 1994 professional community composite also contained a measure of teacher socialization. This latter measure did not exist for the 1997 analysis.

Other School-Level Variables Used in Analyses

Overall reading and math productivity indicators, 1991 to 1996. These variables are the empirical Bayes residuals created by predicting the gain trend in Iowa Tests of Basic Skills (ITBS) scores from the initial status, the initial gain, and the input trend. This variable has been placed on a zero to 100 scale (see Bryk, Thum, et al. 1998).

Student Composition Controls

Predominantly African American, 1994, is a dummy variable that is coded 1 if the percentage of African American students in the school is greater than 85 percent.

Predominantly Hispanic, 1994, is a dummy variable that is coded 1 if the percentage of Hispanic students in the school is greater than 85 percent.

Predominantly minority, 1994, is a dummy variable that is coded 1 if over 85 percent of the student body is a mixed minority.

Racially mixed, 1994, is a dummy variable that is coded 1 if between 15 percent and 30 percent of the student body is white.

Integrated student body, 1994, is a dummy variable that is coded 1 if 30 percent or more of the students in the school are white. This variable is the eliminated category in the analysis.

Concentration of poverty is a composite measure created from 1990 census statistics for each school's census block. This measure consists of two pieces of information: the percentage of males over twenty-one who are employed, and the percentage of families above the poverty line. These are reverse-coded to transform the variable into a concentration-of-poverty indicator.

Percentage low-income students, 1994, is the percentage of students in the school that was eligible for free or reduced-cost lunch.

Stability of student body, 1994, is the log odds of the proportion of students in the school who took the ITBS in spring 1993 and also were tested in the school in spring 1994.

Small school, 1994, is a dummy variable that is coded 1 if the number of students enrolled in the school in 1994 was less than 350.

Prior achievement, 1989, is the log of the mean value of the school's 1988 to 1990 Illinois Goal Assessment Program (IGAP) scores in third-, sixth-, and eighth-grade reading and mathematics.

Teacher Qualification Controls (Measured at the School Level)

Education background of teachers, 1997. This variable is the school mean of a teacher-level Rasch measure. The measure includes whether the teacher has prior teaching experience in private, rural, suburban, or other urban settings; a quality rating of the college or university from which the teacher earned his or her bachelor's degree; and whether or not the teacher graduated from the Chicago Public Schools. These variables were grouped to serve as an indicator of whether a teacher entered the CPS system from outside or was part of a cycle of those who graduated from CPS, attended a local city college, and went straight into the CPS teaching pool. A high score on this measure indicates that a teacher is cosmopolitan or has experience outside of CPS. A low score indicates that a teacher is part of the insular loop described by Orfield and colleagues (1984).

Professional background of teachers, 1997. This variable is the school mean of a teacher-level Rasch measure. The measure includes the teachers' highest degree earned, the number of college-university courses in their primary teaching subject, and whether they have or are eligible to receive tenure. (Teachers not eligible for tenure generally do not have necessary education qualifications.)

Percentage of new teachers hired in first three years of reform is the percentage of teachers hired from 1989 to 1992 as reported by principals in the 1992 Consortium survey of CPS principals.

Average years of teaching in school, 1997, is the mean of the number of years teachers reported they had been in the school. This data is taken from the 1997 Consortium survey of CPS teachers.

Racial conflict among teachers, 1997, is the percentage of teachers in a school that agreed or strongly agreed to the 1997 Consortium survey item, "Racial and ethnic differences among staff members create tensions in this school."

Individual Teacher-Level Variables Used in Analyses

Low grade, 1997, is a dummy variable coded 1 for teachers in primary grades pre-K to 3.

High grade, 1997, is a dummy variable coded 1 for teachers in upper grades 4 to 8.

Grade missing, 1997, is a dummy variable coded 1 for teachers who did not respond to the survey item asking for grade taught.

Female, 1997, is a dummy variable coded 1 if the teacher is female.

Gender missing, 1997, is a dummy variable coded 1 if the teacher did not respond to the survey item asking for gender.

Black, 1997, is a dummy variable coded 1 if the teacher is African American.

Hispanic, 1997, is a dummy variable coded 1 if the teacher is Hispanic.

Race missing, 1997, is a dummy variable coded 1 if the teacher did not respond to the survey item asking for teacher race.

Teaching experience, 1997, is the total number of years teachers have taught.

1991 Composite Measure of Social Trust

This composite trust variable comes from data collected on a 1991 CPS teacher survey conducted by the Consortium. The sampling and data collection procedures were similar to those used in 1994. While this survey was conducted as our work on trust was just beginning, it contained several items that eventually were used in the 1994 and 1997 teacher-parent and teacher-principal measures. This survey also includes several other survey items gathered in 1991 that subsequently were categorized as *teacher collegiality* and *professional community.* Since all items used the same Likert scale response set, we simply standardized each item and created unit-weighted composites. We then estimated the mean of the three standardized composites to create a 1991 omnibus indicator of trust.

Teacher-Principal Items, 1991

- Teachers in this school are evaluated fairly.
- Staff are supported and encouraged in this school.
- The principal lets staff members know what is expected of them.
- Too often, decisions made by staff committees are ignored or reversed by building administrators. [Note: This item was reversed]
- The principal does a good job of getting resources for this school.
- The administration and teaching staff collaborate toward making the school run effectively.
- I feel comfortable voicing my concerns in this school.

Teacher-Parent Items, 1991

- I receive a great deal of support from parents for the work I do.
- Parents respect teachers in this school.
- Teachers respect parents in this school.

Teacher-Teacher Items, 1991

- Most of my colleagues in this school work hard to help their students succeed.
- This school seems like a big family; everyone is close and cordial.
- Staff members support and encourage each other at this school.
- There is a great deal of cooperative effort among staff members.
- Most of my colleagues share my beliefs and values about what the central mission of this school should be.

Appendix C:
Analysis Details

W E CONDUCTED a three-level hierarchical linear model (HLM) analysis that decomposes the variability in teachers' survey responses from the Consortium's 1997 teacher survey into measurement error, variation among teachers within schools, and between-school variance. Level 1 of the HLM is a measurement model. We introduced here information about the unreliability of each individual's measure, which is produced as part of the Rasch scaling. This allowed us to remove from the analysis the variance component associated with measurement error in the outcome variable. Level 2 represented variation among teachers within schools, and level 3 represented variation across schools. From these statistics, we computed the proportion of variance that is between schools.

Results for the Unconditional Hierarchical Linear Model of Relational Trust, 1997

At level 1, we modeled the observed measure for teacher j in school k to predict a "true score" for that person.

$$Y_{jk} = \pi_{jk} + e_{jk} \text{ where we assume } e_{jk} \tag{1}$$
$$\text{is distributed } N(0, \sigma^2_{jk})$$

Y_{jk} is the observed trust measure for teacher j in school k, π_{jk} is the "true" value of the trust measure, and e_{jk} is a random effect that represents the measurement error associated with teacher jk's trust report.

In most linear modeling applications, we assume that measurement error, e_{jk}, is unknown and normally distributed with mean 0 and some constant variance. However, the standard errors estimated for each Rasch outcome measure, s_{jk}, permit us to explicitly represent measurement error in our model. Specifically, we adjusted the measures for their unreliability by multiplying both sides of Equation 1 by the inverse of the standard error estimates $a_{jk} = s^{-1}_{jk}$, so that

$$Y^*_{jk} = a_{jk}\pi_{jk} + e^*_{jk}; e^*_{jk} \sim N(0,1). \tag{2}$$

Note that when we adjust for measurement error, σ^2 is now fixed at 1.

At level 2, teachers' "true scores" are the outcome. Individual teacher variation in the "true scores" is captured in r_{jk}, assumed to be normally distributed with mean 0 and variance T_π

$$\pi_{jk} = \beta_{0k} + r_{jk}; r_{jk} \sim N(0, T_\pi). \tag{3}$$

At level 3, the school means become the outcome

$$\beta_{0k} = \gamma_{00} + u_{0k}; u_{0k} \sim N(0, T_\beta) \tag{4}$$

where γ_{00} is the estimated grand mean of the trust measure and u_{0k} is the variation attributable to school k.

Results for each relational trust measure are shown in tables C.1 to C.3.

Table C.1   Teacher-Parent Trust

Random Effect	Variance Component	df	χ^2	p-value
Teacher (level 2)	1.272			
School (level 3)	0.293	417	1473.734	0.000
Proportion of variance between schools	0.19			

Source: Authors' compilation.

Table C.2   Teacher-Principal Trust

Random Effect	Variance Component	df	χ^2	p-value
Teacher (level 2)	3.447			
School (level 3)	1.174	418	2238.117	0.000
Proportion of variance between schools	0.25			

Source: Authors' compilation.

Table C.3   Teacher-Teacher Trust

Random Effect	Variance Component	df	χ^2	p-value
Teacher (level 2)	1.690			
School (level 3)	0.451	418	1605.770	0.000
Proportion of variance between schools	0.21			

Source: Authors' compilation.

Full Results of the HLM Analyses of School Context Effects on 1997 Relational Trust Measures

We reported in table 6.1 the school-level results of our analyses of the relationship between school context variables and the 1997 measures of relational trust. To be succinct, we did not include the results for the teacher-level variables in that table. The full set of results are reported in table C.4.

The General Hierarchical Multivariate Linear Model (HMLM) Used in Chapter 6

In these analyses, we used measures created from survey data administered at several points in time. Not all schools responded to all surveys at each point. While we have productivity trends for 460 elementary schools, the teacher background variables were available for 397 of those schools, the 1994 measures coming from teacher surveys were available for 254 of those schools, and the changes from 1994 to 1997 for these measures were available for only 221 schools. In ordinary HLM, any school without full data at all time points would be excluded from the analysis. Using HMLM, we were able to use all available data.

To solve this problem, the level-1 data files are arranged with one record per variable. All observed data are copied to a single variable, "outcome." This outcome is linked to a set of indicators that identify which specific variable it is. In essence, level 1 becomes a missing data model with no level-1 variance.

$$Y = \Sigma \beta_{pk} X_{pk} \qquad (1)$$

where Y is the outcome and X_{pk} are a set of indicator variables. If data are missing on some outcome, these records are just absent.

The level-2 equations are simply the coefficients associated with

Table C.4   School Context Effects on 1997 Relational Trust Measures

	Teacher-Parent Trust	Teacher-Principal Trust	Teacher-Teacher Trust
Teacher-level variables, 1997			
Primary grade flag	0.0646	0.1284	0.0879
Upper grade flag	−0.0596	0.0111	−0.0601
Grade missing	−0.1550*	−0.0116	−0.0927
Female flag	0.0699	−0.1752*	−0.0104
Gender missing	0.0418	−0.5902**	−0.2041
Black	0.1699***	0.4042***	0.0263
Hispanic	0.1157	0.2495*	−0.2472**
Race missing	−0.0172	−0.1271	−0.2388*
Teaching experience	0.1398***	−0.2649***	0.0522
School-level variables			
Racial conflict among teachers	−1.1100***	−1.8842***	−2.3065***
Prior school achievement, 1989	0.0027*	0.0061**	0.0021
Percentage low-income	−0.0021	0.0077	0.0033
Small school size	0.1232	0.2930	0.3115*
Stability of student body	0.1829*	0.0527	0.2443**
Racial-ethnic composition			
Predominantly African American	−0.3665***	−0.7036***	−0.3776***
Predominantly Hispanic	0.1649	−0.4505*	−0.0633
Predominantly minority	−0.1117	−0.1094	0.0324
Racially mixed	−0.1622	−0.5154*	−0.2430*

Source: Authors' compilation.
Note: All of the school composition characteristics used in this analysis were from the 1993 to 1994 school year. The data on racial conflict came from the Consortium's 1997 teacher survey.
*p < 0.05.
**p < 0.01.
***p < 0.001.

the indicator variables, which are in turn predicted by an intercept and random error term. These coefficients represent the latent values for each school on each measure at each time point (whether actually observed or not).

$$\beta_{pk} = \gamma_{p0} + u_{pk}; \, u_{pk} \sim N(0, T_\beta) \tag{2}$$

In a latent variable regression, any level-1 parameters, β_{pk}, can become either outcomes or predictors in a structural model. We use this method to make one of our indicator variables the outcome and the others the predictors. The latent variable output then gives us fixed effects for the predictors on whichever outcome we choose (for a further discussion of the general HMLM methodology see Raudenbush et al. 2000; Raudenbush and Bryk 2001).

Details on HMLM Analyses Using Relational Trust to Predict Academic Productivity in Reading and Mathematics

Using the model described in the foregoing, we completed HMLM analyses to examine the relationship between relational trust and academic productivity. (The results of these analyses are discussed and displayed in chapter 6; see tables 6.2 and 6.3.) For these analyses we used latent variable regression making the productivity indicator the outcome and the context and trust variables the predictors.

Results of HMLM Analyses Using Relational Trust to Predict Changes in Core Organizational Conditions

As described in chapter 6, we ran four HMLM models to examine the relationship between relational trust and orientation to innovation, parental outreach, professional community, and school commitment. Our outcomes in these models were the change in each measure from 1994 to 1997. We included in these models school-level composition and context variables along with the 1994 baseline value on the outcome measure. For each outcome, we ran four separate models, one using the trust composite and one for each of the separate role-relationship trust measures. We included both the 1994 base level measure of trust and the change in trust from 1994 to 1997 as predictors. (The results of these models are discussed in chapter 6; see figure 6.13.) Further details on the actual statistical results are presented in tables C.5 to C.8.

Table C.5   Predicting Change in Teacher Innovation, 1994 to 1997, Using Trust Measures

	A	B	C	D
Teacher innovation, 1994	−0.7754***	−0.6220***	−0.6114***	−0.6679***
Context variables				
Racial conflict among teachers	−0.3657*	−1.2305***	−0.9163***	−0.0232
Prior school achievement, 1989	−0.0013	0.0007	−0.0014	0.0015
Percentage low-income students	−0.0032	−0.0005	−0.0023	−0.0031
Racial-ethnic composition Predominantly African American	0.1562	0.0541	0.0278	0.1989*
Predominantly Hispanic	0.1161	−0.0855	0.1260	0.1708
Predominantly minority	0.3172**	0.4751**	0.2402	0.3279**
Racially mixed	0.0705	0.0310	0.0014	0.0350
Small school size	0.0300	−0.0114	0.0216	0.0058
Concentration of poverty	−0.0068	0.0069	−0.0341	−0.0430
Stability of student body	0.0911	0.1196	0.1204	0.0869
Trust measures				
Trust, 1994	1.0865***			
Change in trust, 1994 to 1997	1.0449***			
Teacher-parent trust, 1994		0.8750***		
Change in teacher-parent trust, 1994 to 1997		0.5325***		
Teacher-principal trust, 1994			0.4617***	
Change in teacher-principal trust, 1994 to 1997			0.4641***	
Teacher-teacher trust, 1994				1.0358***
Change in teacher-teacher trust, 1994 to 1997				1.0701***

Source: Authors' compilation.
*p < 0.05.
**p < 0.01.
***p < 0.001.

Table C.6 Predicting Change in Outreach to Parents, 1994 to 1997, Using Trust Measures

	A	B	C	D
Outreach to parents, 1994	−0.7115***	−0.6718***	−0.7286***	−0.5721***
Context variables				
Racial conflict among teachers	0.0152	−0.4464*	−0.3908*	−0.2305
Prior school achievement, 1989	0.0029	0.0046**	0.0023	0.0042*
Percentage low-income students	0.0043*	0.0064**	0.0051*	0.0052
Racial-ethnic composition Predominantly African American	0.1285	0.1170	0.0617	0.1116
Predominantly Hispanic	−0.1285	−0.2688*	−0.1018	−0.1113
Predominantly minority	−0.0584	0.0857	−0.1029	−0.0284
Racially mixed	−0.0539	−0.0511	−0.0779	−0.0599
Small school size	0.1643	0.1524	0.1310	0.0782
Concentration of poverty	−0.0044	0.0374	−0.0365	−0.0644
Stability of student body	0.0534	0.0884	0.0909	0.1269
Trust measures				
Trust, 1994	0.5099***			
Change in trust, 1994 to 1997	0.8484***			
Teacher-parent trust, 1994		0.6279***		
Change in teacher-parent trust, 1994 to 1997		0.8726***		
Teacher-principal trust, 1994			0.2773***	
Change in teacher-principal trust, 1994 to 1997			0.3755***	
Teacher-teacher trust, 1994				0.2202
Change in teacher-teacher trust, 1994 to 1997				0.4600***

Source: Authors' compilation.
*p < 0.05.
**p < 0.01.
***p < 0.001.

Table C.7   Predicting Change in Professional Community, 1994 to 1997, Using Trust Measures

	A	B	C	D
Professional community, 1994	−0.9045***	−0.6456***	−0.7672***	−0.7312***
Context variables				
Racial conflict among teachers	−0.0336	−1.2072***	−0.7309**	0.2281
Prior school achievement, 1989	−0.0039*	−0.0020	−0.0054*	−0.0009
Percentage low-income students	0.0001	0.0034	0.0008	0.0003
Racial-ethnic composition Predominantly African American	0.1451	−0.0256	−0.0296	0.1535
Predominantly Hispanic	−0.0482	−0.2706	−0.0191	0.0278
Predominantly minority	0.0950	0.2666	−0.0409	0.0940
Racially mixed	−0.0517	−0.0800	−0.1087	−0.0849
Small school size	−0.0166	−0.1131	−0.0624	−0.0881
Concentration of poverty	0.0511	0.0580	−0.0080	−0.0134
Stability of student body	0.2482**	0.3370**	0.3357**	0.2889**
Trust measures				
Trust, 1994	1.5720***			
Change in trust, 1994 to 1997	1.4821***			
Teacher-parent trust, 1994		1.0233***		
Change in teacher-parent trust, 1994 to 1997		0.7738***		
Teacher-principal trust, 1994			0.7064***	
Change in teacher-principal trust, 1994 to 1997			0.6728***	
Teacher-teacher trust, 1994				1.2672***
Change in teacher-teacher trust, 1994 to 1997				1.3326***

Source: Authors' compilation.
*p < 0.05.
**p < 0.01.
***p < 0.001.

Table C.8   Predicting Change in Commitment to School Community, 1994 to 1997, Using Trust Measures

	A	B	C	D
Commitment to school community, 1994	−0.9628***	−0.7631***	−0.8150***	−0.7319***
Context variables				
Racial conflict among teachers	0.1080	−1.1024***	−0.5431*	−0.2674
Prior school achievement, 1989	0.0006	0.0026	−0.0010	0.0042
Percentage low-income students	0.0037	0.0070	0.0040	0.0051
Racial-ethnic composition Predominantly African American	−0.2670*	−0.3842*	−0.4077**	−0.2581
Predominantly Hispanic	−0.0680	−0.3318	0.0170	0.0281
Predominantly minority	−0.0986	0.1421	−0.2264	−0.0173
Racially mixed	0.0433	−0.0145	−0.0351	−0.0196
Small school size	−0.0557	−0.1876	−0.1357	−0.2391
Concentration of poverty	−0.0707	−0.0414	−0.1135	−0.1254
Stability of student body	0.2517**	0.2809*	0.2912**	0.2983*
Trust measures				
Trust, 1994	1.5871***			
Change in trust, 1994	1.4902***			
Teacher-parent trust, 1994		1.3240***		
Change in teacher-parent trust, 1994 to 1997		0.8534***		
Teacher-principal trust, 1994			0.7857***	
Change in teacher-principal trust, 1994 to 1997			0.7620***	
Teacher-teacher trust, 1994				1.1286***
Change in teacher-teacher trust, 1994 to 1997				0.9258***

Source: Authors' compilation.
*p < 0.05.
**p < 0.01.
***p < 0.001.

$=$ Notes $=$

Chapter 1

1. For a discussion of these historical developments see Graham 1993.

2. For a summary of Goals 2000 and policies advocating higher standards see Stevenson 1992, 1996. See also McLaughlin and Shepard 1995 for a critique of Goals 2000.

3. See Murnane and Levy 1996; Murnane, Willett, and Levy 1995; and Murphy and Welch 1989.

4. This is the basic argument advanced by Murnane and Levy (1996).

5. At base here is a longstanding argument about the need for universal public education for the effective functioning of a democratic society. See, for example, Dewey's *The Public and Its Problems* (1927). For a more recent account, see Lindblom 1990.

6. See, for example, John Dewey's treatment of this topic in *The Public and Its Problems*.

7. See Meyer, Ramirez, and Soysal 1992 and Psacharopoulos 1984.

8. See Keltner 1998 and RAND Corporation 1995, 1998.

9. For a review of decentralization efforts in six major U.S. school districts, see Bryk et al. 1997. See Hill 1994 for a discussion on contracting, and Wells 1998 for work on charter schools.

10. For an introduction to the literature on the reorganization of teacher and student work, see research studies from the federally funded Center on School Organization and Restructuring at the University of Wisconsin at Madison (Newmann and Wehlage, 1995; Newmann and Associates, 1996). For case study accounts, see Louis and Kruse 1995 and Elmore, Peterson, and McCarthey 1996. See Darling-Hammond 1998 for work on teacher knowledge in English, and Cohen and Hill 1998 and Cohen 1990 on mathematics learning. On the national scale, the best example of implementing best-practices is the work of Robert Slavin (1989) around Success for All. See also Glennan 1998.

11. We refer the reader to the voluminous writings on "systemic reform." For a good introduction see Smith and O'Day 1990. See also Fuhrman and O'Day 1996.

12. In their case study analyses of restructuring schools, Elmore, Peterson, and McCarthey (1996) lay out these contrasting perspectives between a structuralist approach to a reform and a more immediate attack on teachers' knowledge and skill and actual classroom practice.

13. The basic institutional argument here was detailed in Chubb and Moe 1990. For an analysis of this in the context of Chicago School Reform see Bryk, Sebring, et al. 1998.

14. We view this debate as more of a disagreement about strategy for fundamental change than about the scope or dimensions of the changes needed. The structuralists tend to argue that by changing the institutional arrangements, the opportunities created will encourage new and hopefully much more productive forms of behavior. In contrast, those who focus on teacher competence believe that you best start by changing the knowledge and skill of people. These newly empowered professionals will then change the structures to support more productive ends. Under both theories, extensive human resource development and institutional change must occur.

15. On the effects of a communal school organization on the levels of teacher commitment and student engagement in high schools, see Bryk, Lee, and Holland 1993.

16. See Bryk and Driscoll 1988, Bryk, Lee, and Holland 1993, and Bryk and Thum 1989.

17. See ch. 8 in Fullan 1991 for an introductory review of the importance of the principal's role in leading school change.

18. See Louis and Kruse 1995 on the importance of a school-based professional community for school improvement.

19. This phrase is taken from the title of a book by Delpit (1995) that details some of the cultural conflicts in urban schools and classrooms serving African American youth. For an analogous discussion about the education of Latino youth see Valdes 1996.

20. This analysis applies most appropriately to racially isolated, poor African American neighborhoods found in Chicago and other large cities. Wilson's (1987) seminal analysis of the problems of truly disadvantaged communities was based in Chicago. Other minority neighborhoods, although quite poor, tend to maintain a stronger institutional base than these isolated, racially segregated areas. For an elaboration of the themes raised by Wilson, see Mayer and Jencks 1989, Jencks and Peterson 1991, and Mayer and Jencks 1992.

21. This concern about the collective efficacy of neighborhoods to support the rearing of children is a key focus of a major longitudinal study, The Project on Human Development in Chicago Neighborhoods. Sampson, Raudenbush, and Earls (1998) report a strong link between community collective efficacy and concentration of poverty, neighborhood instability, and crime rates.

22. See Hess and Warden 1988.

23. Lightfoot (1978) makes this point in *Worlds Apart: Relationships between Families and Schools*. Comer's work (1980, 1996) also illustrates the problems between urban school teachers and parents in their schools. Ogbu (1978) articulated similar concerns about minority students and teachers' perceptions of each other, a theme that is continued in his more recent work (Gibson and Ogbu 1991).

24. See Payne 1997 for an ethnographic account on how racial differences inside and outside of schools can quickly become an excuse for ignoring the good intentions of others in urban school reform efforts. For a more general discussion of the role of racial-ethnic group identification in social trust, see Kramer, Brewer, and Hanna 1996.

25. One is hard pressed, for example, to find much discussion of this topic in recent back issues of *Sociology of Education*; as Payne (1997) pointed out, even a special issue on sociology and education policy failed to address it with any forcefulness. One notable exception is a decade-long stream of research by Hoy and colleagues focusing on social trust and its relation to school climate. For an overview of this work see Tschannen-Moran and Hoy 1998.

26. See Haynes, Emmons, and Woodruff 1998 for an analysis of the effects of Comer's School Development Program.

27. See ch. 7 in Meier 1995.

28. See, for example, Maloy 1998 and other related materials developed by the Learning Communities Project (Resnick, Elmore, and Alvarado, co-principal investigators).

29. For a review of their overall findings from this center, see Newmann and Wehlage 1995 and Newmann and Associates 1996.

30. See Kruse, Louis, and Bryk 1994, 8.

31. See Spillane and Thompson 1997.

32. Other supporting evidence can also be found in international research on school change. Articles bearing on this topic frequently appear in an international journal, *School Effectiveness and School Improvement*. Work in Australia, for example, by Coleman, Collinge, and Seifert (1993) focuses specific attention on how the relational dynamics among students, parents, and teachers support improvement efforts in schooling.

33. For a further discussion of the Chicago School Reform Act see Moore 1990; O'Connell 1991; Rollow and Bryk 1992, 1993; Bryk et al. 1993; and Hess 1991, 1995.

34. While these powers were given to the LSCs, not all the councils exercised their authority effectively. Similarly, some principals were unable to use effectively the resources and authority granted to them in order to make significant organizational changes in their buildings (see Bryk et al. 1993 and Easton and Storey 1994).

35. For a full discussion of the diverse organizational and political changes wrought by this reform see Bryk, Sebring, et al. 1998.

36. For a further description of the Center's work see Bryk, Rollow, and Pinnell 1996 and the CSI web site at: *www.csi.uchicago.edu*.

Chapter 2

1. One exception is a paper by Bidwell (1970) that offers interesting theoretical observations on trust relations in client-serving organizations. He argues that these principles become modified in schools as a result of the distinctive nature of these contexts (for example, the nonvoluntary nature of association in schools distinguishes them from other client-serving institutions such as medicine or psychotherapy). This work does not appear to have been picked up in subsequent empirical research.

2. Initial studies on trust by Hoy and colleagues (for example, Hoy and Kupersmith 1984, 1985; Tarter, Bliss, and Hoy 1989) focused on school climate and bear little relation to the school organizational perspective we brought to our work. Yet their more recent research (see, for example, Tschannen-Moran and Hoy 1998; Hoy and Tschannen-Moran 1999) has adopted a social-organizational perspective. Like our research, their subsequent empirical work (Goddard, Tschannen-Moran, and Hoy 2001) has sought to measure trust as a school organizational property, examine its variability across schools, and identify its impact on student learning. Their research reinforces the basic conclusions offered herein.

3. Putnam's research focused on the emergence of new democratic institutions in various geographic regions of Italy. As such, his data were at a highly aggregate level. Critiques of this work have focused on the need to articulate mechanisms at the individual interpersonal level that contribute to the formation of this aggregate social capital. See Brehm and Rahn 1997 for a theoretical and empirical response to these concerns.

4. See Putnam 1993, 1995a, 1995b.

5. See Fukuyama 1995. The general theory on the function of trust in the operation of economic institutions can be traced back as far as Simmel (1978).

6. For an extended discussion of the theory of action in the Chicago Reform that linked democratic localism to institutional effectiveness see Bryk, Sebring, et al. 1998.

7. See Coleman 1988, 1990.

8. For a further discussion of human capital theory see Becker 1964 and Schultz 1961.

9. Many researchers working across many different applied fields have appropriated the concept of social capital in their work. In the process, the term has become highly generalized and has come to mean the social resources of some unit (for example, an organization, informal network, workplace, community, nation, and so on) that is rooted in individual

behavior, attitudes, and dispositions. Here, we are less interested in the density of the parent-student social ties within a school community (that is, Coleman's notion of intergenerational closure) and more focused on the qualities that characterize all of the social exchanges that occur (that is, Coleman's conception of trustworthiness).

10. See, for example, Dawes 1988, Hardin 1993, Williamson 1993, Miller 1992, and Sitkin and Roth 1993.

11. Our ideas about relational trust rely heavily on the theory of social exchanges developed in Blau 1986, which assumes that tangible goods (or observable behaviors) are being exchanged. While it may not be possible to place a specific price on these goods, it is nonetheless assumed that the "evidence" is directly manifest on which subsequent judgments about trustworthiness will be made. As we will argue, however, the "goods of education" are diffuse and complex. They may only manifest themselves over a long period of time and, in this regard, can be quite removed from much of the behavior that helped to form them. As a result, judgments about trustworthiness cannot be exclusively outcome-based, but must also entail a broader discernment of intentions underlying any specific behavior.

12. The social-psychological functions of trust is a major cross-cutting theme in the edited volume by Kramer and Tyler (1996). See especially Kramer, Brewer, and Hanna 1996, and Brockner and Siegel 1996. In general, this line of research criticizes the heavy reliance of most rational choice theorists on material self-interest–based explanations for individual behavior. From a group theory perspective, individuals also value personal associations. These researchers note, however, that self-interest and group value theory are not mutually incompatible. Economic (material) rewards are key to self-interest theory, whereas social and psychological benefits play a similar role in group value theory. Our preliminary field note analyses suggested that both kinds of motivations operate in the social dynamics of urban school communities.

13. This is a major theme in the philosophical literature on trust; see, for example, Hertzberg's (1989) analysis of trust in the philosophy of Wittgenstein. Social theorists such as Blau (1986, xvi) also acknowledge this theme:

> The sacred life of religion contrasts with the profane life where exchange reigns. Religious norms demand that exchange considerations be set aside in relation to other human beings, as exemplified by the admonitions to be a Good Samaritan and to give alms to the poor. Other social norms also require treating people in disregard of returns from them, though conformity is usually rewarded by social approval from third parties (for instance, the approval from colleagues that a professional earns for adherence to professional standards).

See also Luhman 1979.

14. An immediate objection to this perspective is the question of who gets to decide what is good, proper, just, right, and so on. In the context of our application of these ideas, it is not necessary to invoke some external moral theory such as Natural Law to justify the judgments that participants make. Our field notes and observations make clear that individuals indeed engage in moral thinking as they articulate their expectations for others and understand their own obligations. A high level of relational trust across an organization entails a moral synchrony in these expectations and obligations. The actual source of these principles need not be known, nor must these understandings be necessarily "moral" in any absolute sense.

15. The classic citation on this point is Lortie 1975. For a more recent study that reaffirms Lortie's conclusions see McLaughlin and Talbert 2001.

16. The significance of procedural fairness (for example, the existence of committee structures that allow teachers to exercise influence over important decisions that affect their work lives) in making trust judgments has been examined in the criminal justice context. While procedural fairness is significant, researchers have found that individuals also rely heavily on assessing other individuals' intentions. In a review article of multiple empirical studies, Brockner and Siegel (1996) argue that participants' discernments about "others'" motivations, more so than the neutrality of the procedures, per se, appear paramount.

17. Blau (1986) makes important distinctions among the economic exchanges of the marketplace where contracts regulate interactions, the personal relations within a family where a love ethic applies, and the broad range of social exchanges that fall somewhere in the middle.

18. See Peshkin 1986.

19. The importance of shared beliefs as a distinctive characteristic of effective schools is extensively documented in the research literature: see, for example, Louis and Miles 1990; Schlechty 1990; Fullan 1982, 1991; and Newmann and Associates 1996. The efforts of leadership to cultivate and maintain these beliefs are also documented in this literature.

20. The distinctive nature of social exchanges in the context of a contractual relationship has been detailed by social theorists. Yamagishi and Yamagishi (1994), for example, describe the expectations of benign behavior from others under these circumstances as assurance, and deliberately distinguish this from trust, which, they argue, requires attention to a partner's intentions. Other social theorists, including Hardin 1993 and Dasgupta 1988 offered similar distinctions. For further discussion see Molm, Takahashi, and Peterson 2000.

21. The importance of the social arrangements of productive workplaces has been intensively detailed. See, for example, Walton 1980; Weisbrod 1991; Peters and Waterman 1982; Ouchi 1981; and Drucker 1989. A key theoretical distinction in this literature is between mechanistic and organic

conceptions of an organization and the conditions under which each is likely to be most effective. For an application of this theory to schools see Rowan 1993.

22. See the discussion in Bryk, Lee, and Holland 1993 about the concept of a school as a community.

23. In its ideal form, as noted in Ashton and Webb 1986 and Waller 1965, a good rapport with students becomes a resource. Yet Powell, Farrar, and Cohen (1985) found that teachers might also demand less from students in exchange for good student behavior.

24. See Epstein and Sanders 2000 and Hoover-Dempsey and Sandler 1997 for a discussion of parental involvement in schools.

25. See Waller 1965.

26. See Louis and Kruse 1995 and Bryk, Camburn, and Louis 1999 for a discussion on professional community and its significance for student learning.

27. This is a common finding in the school change and restructuring literature; see, for example, Newmann and Wehlage 1995. This is also supported by basic findings in organizational research that link the characteristics of the job floor production process to the most effective ways for organizing and controlling the conduct of that work (see, for example, Walton 1980).

28. Interestingly, the theoretical literature on social exchanges (see, for example, Blau 1986) focuses primarily on the distribution of power among participants in a social network and how this in turn influences the structure of the exchanges. As will be shown further, the asymmetry in power distribution across an urban school community has important implications for our theory of relational trust. Nonetheless, we conclude that the key operational feature of a school community is not its power distribution, but rather a set of mutual dependencies and, with them, mutual vulnerability. That is, from the perspective of school reform and improvement, the key concern entails recognizing mutual dependencies among parties. Redistributing power does not by itself address this concern; it may change the specific representation of the dependency and vulnerability in the organization, but it does not eliminate their consideration. Although not a dominant theme in the social science research on trust, discussions of vulnerability and its interplay with beliefs and expectations do appear. See, for example, Luhmann 1979, 1993; and Barber 1983; see also Molm, Takahashi, and Peterson 2000.

29. Merton (1957) developed the basic concept of a role set. Blau (1986, 104) expanded on these ideas, explaining that "Exchange transactions . . . are influenced by the role set of each partner, that is, by the role relations either has by virtue of occupying a social status relevant to the exchange."

30. In adopting this theoretical position, we synthesize positions from both behavioral social scientific research and philosophical argument. Social

scientists have a strong preference for the study of observable behavior rather than the inner mental states of individuals. Thus, in the context of research on trust, social scientists tend to conceptualize trust as principally rooted in the observed behavior of others. In contrast, in the philosophical literature, trust is often viewed as rooted in primary beliefs. Our theory adopts a mixed view: that individuals act in part on behavioral judgments and in part on beliefs.

31. For other discussions about the role of intentions in judgments about trust, see Yamagishi and Yamagishi 1994 and Molm, Takahashi, and Peterson 2000.

32. The idea of trust as a complex, multi-dimensional construct has become well established in the social science literature: see Mayer, Davis, and Schoorman 1995; Mishra 1996; and also Hoy and Tschannen-Moran 1999. The framework deployed in our research closely resembles the one used by Mishra in his study of organizational leaders in times of crises. His four criteria include competence, openness, personal concern, and reliability. Two of the four are identical to ours (that is, competence and personal concern). His openness criterion resembles closely our dimension of respect. We chose the latter term because this was the way many school community actors spoke about their own relationships. Mishra's reliability dimension relates to our integrity factor, but our conception here is a bit broader. By reliability, Mishra means that organizational actors "do the walk that goes along with the talk." We encompass this consideration in our definition of integrity, but also include a discernment of the core value set that underlies this: Can behavior be understood as in the best interests of the children?

33. An excellent example of such formal procedures is the public forum portion of the Chicago Board of Education meetings, as they used to occur prior to 1995. By law, any citizen could request two minutes to present to the board on some issue or concern. As few as one board member might be present during these sessions. Often other conversations among board members were occurring at the same time. While citizens had been afforded a right to speak, whether anyone was really listening was often unclear.

34. Kramer, Brewer, and Hanna (1996) argue that the origins of collective trust are rooted in organizational identification, and that the willingness to trust is tied to the salience and strength of participants' identification with an organization and its members. The study draws on findings from social-psychological experiments that link group identification and cooperation. They argue that personal affirmations of respect play a key role in shaping such organizational identity.

35. Bidwell (1970) posits that parents' social class will affect the nature of this relationship. Higher socioeconomic status (SES) families are more likely to bring expert opinion to bear in evaluating school practice. We expect the competence criteria to play a larger role in trust discernments

in such contexts. In terms of our study of school improvement efforts in very disadvantaged school contexts, however, the modest attention afforded technical expertise seems predictable.

36. This observation runs counter to conventional theory about the basis of trust relations in professional-client settings. See, for example, Bidwell (1970), who argues that the technical expertise with which professionals carry out their role is normally a central component in determining professional-client trust.

37. For an account of this sort, see the prologue to Bryk, Sebring, et al. 1998.

38. Benevolent intention is one of the dimensions in the three-factor model of trust discussed by Mayer, Davis, and Schoorman (1995). We chose the term *personal regard* instead to broaden the concept to include actions that reach beyond what might be thought of in some sense as doing a good job. Expressions of personal regard entail not only reducing vulnerability, but also positive expressions of care and concern.

39. See Seligman 1997 for a discussion of the salience of this idea of moving beyond one's role responsibilities. Also see Noddings 1992 for a discussion of an ethos of caring in the context of schooling.

40. We refer here to the classic distinction from Tonnies 1957 between Gemeinschaft and Gesellschaft. As institutions, schools are unique in that they are deliberately structured to sit part-way between family-small community and the larger society. As such, social relationships within them take on both the intimacy of families (including a love ethic as rationale for action) and formal procedural aspects of organizations. Moreover, the familial aspect of schooling is strongest at the elementary level, where this transition from family to larger society begins. This dimension thus is of special significance in our research, since it is a study of elementary schools. In contrast, we might expect somewhat diminished salience for this dimension in the forming of relational trust in high schools.

41. See Bryk, Lee, and Holland 1993 for an extended illustration of this reciprocal relationship between teacher commitment and student engagement in the context of urban Catholic high schools.

42. Putnam (1993) uses the power relations in a patron-client arrangement (that is, the effects of the Mafia and the Vatican) to describe the historical circumstances of social ties in southern Italy. He links this to low social trust and the subsequent failure of democratic institutions to take deep roots in these regions.

43. In detailing the philosophical basis of trust, Hertzberg (1989) argues that early experiences in the parent-child relationship are primary to any human understanding of trust. Since the elementary school is the major public institution that bridges children's experiences from the family to the larger society, the salience of this transference (or its absence) is arguably quite high.

44. For a detailed ethnographic account along these lines see Haroutunian-Gordon 1991.

45. A notable program in this regard is FAST (Families and Schools Together) at the University of Wisconsin at Madison. The program brings families together at eight weekly meetings in the school for a meal, family activities, and parent group discussion. FAST deliberately aims to strengthen key relational ties among parents, children, and school professionals. Organizational consequences include stronger relational trust and increased social capital (see McDonald et al. 1997 for a description of the program and its effects).

46. Attention to improving the role relations between urban parents and school professionals is a primary feature in James Comer's School Development Program. See Comer 1980.

47. See Walton (1980) and Weisbrod (1991).

48. This is a basic proposition advanced by Fukuyama (1995) in his analysis of the effective functioning of business organizations.

49. We are indebted to Putnam (1993) on this point. Putnam argues that generalized reciprocity constitutes the micro-level behavioral base for normative social trust at the larger community level. The centrality of generalized reciprocity is rooted in turn in assumptions about the exchangeability of roles among individuals within a network. Putnam's exchangeability concept is appropriate in considering citizens in a democratic polity, yet its applicability in schools appears limited to the one role set—teachers with other teachers—that is characterized by relatively symmetric power.

50. One could imagine a group of teachers who engage in intensive, sustained deliberations regarding curricular content and practice. For a real urban school example, see the case study by Raywid in Louis and Kruse 1995.

51. Interestingly, a key provision in the Chicago 1988 Reform Act changed this practice. Under decentralization, principals for the first time were authorized to choose their own faculty, and these choices were not constrained by seniority considerations. In some ways, this was one of the most significant provisions in the entire law. Subsequent research has shown that actively restructuring schools aggressively used this authority to reshape their faculties and catalyze local reform (see Bryk, Sebring, et al. 1998).

52. For an exception on this point, see the Raywid case in Louis and Kruse 1995.

53. See, for example, Jackson, Bookstrum, and Hansen's (1993) account of urban classroom life. See also Bryk 1988.

54. This conceptualization (drawn on ideas presented in Bidwell 1970) is predicated on the assumption of a supportive family socialization expe-

rience, which is typically the case even in very disadvantaged school communities. In instances where a child's early socialization has been traumatic, however (for example, child abuse, removal from the family and placement in foster care), the natural social resources supporting child development may not be present. Clearly, this makes the task of the classroom teacher more difficult. Theorizing the social psychology of trust-relations formation in such situations requires elaboration well beyond the ideas presented here.

55. Empirical support for this decision can also be found in Goddard, Tschannen-Moran, and Hoy 2001. This study of trust in elementary schools attempted to measure separately teachers' trust in parents and students. Their factor analyses, however, indicated that these two dimensions could not be analytically separated.

56. In terms of the organizational management literature see, for example, Ouchi 1981, Peters and Waterman 1982, and Drucker 1989.

57. For a related argument about the importance of trust in times of crisis in corporate settings, see Mishra 1996.

Part II

1. For an introduction to this theory see ch. 2 and 3 in Bryk, Sebring, et al. 1998. For a more detailed treatment see Rollow 1998. See Appendix A for a general discussion of the design and conduct of this field study and the specific analysis strategies that lead to the case studies presented in Part II.

Chapter 3

1. The quotations used here and in the following two cases are taken from typed transcripts of tape-recorded interviews with actual people. Certain minor grammatical changes were made (such as deleting repetitions of "you know," "yeah," and "like") to make the quotations more readable. Names of all individuals in the text were changed to protect their anonymity. Teacher and parent interviews are indexed so that the reader may identify quotations coming from the same individual without revealing that person's identity.

2. For contrasting case study accounts of principal behavior in Chicago in actively restructuring schools during this same period, see Bryk, Sebring, et al. 1998.

3. Formally, under the Reform Act of 1988, councils have no official responsibility to evaluate individual teachers. This authority remains exclusively with the school's principal.

4. For a further elaboration of the complex dynamics of effective school leadership under Chicago's 1988 reform see ch. 6 in Bryk, Sebring, et al. 1998; also Sebring and Bryk 2000.

Chapter 4

1. The Chicago School Reform Act was passed in 1988, but its implementation was delayed until the fall of 1989. In the interim, the central office reassigned a number of staff—primarily Latinos—to fill principal vacancies across the system. Raul Gonzalez was one of these appointments. He thus entered the Thomas School just as Chicago's decentralization reform was beginning. Like all sitting principals at that time, Dr. Gonzalez was responsible for organizing the elections for a local school council that would eventually make a decision on whether to offer him a four-year performance contract (for further details, see Bryk, Sebring, et al. 1998).

2. See the ethnographic study by Guadalupe Valdes (1996) of ten Mexican American families and their relations with public schools.

Chapter 5

1. See Kotlowitz 1991, 93–97.

2. For an analysis of the changing demographic composition of the principalship in the CPS subsequent to the initiation of the decentralization reform, see Bennett et al. 1992.

3. This process of counseling out appears key in many accounts of improved urban schools (see, for example, ch. 6 of Bryk, Sebring, et al. 1998).

4. See ch. 1 of Bryk, Sebring, et al. 1998 for a further discussion of the mobilizing rhetoric for the 1988 reform.

5. This link between community context and local school council capacity was analyzed systematically by Ryan et al. 1996. In general, councils did tap the "elite" of their local neighborhoods for membership. Nonetheless, a strong relationship existed citywide between community characteristics and the overall professional and educational qualifications of council members. These human resources differences, however, seemed to play a negligible role in council effectiveness. More important was the capacity of these individuals to work together, and the external support and training those councils received. Ryan found that indeed, nonfunctional and problematic councils were more common in very disadvantaged neighborhoods like the Holiday community.

6. See Rollow 1998 for an extended case analysis of the actual micropolitics in the Holiday school community during this same period.

7. A stream of studies from the Consortium on Chicago School Research (beginning with Sebring et al. 1995 and 1996 through Bryk, Sebring, et al. 1999) have documented that very disadvantaged, racially isolated, African American schools in Chicago were the least likely to improve during

the early 1990s. These schools were plagued by weak social relations both within the faculty and outwardly with parents and the community.

Part III

1. The data analyzed here were collected by the Consortium on Chicago School Research. In addition to archiving extant data on Chicago schools and their communities, the Consortium also administers broad city-wide surveys of students, teachers and principals on a periodic basis (1991 to 1992, 1994, 1997, 1999). Without such a long-term database on students and schools, to evaluate our analytic claims about relational trust as a resource for school improvement would be impossible. For more information about the Consortium see *www.consortium-chicago.org*.

Chapter 6

1. The first piloting of items was undertaken as part of the school development work of the Center for School Improvement (CSI) at the University of Chicago. A major strand in CSI's work focuses on enhancing the analytic skills of school leadership teams to better understand their organization and its operations. CSI periodically administers school surveys and facilitates conversations about the implications of these data for subsequent school improvement efforts. As our ideas about relational trust were beginning to develop through field study, we initiated an effort in CSI schools to measure these organizational qualities. The initial pilot results convinced us that surveys were capable of assessing reliably some important distinctions that we had observed among these contexts. For a further discussion of CSI's intervention work with Chicago schools see Bryk, Rollow, and Pinnell 1996.

2. As part of an ongoing effort to examine the progress of Chicago school reform, the Consortium on Chicago School Research undertook in the spring of 1994 a survey of elementary and secondary schools to investigate: students' learning opportunities, motivation and engagement, their views of the school environment, and their parents' involvement in their education; and teachers' views of governance, instructional practices, opportunities for growth, and the professional community in their schools. For a complete description of the survey, see King-Bilcer 1996. Classroom teachers administered the student survey during a regular class period. Questionnaires were available in both English and Spanish with teachers determining which version should be given to each student. The teacher survey generally was conducted in a regularly scheduled faculty meeting. The data in this book use information from the elementary school teacher surveys.

   A probability school sample, stratified by percentage of low-income students and geographic location, was drawn. As a check on possible non-response bias, data from the teacher surveys were compared with information from the Chicago Public Schools' universe data files regarding the racial, gender, percentage of low-income composition of the schools, years of teaching experience, and teachers' highest degree. Analyses of these two files indicate that representativeness was achieved.

In addition to the probability sample, all other schools in Chicago were invited to participate in the study. Thus, there are two groups of schools, a probability sample and a volunteer sample. Descriptive analyses on these two groups indicate that overall they had similar characteristics (see Sebring et al. 1995 for a further discussion). In all, 266 of the 477 elementary schools in the Chicago Public Schools system participated in either or both of the teacher or student surveys. Within the responding sample of schools, 54 percent of elementary school teachers returned surveys.

3. The Consortium also had conducted a large-scale teacher survey in 1991. Since the theory development for relational trust had not yet begun, no items were explicitly written to tap this domain. Retrospectively, however, we were able to extract some items from these surveys that provide more general information about the school's quality of relationships. We use these items later in this chapter as "base state" indicators in longitudinal analyses that link changes in relational trust and improvements in student learning.

Four hundred fifty of the 473 elementary schools in Chicago participated in the 1991 teacher survey, a 95 percent response rate. Nearly 70 percent of teachers responded overall.

4. The Consortium used the same general procedure in its 1997 survey as in 1994. In 1997, however, the sample was stratified only by neighborhood. Again, the Consortium conducted an analysis of non-response bias, which found no evidence of systematic errors. Of the 477 elementary schools in the system, 422 participated in either or both the student and teacher surveys in 1997. Within the sample of responding schools, 63 percent of elementary school teachers returned a survey (see King-Bilcer 1997 for further details).

5. In general, after controlling for measurement error, the proportion of variance between schools is about 20 percent, with the greatest between-school variance, 25 percent, occurring for teacher-principal trust. These results indicate that there are significant differences between schools in how teachers perceive their work environments, lending credibility to treating relational trust as an organizational property. The amount of between-school variability here is greater than for any other school-level indicators developed to date using these Consortium data (Sebring et al. 1995). Also see appendix C for further details on this Hierarchical Linear Model analysis.

On balance, a substantial portion of the variability in teachers' reports about trust relations is within schools. This substantial within-school variability may be related to other unmeasured characteristics of teachers and their roles in the organization. This variability also may be a function of the informal social organization within the school (Frank 1993, 1995).

6. See Wright and Masters 1982 for a full description of Rasch Rating Scale Analyses.

7. Bryk and Driscoll (1988) documented the positive effects of small school size on student engagement and teacher commitment. See also Bryk, Lee, and Holland 1993 for research on the effectiveness of urban Catholic high schools. Small school size was identified as a key facilitating factor in the early implementation of Chicago school reform (see Easton and Storey 1994; Bryk et al. 1993; and Sebring et al. 1995). Small school size has also been documented as a key structural feature supporting successful school restructuring (Newmann and Wehlage 1995). See also Lee and Smith 1996.

8. Sebring et al. (1995) document the prevalence of such tensions in a small proportion of Chicago school communities. Although these animosities were not widespread, they did constitute a significant impediment to school improvement when present.

    More generally, shared racial-ethnic identity forms a natural basis for trust relations. Kramer, Brewer, and Hanna (1996) argue that people tend, at least initially, to perceive members of their own group as trustworthy until counter evidence arises. Due to enhanced perceptions of similarity, individuals presume that other members of a collective will perceive a given situation in a similar way. Thus, common social group membership tends to support trust and highly differentiated membership tends to undermine it. The results reported in Sebring et al. 1995 are consistent with this general social-psychological theory.

9. These results are based on a 3-level HLM analysis. Level 1 consists of a measurement model that takes into account the error variability in teacher reports about trust relations. At level 2, teacher-level variables are considered. Each of these is entered as fixed and grand-mean centered. The random intercept, the average school trust level adjusted for differences among schools in teacher characteristics, became the outcome variable at level 3. This is modeled as a function of the school characteristics. Table 6.1 presents the level 3 results.

    A number of school-level variables were introduced in the analyses that control for aspects of student composition, including race and ethnicity mix, and the proportion of students from low-income families. We also considered in preliminary analyses a range of variables derived from Census Block Group information that was geo-coded by the Consortium onto student records. This included information about neighborhood poverty, education levels, percentage single-family households, and employment. None of these variables, however, explained significant variation in the organizational outcomes given the other factors already included in the model.

For teacher-level covariates, we included basic individual characteristics, such as race and ethnicity and gender. Since we thought that teacher responses might also depend on their status and role within the organization, we included grade level taught and years of experience in the school. In general, the teacher's race was a significant predictor of trust levels for all three trust measures. African American teachers reported higher levels of teacher-parent trust while Hispanic teachers reported lower levels of teacher-teacher trust. These results are expected considering the predominance of African American students and families in the system and the divisive nature of some bilingual programs (as seen in the Thomas case). Both African American and Hispanic teachers report higher levels of teacher-principal trust. Female teachers reported lower levels of teacher-principal trust. Teaching experience also was a significant predictor leading to increased teacher-parent trust and decreased teacher-principal trust.

10. See Sebring et al. 1995, 58.

11. See Payne 1997.

12. See Bryk, Sebring, et al. 1999.

13. The ITBS, like most standardized tests, is a nationally norm-referenced assessment. All of the basic score reports, such as grade equivalents and percentile ranks, compare student performance against a national sample of students who took the same form and test level. Strictly speaking, scores from different forms and levels are not directly comparable, but this is precisely what we have to do in any study of test score trends over time. The solution to this problem entailed an Item Response Theory equating of the various forms and levels of the ITBS used by the Chicago Public Schools between 1990 and 1996. The Consortium on Chicago School Research undertook such an equating study (see Bryk, Thum, et al. 1998 for further details).

14. Meyer (1996) conducted a systematic study of efforts to judge school improvement from only cross-sectional data. He demonstrated that, in some cases, average annual test score reports for a school could indicate declining student achievement, even though the school is having a very positive impact on the children it has the opportunity to educate. The high mobility port-of-immigration school is a prototype case in this regard.

15. Figure 6.5 is based on actual data from a Chicago public elementary school. The name, however, is fictitious.

16. See Bryk, Thum, et al. 1998 for a further description of the technical details of the 3-level HLM used here.

17. The dependent variable in this study—the overall academic productivity indicator—is the empirical Bayes residual created by predicting the gain trend from the initial status, the initial gain, and the input trend. These were computed separately for each grade and then averaged into an overall school index.

18. See Weick 1984 for a further discussion of how "small wins" can help build social resources for an organization.

19. These statistics are drawn from Bennett et al. 1992. Although the Reform Act was passed in 1988, its implementation was delayed until the 1989 to 1990 academic year. The first year was spent almost entirely on establishing the logistics of local school governance and electing the first local school councils. Half of these LSCs made a decision on a school principal in the spring of 1990; the other half undertook this activity in the spring of 1991. For this reason, the 1990 to 1991 academic year represents the first real experiences with local control. (For a further discussion of these early efforts, see Bryk, Sebring, et al. 1998.)

20. It is important to note that the categorization of schools as improving is based on the full-time trends in student learning from 1991 through 1996. The distinction between these two groups is not readily apparent if we look at test data only for the first three years. Most of the actual differences in school productivity improvements emerged over the last three years of the study period. For this reason, we refer to schools as "eventually categorized" as improving or non-improving.

21. For the purposes of this descriptive comparison, we classified schools with a composite trust measure in the top quartile as strongly positive; schools in the bottom quartile on the composite measure were classified as very weak or negative.

22. Only one school out of nineteen with this combination of reports improved in math, and only two schools out of nineteen improved in reading. These anomalous positive results are very close to what we expect simply as a function of the unreliability of measurement in the productivity indicator and the composite trust measure. For a further discussion of this latter point see Sebring, Bryk, and Associates (forthcoming).

23. To elaborate, if the trust trends (and their observed effects on improving academic productivity) were primarily a result of recruiting better teachers, we would expect that by the end of our study in 1997, improving schools would have substantially better personnel. In addition, earlier research on Chicago School Reform (Bryk, Sebring, et al. 1998) identified a specific mechanism at work in initiating reform in actively restructuring schools. Typically, new school leadership brought new energy and vision to local reform initiatives. Some of the more resistant teachers that they encountered left for other schools and were replaced with new, eager recruits. In addition, the increasing amounts of local discretionary money in the first years of reform meant that principals could hire additional new faculty committed to their particular vision of local reform. In actively restructuring schools, these high initial rates of teacher turnover eventually subsided and a stable faculty core emerged. This suggests that we should find a positive relationship with teacher turnover in the early years and a positive relationship with teacher longevity in the school by 1997. That is, if teacher turnover were still high in 1997, we would not expect to find an improving school.

24. Since the items used in the 1991 trust measure were not identical to those used in 1994 and 1997, we could not create a simple change in trust score between 1991 and 1994. Thus, the base level in 1991 is entered into the analysis as a covariate.

25. The outcome metric for these analyses is the rate of productivity improvement per grade per year. To estimate the actual cumulative effect on student learning of a one-unit change in any predictor, we would have to multiply the estimated coefficient by thirty-five (that is, five years and seven grades). This would tell us how much more learning would occur over the elementary grades (2 through 8) for a student beginning second grade in a school in 1996 as compared to a student who entered in 1990. Although the numbers reported in the tables may appear small, when re-expressed in terms of their actual cumulative effects on student learning some of these are quite large.

26. See for example, Easton et al. 1991, Bennett et al. 1992, and Sebring et al. 1995. Also see Bryk, Sebring, et al. 1998.

27. We are cautious in our interpretation given the limited data on teacher qualifications available. The measures used are common in large-scale studies of school effectiveness. Included in this variable set are information about the quality of the undergraduate institution teachers attended, whether teachers held an advanced degree, and the amount of course work taken in the subject matter that they primarily teach. Since we did not observe big differences between schools that improved and those that did not on these variables, it seems unlikely that additional analyses with other teacher personnel variables would negate the basic findings presented here.

    Moreover, our theory of relational trust provides good reason as to why this should be the case. Unless deliberate efforts are undertaken to strengthen the social ties in a school community, good teachers are unlikely to accept a post in such schools or to stay in these contexts even if recruited. That is, even if the quality of teacher human resources is a major causal factor in advancing student learning (as other research evidence suggests) we would argue that a school is unlikely to be able to maintain such human resources in the presence of weak relational ties.

28. The simple correlation of trust (1991) with the overall academic productivity index was weakly positive. The relation becomes significantly negative only when trust (1994) and the change in trust (1994 to 1997) enter the model. Thus, trust 1991, 1994, and 1997 worked in our analysis as a system of relations. Interpreting the 1991 effect by itself would be misleading.

29. To create figure 6.12, we calculated the average trust level for schools in the bottom quartile on this measure in 1991, 1994, and 1997. We also calculated the median for the composite measure of trust in 1994 and the average trust for schools in the top quartile on the composite measure of trust in 1997. We estimated the change in trust from 1994 to 1997 by

taking the difference of trust (1997) and trust (1994) for schools that remained low in trust and for schools that went from the median to the top quartile in trust. We then multiplied the values for trust (1991), trust (1994), and change-in-trust (1994 to 1997) by the coefficients from our models for both reading and mathematics, multiplied the CPS average value for the remaining variables by the corresponding coefficients, and summed the results with the intercept to estimate the productivity indicator. We estimated a value of -0.0205 for consistently low trust schools in reading and -0.0253 in mathematics. Schools that went from low trust in 1991 to median in 1994 and high in 1997 had values of 0.0658 in reading and 0.0940 in mathematics. We then located these results among the actual percentile rankings for each productivity indicator.

30. See for example, Rosenholtz 1989, Louis and Miles 1990, Fullan 1991, Louis and Kruse 1995, and McLaughlin and Talbert 2001.

31. For urban teachers to ascribe school failure to disadvantaged community conditions and family problems is both easy and understandable. Unless teachers genuinely believe that they can make a difference in student learning, regardless of the difficult circumstances in which they work, change will not occur. For a further discussion of this theory of local school change and the supporting empirical evidence in the context of Chicago school reform, see ch. 6 in Bryk, Sebring, et al. 1998. Also see Sebring and Bryk 2000.

32. See the discussion in ch. 1 on the rationale for the School Development Project (Comer 1988). More generally on this point see Epstein and Sanders 2000.

33. See Louis and Kruse 1995 for a discussion of the role of trust in the formation of a school-based professional community.

34. Supportive empirical evidence on this point can be found in Smith, Smith, and Bryk 1998. In general, disadvantaged urban schools tend to report weaker curricular alignment and instructional coherence. Schools organized as strong professional communities, however, significantly moderated these effects.

35. See Rowan 1993 for a further discussion of this idea of normative control in the organizational design of schools. For more general organizational theory account on this point see Walton 1980 and Weisbrod 1991. For empirical evidence specifically on the role of professional community in supporting instructional improvement see Newmann and Wehlage 1995 and Newmann and Associates 1996.

36. See also Cohen, McLaughlin, and Talbert 1993 and McLaughlin and Talbert 2001.

37. A school-based professional community involves both specific work practices, such as collaborative adult work, and a normative-based control mechanism (Louis and Kruse 1995). Relational trust facilitates both the structural and normative aspects of professional community formation.

38. See Kramer, Brewer, and Hanna (1996) for a more general discussion of this hypothesis and the extant social-psychological research evidence that supports it.

39. Owing to the length of the teacher surveys administered by the Consortium on Chicago School Research, each teacher answers only half of the questions. The survey is subdivided by content area (for example, parent community relations, professional work life, instructional practices in math versus reading, and so on) with each teacher asked to respond to only half of the content areas. Of particular importance to the analyses presented here, the measure of outreach to parents was answered by a different sub-sample of teachers in each school than the teachers who responded to the trust items and to the other three workplace measures considered in this section. The fact that the results for changes in outreach to parents are virtually identical to those found for school commitment, innovation, and professional community strengthens our claim that we are observing a structural school effect rather than some measurement artifact. That is, the changes in parental involvement are reported by one subset of teachers in each school, and the key predictors—trust in 1994 and 1997—are reported by an another independent subset of teachers in the same school. If this were just a social-psychological effect (that is, positive individual teachers being positive about everything and negative individual teachers being negative about everything), we would not expect to find this cross sub-group correlation. Only an effect at the organizational rather than personal level could produce these results.

40. The 1994 professional community factor also includes a two-item measure of teacher socialization. These items, unfortunately, were not asked in the 1997 survey (see appendix B for details on the 1994 teacher socialization measure).

41. This composite measure developed out of an earlier collaboration of one of the authors (Bryk) as a co-principal investigator with the Center on School Organization and Restructuring at the University of Wisconsin at Madison. The basic theory of a school-based professional community with illustrative cases is set out in Louis and Kruse 1995 and Kruse, Louis, and Bryk 1994. Its links to authentic achievement have been documented in Newmann and Wehlage 1995 and Newmann and Associates 1996. For further details about this theory as elaborated in our Chicago research and supplemental empirical results, see Bryk, Camburn, and Louis 1999.

42. In addition to evidence from prior research that links these four organizational conditions to improving academic achievement, these links also have been documented in other Consortium research using this same data set and measures (see Bryk et al. 1999; Sebring, Bryk, and Associates, forthcoming).

43. To create figure 6.13, we calculated the change in trust from 1994 to 1997 for a school that was average in trust in 1994 and stayed average in 1997

by taking the average trust in 1997 and subtracting the average trust in 1994. We then inserted this value in the equation for each organizational outcome along with the CPS average values for all other variables, thereby calculating the change in the organizational outcome from 1994 to 1997 for such a school. We added this change to the average 1994 value for the organizational outcome to calculate the predicted 1997 value of this type of school. We then placed the predicted 1997 value on the percentile ranking for the 1997 organizational outcome. Next we calculated the change in trust (1994 to 1997) for a school that was average in trust in 1994 and moved to the top quartile in trust in 1997 by finding the average trust score for schools in the top quartile of trust in 1997 and subtracting the average trust score in 1994. We then followed the same method as described earlier of inserting this value into the models along with average values on all other variables, adding the result to the average 1994 value of each organizational outcome and placing the sum on the percentile ranking of the 1997 organizational outcome. A school that remained average in trust in 1997 had a predicted score of 5.4003 in 1997 teacher innovation, 5.8902 in school commitment, 5.4174 in outreach to parents, and -0.1043 in professional community. (Since professional community is a composite measure, it is reported here in a standard deviation metric rather than a 10-point scale.) A school that moved from average trust in 1994 to high trust in 1997 had a predicted score of 6.1380 in teacher innovation, 6.9425 in school commitment, 6.0165 in outreach to parents, and 0.9422 in professional community.

44. Empirical results from Chicago supporting this conclusion can be found in Bryk et al. 1999 and Sebring, Bryk, and Associates, forthcoming. They have examined the link between each of these organizational conditions and actual changes in school productivity from 1990 to 1996. Schools with strong reports in 1994 on all four of these organizational conditions had probabilities approaching 0.70 of improving academic productivity in reading and mathematics.

45. For a lay audience review of the accumulated empirical evidence and clinical wisdom on this account, see Fullan 2000.

Chapter 7

1. The centrality of school-based professional communities in improving student learning emerged independently in the research of two separate federally funded research centers, the Center on School Context at Stanford University and the Center on School Organization and Restructuring at the University of Wisconsin at Madison. For an overview of the Stanford findings see McLaughlin and Talbert 2001; for the Wisconsin work see Newmann and Associates 1996.

2. These are the simple relative odds of a school being among the 100 most improved in academic productivity between 1990 and 1996. As noted in chapter 6, less than 15 percent of schools in the bottom quartile on the composite measure of trust in 1997 fell into this group. In contrast, about

50 percent of the schools with composite trust reports in the top quartile demonstrated improvements.

3. In addition to the growing body of research on the importance of school-based professional community cited earlier, see also the more general research on teacher collaboration, including Rosenholtz 1989 and Ashton and Webb 1986.

4. For a further elaboration on this theme see Bryk 1988; see also Jackson, Bookstrum, and Hansen 1993.

5. All of the parent and community representatives on the LSC at this field site held professional jobs with master's degrees or better. Adverse faculty reactions arose when this LSC began on its own to research program initiatives and suggest specific instructional changes to the faculty. In a fundamental sense, teachers' expectations about appropriate parental behavior had been violated here as well.

6. See Bryk et al. 1998 and Sebring, Bryk, and Associates, forthcoming.

7. For a further discussion of this point see ch. 1 in Bryk et al. 1998.

8. The comments on Chicago School Reform, referenced in this closing chapter, draw on results established in a ten-year research program of the Center for School Improvement at the University of Chicago and the Consortium on Chicago School Research. For a summary of what was learned during the first phase of Chicago School Reform (up through the mayoral takeover in 1995 to 1996) see Bryk et al. 1998 and Hess 1995.

9. The contrasts presented at Ridgeway and Holiday schools illustrate why this was the case. Key is how the newfound local power established in the 1988 reform was eventually utilized. The expanded local authority at Holiday led to a deepening of ties among school staff, parents, and the local community. No similar efforts occurred at Ridgeway, and the social resources to support improvement remained limited.

We note that Bryk, Sebring, et al. (1998) identified a second pattern of dysfunctional local politics. In contrast to the adversarial politics at Ridgeway, some school communities were characterized by consolidated principal power. Relational trust remained weak in these schools too as principals exercised authoritarian control and undermined any incipient efforts by parents, staff, or community leaders to collectively advance reform. In essence, democratic localism was never implemented in these sites.

10. For a further discussion of this idea of an urban school as a bridging institution see Bryk, Lee, and Holland 1993, 316.

11. For a further discussion of this aspect of the Chicago reform, see ch. 6 in Bryk, Sebring, et al. 1998.

12. This comment assumes direct public bureaucratic control over these school improvement mechanisms. Were a contracting option chosen instead, a very different power dynamic might be enjoined.

13.   The relationship between residential and school moves has received limited attention in the literature. It is generally assumed that residential changes drive school changes. Yet, some evidence points to the quality of social ties families have with schools as an integral contributing factor. In a study of the patterns of mobility in elementary schools in Chicago, Kerbow (1996) found that 60 percent of school changes were prompted by residential changes—leaving 40 percent due to school-related factors. The majority were exit moves associated with safety concerns or conflict at the school. Rather than resolving such issues with the school, families chose to transfer. Consequently, the opportunity to build social trust for students and parents must begin again in a new context. At the high school level, a study of California students also found that as much as 40 percent of school changes were not associated with a residential move (Rumberger et al 1999). (For additional evidence see also Swanson and Schneider, 1999.) Finally, the impact of mobility on student achievement also has been connected to the disruption of social relationships experienced by students and families who move. That is, the differences in achievement between movers and non-movers are partially a result of declines in social networks and personal relationships with teachers and other students that movers experience (Pribesh and Downey 1999).

14.   For earlier work on this topic in the context of effective urban Catholic high schools see Bryk, Lee, and Holland 1993. For other accounts of good schools that share these features, see Lightfoot 1983; Meier 1995; and Sizer 1996, 1999. For a general discussion of intentional communities, see Shenker 1986.

15.   For a further discussion on this point see Bryk, Sebring, et al. 1998.

= References =

Arrow, K. 1974. *The Limits of Organization*. New York: Norton.

Ashton, P. T., and R. B. Webb. 1986. *Making a Difference: Teachers' Sense of Efficacy and Student Achievement*. White Plains, N.Y.: Longman.

Barber, B. 1983. *The Logic and Limits of Trust*. New Brunswick, N.J.: Rutgers University Press.

Becker, G. 1964. *Human Capital*. New York: National Bureau of Economic Research, Columbia University Press.

Bennett, A. L., A. S. Bryk, J. Q. Easton, D. Kerbow, S. Luppescu, and P. A. Sebring. 1992. *Charting Reform: The Principal's Perspective*. Chicago: Consortium on Chicago School Research.

Bidwell, C. E. 1970. "Students and Schools: Some Observations on Client Trust in Client-Serving Organizations." In *Organizations and Clients: Essays in the Sociology of Service*, edited by W. R. Rosengren and M. Lefton (37–69). Columbus, Ohio: Charles E. Merrill.

Blau, P. 1986. *Exchange and Power in Social Life*. New York: John Wiley and Sons.

Brehm, J., and W. Rahn. 1997. "Individual-Level Evidence for the Causes and Consequences of Social Capital." *American Journal of Political Science* 41(3): 999–1023.

Brockner, J. and P. Siegel. 1996. "Understanding the Interaction Between Procedural and Distributive Justice: The Role of Trust." In *Trust in Organizations*, edited by R. M. Kramer and T. R. Tyler. Thousand Oaks, Calif.: Sage.

Bryk, A. S. 1988. "Musings on the Moral Life of Schools." *American Journal of Education* 96(2): 256–90.

Bryk, A. S., E. Camburn, and K. S. Louis. 1999. "Professional Community in Chicago Elementary Schools: Facilitating Factors and Organizational Consequences." *Educational Administration Quarterly* 35: 750–80.

Bryk, A. S., and M. E. Driscoll. 1988. *The School as Community: Theoretical Foundation, Contextual Influences, and Consequences for Teachers and Students*. Madison, Wisc.: National Center for Effective Secondary Schools.

Bryk, A. S., J. Q. Easton, D. Kerbow, S. G. Rollow, and P. B. Sebring. 1993. *A View from the Elementary Schools: The State of Reform in Chicago*. Chicago: Consortium on Chicago School Research.

Bryk, A. S., V. E. Lee, and P. B. Holland. 1993. *Catholic Schools and the Common Good*. Cambridge, Mass.: Harvard University Press.

Bryk, A. S., S. G. Rollow, and G. S. Pinnell. 1996. "Urban School Development: Literacy as a Lever for Change." *Educational Policy* 10(2): 172–201.

Bryk, A. S., and B. Schneider. 1996. *Social Trust: A Moral Resource for School Improvement*. Chicago: Consortium on Chicago School Research.

Bryk, A. S., P. B. Sebring, E. Allensworth, J. Q. Easton, and S. Luppescu. 1999. "Long-Term Academic Productivity Gains in Chicago Elementary Schools: A Theory of Five Essential Supports." Paper presented at the annual Consortium on Chicago School Research ASA Presentation, Chicago.

Bryk, A. S., P. B. Sebring, D. Kerbow, S. Rollow, and J. Q. Easton. 1998. *Charting Chicago School Reform: Democratic Localism as a Lever for Change*. Boulder, Colo.: Westview Press.

Bryk, A. S., D. Shipps, P. T. Hill, and R. Lake. 1997. *Decentralization in Practice: Toward a System of Schools*. Final report to the Annie E. Casey Foundation, Baltimore, Md.

Bryk, A. S., and Y. M. Thum. 1989. "The Effects of High School Organization on Dropping Out: An Exploratory Investigation." *American Educational Research Journal* 26(3): 353–84.

Bryk, A. S., Y. M. Thum, J. Q. Easton, and S. Luppescu. 1998. "Assessing School Academic Productivity: The Case of Chicago School Reform." *Social Psychology of Education* 2: 103–42.

Chubb, J. E., and T. M. Moe. 1990. *Politics, Markets and America's Schools*. Washington, D.C.: The Brookings Institution.

Cohen, D. K. 1990. "A Revolution in One Classroom: The Case of Mrs. Oublier." *Educational Evaluation and Policy Analysis* 12(3): 311–30.

Cohen, D. K., and H. C. Hill. 1998. *State Policy and Classroom Performance: Mathematics Reform in California*. Philadelphia: Consortium for Policy Research in Education.

Cohen, D. K., M. W. McLaughlin, and J. E. Talbert. 1993. *Teaching for Understanding*. San Francisco: Jossey-Bass.

Coleman, J. S. 1988. "Social Capital and the Creation of Human Capital." *American Journal of Sociology* 94: 95–120.

———. 1990. *Foundations of Social Theory*. Cambridge, Mass.: The Belknap Press of Harvard University Press.

Coleman, P., J. Collinge, and T. Seifert. 1993. "Seeking the Levers of Change: Participant Attitudes and School Improvement." *School Effectiveness and School Improvement* 41: 59–83.

Comer, James P. 1980. *School Power: Implications of an Intervention Project*. New York: The Free Press.

———. 1988. "Educating Poor Minority Children." *Scientific American* 259(5): 42–48.

Comer, James P., Norris M. Haynes, Edward T. Joyner, and Michael Ben-Avie. 1996. *Rallying the Whole Village: The Comer Process for Reforming Education*. New York: Teachers College Press.

Darling-Hammond, L. 1998. "Teacher Learning That Supports Student Learning." *Educational Leadership* 55(5): 6–11.

Dasgupta, P. 1988. "Trust as a Commodity." In *Trust: Making and Breaking of Cooperative Relations*, edited by D. Gambetta. Oxford: Blackwell.

Dawes, R. M. 1988. *Rational Choice in an Uncertain World*. San Diego: Harcourt Brace Jovanovich.

Delpit, L. D. 1995. *Other People's Children: Cultural Conflict in the Classroom*. New York: New Press.

Dewey, J. 1927. *The Public and Its Problems*. New York: Holt.

Drucker, P. 1989. *The New Realities*. New York: Harper and Row.

Easton, J. Q., A. S. Bryk, M. E. Driscoll, J. G. Kotsakis, P. Sebring, and A. J. van der Ploeg. 1991. *Charting Reform: The Teachers' Turn*. Chicago: Consortium on Chicago School Research.

Easton, J. Q., and S. L. Storey. 1994. "The Development of Local School Councils." *Education and Urban Society* 26(3): 220–37.

Elmore, R. E., P. L. Peterson, and S. J. McCarthey. 1996. *Restructuring in the Classroom: Teaching, Learning, and School Organization*. San Francisco: Jossey-Bass.

Epstein, J. L., and M. G. Sanders. 2000. "Connecting Home, School, and Community: New Directions for Social Research." In *Handbook of Sociology of Education*, edited by M. Hallinan. New York: Plenum.

Frank, K. A. 1993. *Identifying Cohesive Subgroups*. Ph.D. diss., University of Chicago.

———. 1995. "Identifying Cohesive Subgroups." *Social Networks* 17: 27–56.

Fuhrman, S. H., and J. A. O'Day. 1996. *Rewards and Reform: Creating Educational Incentives That Work*. San Francisco: Jossey-Bass.

Fukuyama, F. 1995. *Trust: Social Virtues and the Creation of Prosperity*. New York: The Free Press.

Fullan, M. G. 1982. *The Meaning of Educational Change*. New York: Teachers College Press.

———. 1991. *The New Meaning of Educational Change*. New York: Teachers College Press.

———. 2000. "The Three Stories of Education Reform." *Phi Delta Kappan* 81(8): 581–84.

Gambetta, D. 1988. *Trust: Making and Breaking Cooperative Relations*. New York: Blackwell.

Gibson, M. A., and J. U. Ogbu. 1991. *Minority Status and Schooling: A Comparative Study of Immigrant and Involuntary Minorities*. New York: Garland.

Glennan, T., Jr. 1998. *New American Schools After Six Years*. Santa Monica, Calif.: RAND Corporation.

Goddard, R. D., M. Tschannen-Moran, and W. Hoy. 2001. "A Multilevel Examination of the Distribution and Effects of Teacher Trust in Students and Parents in Urban Elementary Schools." *Elementary School Journal* 102(1): 3–19.

Graham, P. A. 1993. "What America Has Expected of Its Schools Over the Past Century." *American Journal of Education* 101(2): 83–98.

Granovetter, M. 1985. "Economic Action and Social Structure: The Problem of Embeddedness." *American Journal of Sociology* 91: 481–511.

Hardin, R. 1993. "The Street-Level Epistemology of Trust." *Politics and Society* 21(4): 505–29.

———. 1998. *Conceptions and Explanations of Trust*. New York: Russell Sage Foundation.

Haroutunian-Gordon, S. 1991. *Turning the Soul: Teaching Through Conversation in the High School.* Chicago: University of Chicago Press.

Haynes, N. M., C. L. Emmons, and D. W. Woodruff. 1998. "School Development Program Effects: Linking Implementation to Outcomes." *Journal of Education for Students Placed at Risk* 3(1): 71–85.

Hertzberg, L. 1989. "On the Attitude of Trust." *Inquiry* 31: 307–22.

Hess, G. A., Jr. 1991. *School Restructuring, Chicago Style.* Newbury Park, Calif.: Corwin.

———. 1995. *Restructuring Urban Schools: A Chicago Perspective.* New York: Teachers College Press.

Hess, G. A., Jr., and C. Warden. 1988. "Who Benefits from Desegregation?" *Journal of Negro Education* 57(4): 536–51.

Hill, P. 1994. "Public Schools by Contract: An Alternative to Privatization." In *Privatizing Education and Educational Choice,* edited by S. Hakim, P. Seidenstat, and G. W. Bowman. Westport, Conn.: Praeger.

Hoover-Dempsey, K., and H. Sandler. 1997. "Why Do Parents Become Involved in Their Children's Education?" *Review of Educational Research* 67: 3–42.

Hoy, W. K., and W. J. Kupersmith. 1985. "The Meaning and Measure of Faculty Trust." *Educational and Psychological Research* 5: 1–10.

———. 1984. "Principal Authenticity and Faculty Trust: Key Elements in Organizational Behavior." *Planning and Change* 15(2): 80–88.

Hoy, W. K., and M. Tschannen-Moran. 1999. "Five Faces of Trust: An Empirical Confirmation in Urban Elementary Schools." *Journal of School Leadership* 9: 184–208.

Jackson, P. W., R. E. Bookstrum, and D. T. Hansen. 1993. *The Moral Life of Schools.* San Francisco: Jossey-Bass.

Jencks, C., and P. E. Peterson. 1991. *The Urban Underclass.* Washington, D.C.: The Brookings Institution.

Keltner, B. 1998. *Funding Comprehensive School Reform.* Santa Monica, Calif.: RAND Corporation.

Kerbow, D. 1996. "Patterns of Student Mobility and Local School Reform." *Journal of Education for Students Placed at Risk* 1: 147–70.

King-Bilcer, D. 1996. *User's Manual, Version 1 for 1994 Surveys: Charting Reform: Chicago Teachers Take Stock and Charting Reform: The Students Speak.* Chicago: Consortium on Chicago School Research.

———. 1997. *User's Manual, Version 1 for Improving Chicago's Schools: The Teacher's Turn, 1997.* Chicago: Consortium on Chicago School Research.

Kochanek, J. R. 1999. *The Personal Side of Schooling: Linking Relational Trust and Achievement.* Master's thesis, University of Chicago.

Kotlowitz, A. 1991. *There Are No Children Here: The Story of Two Boys Growing Up in the Other America.* New York: Doubleday.

Kramer, R. M., M. B. Brewer, and B. A. Hanna. 1996. "Collective Trust and Collective Action." In *Trust in Organizations,* edited by R. M. Kramer and T. R. Tyler (357–89). Thousand Oaks, Calif.: Sage.

Kramer, R. M., and T. R. Tyler. 1996. *Trust in Organizations: Frontiers of Theory and Research.* Thousand Oaks, Calif.: Sage.

Kruse, S., K. S. Louis, and A. S. Bryk. 1994. *Building Professional Community in Schools*. Madison, Wisc.: Center on Organization and Restructuring of Schools.

Lee, V. E., and J. B. Smith, 1996. *High School Size: Which Works Best, and for Whom?* Unpublished paper. University of Michigan, Ann Arbor.

Lightfoot, S. L. 1978. *Worlds Apart: Relationships Between Families and Schools*. New York: Basic Books.

———. 1983. *The Good High School: Portraits of Character and Culture*. New York: Basic Books.

Lindblom, C. E. 1990. *Inquiry and Change: The Troubled Attempt to Understand and Shape Society*. New Haven: Yale University Press.

Lortie, D. 1975. *Schoolteacher*. Chicago: University of Chicago Press.

Louis, K. S., and S. D. Kruse. 1995. *Professionalism and Community: Perspectives on Reforming Urban Schools*. Thousand Oaks, Calif.: Corwin Press.

Louis, K. S., and M. B. Miles. 1990. *Improving the Urban High School: What Works and Why*. New York: Teachers College Press.

Luhmann, N. 1979. *Trust and Power*. New York: John Wiley.

———. 1993. *Risk: A Sociological Theory*. New York: W. de Gruyter.

Maloy, K. 1998. *Building a Learning Community: The Story of New York City Community School District #2*. Pittsburgh, Pa.: Learning Research and Development Center, University of Pittsburgh.

Mayer, R. C., J. H. Davis, and F. D. Schoorman. 1995. "An Integrative Model of Organizational Trust." *Academy of Management Review* 20(3): 709–34.

Mayer, S. E., and C. Jencks. 1989. "Growing Up in Poor Neighborhoods: How Much Does It Matter?" *Science* 243(4897): 1441–45.

———. 1992. *Recent Trends in Economic Inequality in the United States: Income vs. Expenditures vs. Material Well-Being*. Evanston, Ill.: Center for Urban Affairs and Policy Research, Northwestern University.

McDonald, L., S. Billingham, T. Conrad, N. O. Morgan, and E. Payton. 1997. "Families and Schools Together (FAST): Integrating Community Development with Clinical Strategies." *Families in Society: The Journal of Contemporary Human Services* 78(2): 140–55.

McLaughlin, M. W., and L. A. Shepard. 1995. *Improving Education Through Standards-Based Reform*. Stanford, Calif.: National Academy of Education Panel on Standards-Based Education Reform.

McLaughlin, M. W., and J. E. Talbert. 2001. *Professional Communities and the Work of High School Teaching*. Chicago: University of Chicago Press.

Meier, D. 1995. *The Power of Their Ideas: Lessons for America from a Small School in Harlem*. Boston: Beacon Press.

Merton, R. K. 1957. *Social Theory and Social Structure*. Glencoe: Free Press.

Meyer, J., F. Ramirez, and Y. Soysal. 1992. "World Expansion of Mass Education, 1870–1980." *Sociology of Education* 65(2): 128–49.

Meyer, R. H. 1996. "Value-Added Indicators of School Performance." In *Improving the Performance of America's Schools*, edited by E. Hanushek and D. W. Jorgensen (197–223). Washington, D.C.: National Academy Press.

Miller, G. J. 1992. *Managerial Dilemmas: The Political Economy of Hierarchy*. Cambridge: Cambridge University Press.

Mishra, A. K. 1996. "Organizational Responses to Crisis: The Centrality of Trust." In *Trust in Organizations*, edited by R. M. Kramer and T. R. Tyler (261–87). Thousand Oaks, Calif.: Sage.

Molm, L. D., N. Takahashi, and G. Peterson, 2000. "Risk and Trust in Social Exchange: An Experimental Test of a Classical Proposition." *American Journal of Sociology* 105(5): 1396–427.

Moore, D. R. 1990. Voice and Choice in Chicago. In *Choice and Control in American Education*. Vol. 2. *The Practice of Choice, Decentralization, and School Restructuring*, edited by W. H. Clune and J. F. Witte (153–98). Philadelphia: Falmer.

Murnane, R. J., and F. Levy. 1996. *Teaching the New Basic Skills: Principles for Educating Children to Thrive in a Changing Economy*. New York: Free Press.

Murnane, R. J., J. B. Willett, and F. Levy. 1995. "The Growing Importance of Cognitive Skills in Wage Determination." *Review of Economics and Statistics* 77(2): 251–66.

Murphy, K. M., and F. Welch. 1989. "Wage Premiums for College Graduates." *Educational Researcher* 19(4): 17–26.

Newmann, F. M., and Associates. 1996. *Authentic Achievement: Restructuring Schools for Intellectual Quality*. San Francisco: Jossey-Bass.

Newmann, F. M., and G. G. Wehlage. 1995. *Successful School Restructuring: A Report to the Public and Educators*. Madison, Wisc.: Center on Organization and Restructuring of Schools.

Noddings, N. 1992. *The Challenge to Care in Schools: An Alternative Approach to Education*. New York: Teachers College Press.

O'Connell, M. 1991. *School Reform Chicago Style: How Citizens Organized to Change Public Policy* (A Special Issue of *The Neighborhood Works*). Chicago: Center for Neighborhood Technology.

Ogbu, J. U. 1978. *Minority Education and Caste: The American System in Cross-Cultural Perspective*. New York: Academic Press.

Orfield, G., and Associates. 1984. *The Chicago Study of Access and Choice in Higher Education: A Report to the Illinois Senate Committee on Higher Education*. Chicago: Illinois Committee on Public Policy Studies.

Ouchi, W. G. 1981. *Theory Z: How American Business Can Meet the Japanese Challenge*. Reading, Mass.: Addison-Wesley.

Payne, C. M. 1997. *"I Don't Want Your Nasty Pot of Gold": Urban School Climate and Public Policy*. Evanston, Ill.: Institute for Policy Research.

Peshkin, A. 1986. *God's Choice: The Total World of a Fundamentalist Christian School*. Chicago and London: University of Chicago Press.

Peters, T. J., and R. H. Waterman, Jr. 1982. *In Search of Excellence: Lessons from America's Best-Run Companies*. New York: Harper and Row.

Powell, A., E. Farrar, and D. K. Cohen. 1985. *The Shopping Mall High School: Winners and Losers in the Educational Marketplace*. Boston: Houghton Mifflin.

Pribesh, S., and D. B. Downey. 1999. "Why Are Residential and School Moves Associated with Poor School Performance?" *Demography* 36: 521–34.

Psacharopoulos, G. 1984. "The Contribution of Education to Economic Growth: International Comparisons." In *International Comparisons of Productivity and Causes of Slowdown*, edited by John Kendrick (300–55). Cambridge: Ballner.

Putnam, R. D. 1993. *Making Democracy Work: Civic Traditions in Modern Italy.* Princeton, N.J.: Princeton University Press.

Putnam, R. D. 1995a. "Bowling Alone: America's Declining Social Capital." *Journal of Democracy* 6(1): 65–78.

———. 1995b. "Tuning In, Tuning Out: The Strange Disappearance of Social Capital in America." *PS: Political Science and Politics* 28: 664–83.

RAND Corporation. 1995. *Contracting: The Case for Privately Operated Public Schools.* Santa Monica, Calif.: RAND Corporation.

———. 1998. *Reforming America's Schools: Observations on Implementing "Whole School Designs."* Santa Monica, Calif.: RAND Corporation.

Raudenbush, S. W., and A. S. Bryk. 2001. *Hierarchical Linear Models: Applications and Data Analysis Methods.* 2d ed. Newbury Park, Calif.: Sage.

Raudenbush, S. W., A. S. Bryk, F. Cheong, and R. Congdon. 2000. *Hierarchical Linear and Nonlinear Modeling.* Lincolnwood, Ill.: Scientific Software Institute.

Raywid, M. A. 1995. "Professional Community and Its Yield at Metro Academy." In *Professionalism and Community: Perspectives on Reforming Urban Schools,* edited by K. S. Louis and S. D. Kruse (45–75). Thousand Oaks, Calif.: Corwin Press.

Rollow, S. G. 1998. *Grounding a Theory of School Community Politics.* Unpublished Ph.D. diss., University of Chicago.

Rollow, S. G., and A. S. Bryk. 1992. *Democratic Politics and School Improvement: The Potential of Chicago School Reform.* Chicago: Center for School Improvement.

———. 1993. "The Chicago Experiment: The Potential and Reality of Reform." *Equity and Choice* 9(3): 22–32.

Rosenholtz, S. J. 1989. *Teachers' Workplace: The Social Organization of Schools.* White Plains, N.Y.: Longman.

Rowan, B. 1993. "Commitment and Control: Alternative Strategies for the Organizational Design of Schools." *Review of Research in Education* 16: 353–89.

Rumberger, R. W., K. A. Larson, R. K. Ream, and G. J. Palardy. 1999. *The Educational Consequences of Mobilty for California Students and Schools.* Berkeley: Policy Analysis for California Education, University of California.

Ryan, S., A. S. Bryk, G. Lopez, K. P. Williams, K. Hall, and S. Luppescu. 1996. *Charting Reform: Local Leadership at Work.* Chicago: Consortium on Chicago School Research.

Sampson, R. J., S. W. Raudenbush, and F. Earls. 1998. *Neighborhood Collective Efficacy: Does It Help Reduce Violence?* Washington: U.S. Department of Justice.

Schlechty, P. 1990. *Schools for the 21st Century.* San Francisco: Jossey-Bass.

Schneider, B., and A. S. Bryk. 1995. "Social Trust: A Moral Resource for School Improvement." Paper presented at the University of Wisconsin Invitational Conference on Social Capital, Madison, Wisconsin.

Schultz, T. 1961. "Investment in Human Capital." *American Economic Review* 51: 1–17.

Sebring, P. B., and A. S. Bryk. 2000. "School Leadership and the Bottom Line in Chicago." *Phi Delta Kappan* 81(6): 440–43.

Sebring, P. B., A. S. Bryk, J. Q. Easton, S. Luppescu, Y. M. Thum, W. Lopez, and B. Smith. 1995. *Charting Reform: Chicago Teachers Take Stock*. Chicago: Consortium on Chicago School Research.

Sebring, P. B., A. S. Bryk, M. Roderick, E. Camburn, S. Luppescu, Y. M. Thum, B. Smith, and J. Kahne. 1996. *Charting Reform in Chicago: The Students Speak*. Chicago: Consortium on Chicago School Research.

Sebring, P. B., A. S. Bryk, and Associates. Forthcoming. "Organizing Schools to Improve Student Learning." Chicago: Consortium on Chicago School Research.

Seligman, A. B. 1997. *The Problem of Trust*. Princeton, N.J.: Princeton University Press.

Shenker, B. 1986. *Intentional Communities*. London: Routledge and Kegan Paul.

Simmel, G. 1978. *Philosophy of Money*. London: Routledge and Kegan Paul.

Sitkin, S. B., and N. L. Roth. 1993. "Explaining the Limited Effectiveness of Legalistic 'Remedies' for Trust/Distrust." *Organizational Science* 4: 367–92.

Sizer, T. R. 1996. *Horace's Hope: What Works for the American High School*. Boston: Houghton Mifflin.

———. 1999. "No Two Are Quite Alike." *Educational Leadership* 57(1): 6–11.

Slavin, R. E. 1989. "What Works for Students at Risk: A Research Synthesis." *Educational Synthesis* 46(5): 4–18.

Smith, J. B., B. Smith, and A. S. Bryk. 1998. *Setting the Pace: Opportunities to Learn in Chicago's Elementary Schools*. Chicago: Consortium on Chicago School Research.

Smith, M. S., and J. A. O'Day. 1990. *Systemic School Reform: Politics of Education Yearbook*. Washington, D.C.: Falmer.

Spillane, J., and C. L. Thompson. 1997. "Reconstructing Conceptions of Local Capacity: The Local Education Agency's Capacity for Ambitious Instructional Reform." *Education Evaluation and Policy Analysis* 19 (2): 185–203.

Stevenson, D. L. 1992. *Raising Standards for American Education: A Report to Congress, the Secretary of Education, the National Education Goals Panel, and the American People*. Washington, D.C.: National Center for Educational Statistics (NCES).

———. 1996. "Standards and Assessments." In *Goals 2000: Implementing Educational Reform*, edited by K. M. Borman, P. W. Cookson, A. R. Sadovnik, and J. Z. Spade. Norwood, N.J.: Ablex.

Swanson, C., and B. Schneider. 1999. "Students on the Move: Residential and Educational Mobility in American Schools." *Sociology of Education* 72(1): 54–67.

Tarter, C. J., J. R. Bliss, and W. Hoy. 1989. "School Characteristics and Faculty Trust in Secondary Schools." *Educational Administration Quarterly* 25(3): 294–308.

Tonnies, F. 1957. *Gemeinschaft und Gesellschaft*. East Lansing: Michigan State University Press.

Tschannen-Moran, M., and W. Hoy. 1998. "Trust in Schools: A Conceptual and Empirical Analysis." *Journal of Educational Administration* 36(4): 334–52.

Tyler, T. R., and R. M. Kramer. 1996. "Whither Trust?" In *Trust in Organizations: Frontiers of Theory and Research*, edited by R. M. Kramer and T. R. Tyler (1–38). Thousand Oaks, Calif.: Sage.

Valdes, G. 1996. *Con Respeto: Bridging the Distances Between Culturally Diverse Families and Schools*. New York: Teachers College Press.

Waller, W. 1965. *The Sociology of Teaching*. New York: J. Wiley.

Walton, R. E. 1980. "Establishing and Maintaining High Commitment Work Systems." In *The Organization Life Cycle*, edited by J. R. Kimberly, R. H. Miles, and Associates. San Francisco: Jossey-Bass.

Weick, K. 1984. "Small Wins: Redefining the Scale of Social Problems." *American Psychologist* 39(1): 40–49.

Weisbrod, M. 1991. *Productive Workplaces: Organizing and Managing for Dignity, Meaning and Community*. San Francisco: Jossey-Bass.

Wells, A. S. 1998. "Charter School Reform in California: Does It Meet Objectives?" *Phi Delta Kappan* 80(4): 305–12.

Williamson, O. E. 1993. "Calculativeness, Trust, and Economic Organization." *Journal of Law and Economics* 34: 453–502.

Wilson, W. J. 1987. *The Truly Disadvantaged: The Inner City, the Underclass, and Public Policy*. Chicago: University of Chicago Press.

Wright, B. D., and G. N. Masters. 1982. *Rating Scale Analysis*. Chicago: Mesa Press.

Yamagishi, T., and M. Yamagishi. 1994. "Trust and Commitment in the United States and Japan." *Motivation and Emotion* 18(2): 129–66.

= Index =

Boldface numbers refer to figures and tables.